Tackling Behaviour in your Primary School

Tackling Behaviour in your Primary School provides ready-made advice and support for classroom professionals and can be used, read and adapted to suit the busy everyday lives of teachers working in primary schools today.

This valuable text sets the scene for managing behaviour in the primary classroom in the context of the Children Act, 2004 agenda, making it highly relevant to trainee primary teachers, learning school mentors, classroom assistants, behaviour specialists and senior management teams. As experts in the field of behaviour management, the authors draw on their many years of experience to provide evidenced whole-school strategies, extensively-researched concepts and step-by-step behaviour programmes. Topics covered include:

- understanding behaviour;
- how to measure behaviour and why this can be an effective approach;
- using and implementing whole-school behaviour policies;
- honing your classroom management skills;
- managing bullying;
- dealing with specific classroom difficulties;
- working effectively and supportively with parents.

Drawing on case studies throughout, this Handbook will help you to understand and deal with the most confrontational of classroom behaviour. *Tackling Behaviour in your Primary School* provides all staff, parents and carers engaged in health, education and social services with a ready-made resource packed full of strategies, ideas, activities and solutions to help manage behaviour in even the toughest of classrooms.

Ken Reid (OBE) is presently the Adviser to the Welsh Government on Behaviour and Attendance. He was formerly the Deputy Vice Chancellor and Research Professor at Swansea Metropolitan University.

Nicola S. Morgan is a qualified teacher and behaviour management consultant.

To Becky, Nick and Jo from Dad!

To my grandmother Eileen Knight for her love, support, creativity and spirit.
(Nicola S. Morgan)

Tackling Behaviour in your Primary School

A practical handbook for teachers

Ken Reid and Nicola S. Morgan

 Routledge
Taylor & Francis Group

LONDON AND NEW YORK

First published 2012
by Routledge
2 Park Square, Milton Park, Abingdon, Oxon OX14 4RN

Simultaneously published in the USA and Canada
by Routledge
711 Third Avenue, New York, NY 10017

Routledge is an imprint of the Taylor & Francis Group, an informa business

British Library Cataloguing in Publication Data
A catalogue record for this book is available from the British Library

Library of Congress Cataloging-in-Publication Data
Reid, Ken.
Tackling behaviour in your primary school: a practical handbook for teachers/Ken Reid and Nicola S. Morgan.
p. cm.
Includes bibliographical references and index.
1. Classroom management. 2. Behavior modification--Education (Primary) 3. Education, Primary. I. Morgan, Nicola S. II. Title.
LB3013.R38 2012
371.102'4--dc23
2011045341

ISBN: 978-0-415-67023-4 (pbk)
ISBN: 978-0-203-11985-3 (ebk)

Typeset in Bembo by Fakenham Prepress Solutions, Fakenham, Norfolk NR21 8NN

Printed and bound in Great Britain by the MPG Books Group

Contents

Illustrations

Foreword

Nicola and I have enjoyed the preparation and research for this Handbook. The idea started during my period as Chair of the National Behaviour and Attendance Review (NBAR) in Wales between 2006 and 2008 when any amount of evidence was given by a wide range of primary-level professionals about their training needs and practical deficits on managing behaviour in their schools and classrooms and which impacted negatively on their professional enjoyment in their daily lives and, in extreme cases, led to serious levels of stress. We heard from many different teachers, head teachers, professional support staff, caring professionals, local authority and voluntary body staff not only about their needs but also about the inadequacy of their initial teacher training, induction and in-service training needs at both an individual and a school or service level. Most staff considered that they had learnt 'on-the-job'; some better than others.

After the publication of the NBAR Report in 2008 and the follow-up Report on Behaving and Attending a year later (Welsh Government, 2009), Nicola and I started to work together on a range of projects in the field of behaviour management, often supported by Gill Ellis, Head Teacher of Coed Eva Primary School in Torfaen, who is herself a highly proficient practitioner and behavioural consultant. We are continuing to develop this collaboration; not least on a new book entitled *Better Behaviour through Home–School Relations: Using Values-Based Education to Promote Positive Learning*, shortly also to be published by Routledge (2012).

The idea behind this book which Nicola and I have written jointly is to provide a practically-based text which can be used by readers in several different ways. First, it can be read, used and adapted by a wide range of primary professionals. These include head teachers, deputies, promoted, experienced and new staff, including those engaged in initial teacher training, irrespective of route. It is intended also for use by a wide range of para-professional and support staff, including classroom assistants, learning support mentors, home–school liaison officers, and a wide variety of behaviour and attendance support staff. These include education welfare officers, education social workers, attendance officers, advisers, consultants, educational psychologists, initial and in-service training tutors, voluntary service staff, health and social service professionals, as well as interested parents and carers.

Second, the contents of the book can be read cover to cover or dipped into for particular ideas. Explicitly, the evidence and practical activities outlined in the text can be used in senior management meetings or by behaviour support or behaviour management leadership teams within schools or local authorities or in other settings. They can inform agendas or be used to help draft or amend relevant documentation. Alternatively, they may provide a wide range of useful material for in-service or professional development events.

Third, the book may help more seasoned professionals to update their knowledge and skills in the field of behaviour management. This field is currently changing rapidly and significantly. The area has moved away from the old notions of control and discipline to one where pupils' views and rights are respected and incorporated into the planning. The new philosophy includes such concepts as values education, multidisciplinary and interdisciplinary practice, the Children Act agenda, inclusivity, diversity, individualised learning plans, well-being and respect and relationship policies, the role of the school council and parents' and carers' views, teachers' rights, restorative justice schemes, pupil support plans, sharing good practice and the use of websites and cyber bullying, to name but some of the emerging fields and issues. Long gone are the days when the emphasis was solely upon discipline, compliance and punishment.

Fourth, the content of the book focuses upon a wide range of responsibilities which schools, teachers, pupils, parents and local authorities manage, as well as considering such practical issues as managing case conferences, the role and use of nurture groups, improving school attendance, preventing bullying and the purpose of whole-school behaviour policies. Therefore, the content of the book is both substantial and broad. It concentrates, however, upon everyday practical life in primary schools. This Handbook does not attempt to provide in-depth specialist advice for those professionals who are concerned with serious psychological, specialist behavioural or mental health disorders such as school phobia, ADHD or Asperger's Syndrome. The authors strongly recommend the work of the Social, Emotional and Behavioural Difficulties Association (SEBDA) in this regard as well as such journals as *Emotional and Behavioural Difficulties* and the *British Journal of Educational Psychology*, in addition to specialist texts and websites.

Fifth, some of the chapters contain evidence and ideas based on our own work, such as the Family Values Scheme and the 5-Step Behaviour Programme. We have also incorporated some ideas from schools and local authorities with whom we have worked, with their prior agreement and consent.

Finally, Nicola and I hope very much that you will enjoy reading our book and using and playing around with the text for your own professional benefits.

Ken and Nicola, South Wales

Acknowledgements

Ken and Nicola would like to thank the following for their help, advice and support: Gill Ellis, Mark Provis, selected members of the NBAR Group, various head teachers and staff within selected primary schools and local authorities including the City and County of Cardiff, Torfaen, Hereford and Derby, Nant Celyn Primary and the Ysgol Plasmawr Cluster. In some cases we have used the actual names of individual schools or local authorities with their prior knowledge and consent (e.g. Coed Eva Primary School). In others, with the prior agreement of staff, we have changed the name of a particular school to avoid identification whilst retaining the authenticity of the documentation. Case names referred to in the text have all been changed to avoid any risk of identification.

Part I

Setting the scene

Chapter 1

New approaches 1
Managing behaviour in the primary school

Introduction

Managing behaviour in the primary school is a fast evolving field. The subject has moved quickly away from the old notions of control and discipline to the point where pupils' rights and views are respected and incorporated into the planning processes. The whole concept of both the meaning and content of primary school management has changed. The new philosophy incorporates such concepts and topics as values education, multidisciplinary and interdisciplinary practice, inclusivity, diversity, individualised learning plans, well-being and respect and relationship policies, the role of the school council and respecting parents' and teachers' views and rights, the creation of pupil support plans, restorative justice, sharing good practice, the use of specific websites, e-mail and the combating of unfortunate acts of cyber bullying, to name but a few of the emergent fields.

Reading the texts of thirty, forty or fifty years ago, you would find none of these ideas. In fact, in those days very few books on primary school management even existed. The area was largely represented and dominated by secondary textbooks written about discipline, control and punishment, with the ideas applied to primary schools. Today, everything has changed to the extent that it is possible to find whole texts written solely about individual aspects of primary school management such as applying restorative justice schemes or understanding cyber bullying and children's rights.

Similarly, thirty, forty or fifty years ago the whole landscape of primary school classrooms was different. For the average practitioner it was about teaching your class of perhaps thirty to thirty-five pupils on your own on a daily basis, finding time to undertake reading sessions with individual pupils, mounting classroom displays and, occasionally, talking to parents. Operating at a higher level above you as your inspiration and mentor was your experienced teaching head teacher or, in the larger primaries, your non-teaching head as a full-time administrator or manager. There were no computers, word-processors, laptops, mobile phones or the ilk. The curriculum was largely unstructured and open-ended. How staff of that era would feel looking inside the modern primary school classroom of today would be difficult to imagine. Would they be envious? Would they revel in the challenge?

Today's primary school classrooms are about much more than the teacher and her class. They are about the teacher, her class and her support team, and how together they manage the curriculum, behaviour and the pupils' learning and workloads. Your school, its size and location and where and how you teach, as well as the composition of your class (e.g. pupils with special or additional learning needs), may determine the culture and teaching styles inside your classroom. Your class may involve, in addition to the class teacher, such staff as one or more of the following: classroom assistant (CA), learning school mentor (LSM), home–school liaison officer (HSLO) or specialist behaviour or attendance support professionals. The teacher and head teacher can be involved regularly with a range of support or caring professionals such as education welfare officers, education social workers, advisers, consultants, educational psychologists, initial training or in-service tutors, voluntary support staff, health and social service professionals, parent helpers or parent/carer groups, local authority (LA) support staff, playground assistants, amongst many more. The head teacher and classroom teacher will play the leading professional roles, managing the school or playing the role of extended leader in the classroom, guiding a specialist team in implementing the National Curriculum, and supporting the pupils' diverse learning support and developmental needs. Included in these latter tasks is the management of pupils' behaviour and this is what the rest of this Handbook is about.

The position is complicated further by the contrasting educational frameworks and policies being implemented and carried out by different United Kingdom governments and by different administrations, local governments and states around the world, such as in Australia, Europe, Canada and the United States. For example, in Wales primary schools now follow the Foundation Phase National Curriculum, which is play-led and pupil-centred for pupils aged between three and seven, and all of these different national policies and strategies have an effect upon the ethos, organisation and culture of primary schools and teachers' classrooms.

There is abundant evidence also that many primary school teachers and head teachers and primary-support professionals (NBAR, 2007, 2008) feel strongly that they have a wide range of training needs and practical deficits on aspects of managing behaviour in their schools and classrooms. In extreme circumstances, these deficits and their inabilities to manage challenging pupils in their classrooms can impact negatively not only their professional lives but also their personal daily lives and even lead to some teachers leaving the profession, which is, if nothing else, a waste of scarce resources in these difficult financial times. The failure to be able to manage challenging pupils is regularly reported to be the number one cause of stress amongst teachers in frequent teacher-based surveys conducted by both professional organisations and researchers. Other reports and surveys often refer to the inadequacies in or lack of training provided on school behaviour management at the initial teacher education, induction and in-service phases, whilst requests for specific training on aspects of primary school management feature at the top of surveys into teachers' professional development needs (DfES, 2005; Cole, 2007).

For all these reasons, the content included in the rest of this book is broad, practical and intended to be both informative and helpful to all those staff interested in managing primary schools effectively as well as interested professionals and parents. The content covered in the remainder of this book includes: tips for classroom professionals; the use of whole-school strategies on a range of issues, including well-being, respect and relationships policies, nurture groups, and the management of challenging behaviour and serious incidents; implementing the 5-Step Behaviour Programme and effective whole-school and classroom management skills; dealing with specific classroom difficulties and behaviour; managing positive behaviour in the playground; forming effective partnerships with parents; the Family Values Scheme (Ellis et al., 2012); and managing school attendance and bullying.

The Handbook has been divided into two convenient sections. Part I provides essential background information on managing behaviour in the primary school. The content of the rest of this chapter covers:

- the role of the head teacher and senior management team (SMT);
- values-based education;
- social and emotional learning;
- defining social, emotional and behavioural difficulties;
- responding to pupils with social, emotional and behavioural difficulties;
- SEAL, Webster-Stratton and the Solihull Approach;
- the challenge of bad behaviour;
- SEBDA;
- the Children Act, 2004, and the Every Child Matters agenda;
- related interdisciplinary and multidisciplinary approaches;

- pupils' rights;
- research into pupils' views;
- how to elicit pupils' views;
- inclusivity, equal opportunities, diversity;
- the school council;
- how to use the school council effectively;
- the role of governors;
- the use of nurture groups.

In Chapter 2, we will consider the five levels at which to address behaviour management, from the national to the individual level. Then in Chapter 3 we will discuss the following:

- respect and relationships policies;
- a well-being policy document;
- the various categories for classifying pupils' behaviour;
- the role of the primary behaviour support team.

Finally, in the introductory section for this book, we will present and discuss the following related issues by way of bringing our essential background information to a close:

- school-based case conferences and the use of case studies and case histories;
- making home visits;
- monitoring and follow-up;
- links with secondary schools;
- sharing good practice;
- the use of websites;
- leading aspect awards;
- TES Schools awards;
- training in behavioural management;
- the role of inspectors;
- the role of classroom assistants, learning school mentors and home–school liaison officers;
- the role of playground assistants;
- time management, decision-making and record keeping;
- restorative justice;
- the role of parents and carers.

The role of the head teacher and the SMT

All good primary schools have a senior management team (SMT) unless they are a very small one- or two-teacher school, and these are often found in extremely rural areas. SMTs vary in their meeting arrangements. Some meet weekly; others fortnightly. These meetings are normally augmented by full staff meetings, which usually take place before the start of each new term/year, at the end of sessions and as and when necessary (e.g. before or after half-terms). Sometimes they occur more frequently, as when, for example, there are major changes to the National Curriculum (NC), or in the period leading up to a school inspection or when a school is suffering from an outbreak of disaffection amongst its pupils.

Partly because the management of pupils' behaviour has become so important, many schools now have a separate behaviour management team (BMT). Whereas the composition of the senior management team is fairly obvious (normally head teacher, designated deputy and one or two senior members of staff), the make-up of the BMT appears to vary much more, often from school to school, partly because the composition might be dependent upon location, a school's history and ethos, its record on attendance, behaviour, bullying, exclusions (both fixed and permanent), and parental–school interaction and out-of-school and community links.

Take these two examples. School A has 550 pupils and is based in the heartlands of the South Wales Valleys. It has an overall attendance rate of 88 per cent and has excluded thirty-seven pupils for fifty-three separate major incidents over the course of the previous year. Over 95 per cent of the parents emanate from two deprived neighbouring estates which are riddled with poverty, vandalism and serious cases of familial breakdown. Its BMT consists of the head teacher (chair), two deputies, a senior member of staff, the special educational needs co-ordinator (SENCO), an external consultant and a senior member of the LA's Behaviour Support Team. It has a lot of regular business to attend to and meets at least fortnightly. Writing referrals on pupils' attendance or behaviour is a routine daily event. Bullying incidents within school, within the community and on the way to and from school are regular events. So is maintaining interview notes with pupils and/or parents or carers and a wide range of external bodies such as the police, social services, health, voluntary agencies, health visitors and relevant LA staff, such as the education welfare service and educational psychology service. The BMT currently feels unable to incorporate pupils because of the serious and confidential nature of its work/tasks.

School B is located in Leicestershire. It has eighty pupils drawn mainly from middle-class and reasonably educated backgrounds. It is located on the edge of a small rural town not too far from Rutland Water. Its overall attendance rate is 98.5 per cent. In the previous twelve months there were no recorded incidents of bullying, truancy or the need for any exclusions. The BMT is composed of the head, deputy and a pupil representative.

Clearly, the length of the BMT agenda and the amount of time devoted to the issues differ significantly between the two schools. So do the teachers' stress and tolerance levels, their time management needs, the extent of the form filling and their overall in-school duties and responsibilities.

In fact, some might argue that School B hardly requires a BMT, apart from its Children Act responsibilities. This is why in so many primaries the SMT actually doubles up as the BMT and, in some schools, holds alternative management meetings or complete separate agendas in the same meeting.

The truth is that being a teacher, classroom assistant, learning school mentor or SENCO in School A bears little resemblance to being one in School B, although, in theory at least, both perform the same tasks. Also, both schools require a school council, a behaviour, school attendance and anti-bullying policy, and, again, in theory, a well-being and respect and relationships policy. You can probably guess which school of the two needs and uses them most. Record keeping strategies and the updating of pupils' records, agenda setting, pupils' progress reports, school-based and externally held pupils' case conferences are all part of thinking about, planning and carrying out daily activities and events within School A, and these tasks can test the patience and abilities of even the most competent head teacher on occasion.

It seems almost superfluous, then, to point out that the leadership skills and managerial competence of the head teacher and her SMT are probably the single most important element in a school's success or failure; not least in terms of conducting its behaviour management policies, strategies, follow-up actions and home–school liaison, as Heal (1978), in his study of primary pupils' misbehaviour, and Rutter *et al.* (1979) all those years ago first showed.

Values education

Values Education is a way of conceptualising education that places the search for meaning and purpose at the heart of the educational process. It recognises that the recognition, worth and integrity of all involved in the life and work of the school are central to the creation of a values-based learning community that fosters positive relationships and quality in education.

Behind my thinking lies an understanding and assumption that values-based education is far more than a process of instilling values in pupils. It is concerned with the very meaning and purpose of education; a statement about the quality of education can be achieved and the impact that this can have on society and the world. With this view of the role and purpose of education, schools that adopt a values-based approach can positively influence the development of positive values, which sustain a civil, caring and compassionate society.

(Dr Neil Hawkes, International Consultant)

Schools which have introduced values education into their vision for their schools have placed values at the heart and soul of their schools. In practice, having a values-based approach in school begins with the element of forging high-quality personal relationships. This means establishing good relationships not just between staff, pupils and parents but between all three groups. A values-based school is one where these high-quality values are lived on a daily basis and this is evident in a culture which is open, honest and harmonious. As adults we need to be the role models for the pupils in our care. When staff show and demonstrate these values to each other, this important message will be transmitted to the pupils, parents and carers alike. We will develop this theme further in Chapter 12.

Social and emotional learning

Social and emotional learning is the process through which children acquire the knowledge, attitudes and skills they need to recognise and manage their emotions, demonstrate caring and concern for others, establish positive relationships, make responsible decisions and handle challenging situations constructively. Research indicates that large numbers of children are contending with significant social, emotional and mental health barriers to their success in primary school and in later schooling and life.

Defining emotional, social and behavioural difficulties

There are many definitions of children who are perceived as having emotional, social and behavioural difficulties. For the purpose of this Handbook, these academic arguments are less important than having an appropriate understanding of the concepts involved.

Social, emotional and behavioural difficulties can arise from interactions in the home, peer group, school and community as they affect the individual child. They are frequently a sign of environmental pressure, unmet needs, emotional difficulties or the development of behaviour that enables the individual to cope under pressure.

Emotional, social and behavioural difficulties can manifest themselves in a variety of ways. These include acts of aggression, disruption, attention-seeking, anxiety, passivity, low motivation, withdrawal and depression.

Certain points stand out. First, the problems faced are unique to each person. Second, a school's ethos, culture and management of learning and discipline can have a significant impact upon individuals. Third, few children are inclined to express their difficulties in every setting all of the time and some are either unable or unwilling to do so, especially when it involves their home or family members. It is often the frequency, severity and persistence of this expression of their difficulties that defines the need for intervention.

Fourth, professional support and interventions should reflect the degree of difficulty experienced by the individual as well as the range of factors that caused these difficulties. Finally, help and support should aim to resolve the causes of these difficulties. It is important not to simply contain an individual's troubled behaviour. Otherwise, it is likely to recur.

Responding to pupils with emotional, social and behavioural difficulties

All primary teachers will from time to time have contact with some pupils whose behaviour is difficult, unusual or exceptional. Successful teaching and successful interventions are more likely when teachers, classroom assistants (CAs), learning school mentors (LSMs) and/or others:

- show a good understanding of the causes of such behaviour;
- plan preventively to reduce the potential 'trigger points' for pupils to misbehave;
- manage their interaction with their classes empathetically and effectively;
- make low-key responses to troubled behaviour (e.g. avoid knee-jerk reactions).

Where such behavioural difficulties persist, it is likely that the skilled and appropriate profes-sional intervention of supportive class teachers will provide pupils with their best chance of securing success.

When individual pupils persist in manifesting emotional, social and behavioural diffi-culties, class teachers should refer them to either their head teacher or the behaviour support tutor. Sometimes a school-based case review is necessary, possibly as a precursor to making a referral to the local authority or another support agency. Sometimes full-scale need assessments are undertaken, possibly involving an educational psychologist, social worker, education welfare officer or behaviour support adviser, amongst others.

Many schools now utilise specialist curriculum materials to help staff teach pupils with emotional, social and behavioural difficulties. There are many such packs available to schools. Three of the best known and most widely used are the SEAL and Webster-Stratton materials and the Solihull Approach.

SEAL, Webster-Stratton and the Solihull Approach

SEAL materials

Presently, many primary schools utilise the Social and Emotional Aspects of Learning Materials (SEAL). These materials are intended to provide a whole-school approach to promoting social, emotional and behavioural skills for pupils. The materials provide a wide range of resources that can be used across the whole school for managing behaviour and emotional learning. These include such facets as working in partnership with parents and carers, problem-solving, assertiveness and circle time. The contents provide posters and photo-capable resources as well as CD-ROMs on issues such as children's emotional barom-eters, 'the feelings fan', ways to calm down, fireworks, working together (with self-review checklists) and feelings and thoughts on behaviour. The CD-ROMs include practical kits for drawing, listening to music and guidance on themed tasks.

SEAL resources are often incorporated in packs provided by local authorities for use by primary teachers in schools. These resources are aimed at providing schools with an explicit, structured whole-curriculum framework along with practical ideas for teaching social, emotional and behavioural skills to all children.

The Webster-Stratton Programme

Some other schools use the Webster-Stratton materials. These can be found in the book *How to Promote Children's Social and Emotional Competence*, written by Carolyn Webster-Stratton, published by Sage in 2000 and reprinted since.

The Webster-Stratton Programmes are internationally developed schemes for use with parents, teachers and children which offer a wide range of schemes at both primary and secondary levels. These schemes include programmes on parent training, teacher training and child social skills training. Taken collectively, they are known as 'The Incredible Years Programmes' (Webster-Stratton, 2006).

The Webster-Stratton philosophy is based on the idea that a child is the most precious of all human beings and his or her ability to withstand emotional and social challenges clearly rests upon a caring relationship between parent, teacher and child.

The Incredible Years Series Programmes have two related long-term goals. The first is to develop comprehensive treatment programmes for young children with early onset conduct problems. The second goal is the development of cost-effective, community-based, universal prevention programmes. These are intended for use by families and teachers of young children in order to promote social competence; and to prevent children from developing conduct disorders in the first place. The Incredible Years Programme aims to reduce conduct disorders in children by:

- decreasing negative behaviour and non-compliance with parents at home;
- decreasing peer aggression and disruptive behaviour in the classroom.

The Programme is also used to promote social, emotional and academic competence in children by increasing the following:

- children's social skills;
- children's understanding of their own feelings;
- children's conflict self-management skills by decreasing negative attributions;
- children's academic engagement, school readiness and co-operation with teachers.

The Solihull Approach

The Solihull Approach is an evidence-based theoretical model for working with children and their families, supported by training and comprehensive resource packs. Thousands in the children's workforce are using it across the UK and it has recently been adapted for use in primary schools. It provides a framework for behavioural interventions across a wide range of possible difficulties and leads to professionals making considered choices to help a child to learn and develop effectively. Many schools and children's centres also utilise the Solihull Approach methods and materials for their evidence-based parenting group work on 'Understanding Your Child's Behaviour'. Together, they provide a shared understanding for teachers and parents to work together.

In the boroughs where educational psychologists, school nurses and other practitioners are also trained in the Solihull Approach there are additional advantages from sharing the same language and understanding. The Solihull Approach provides all staff within primary schools with an understanding of brain development and how this development takes place within the context of relationships. It introduces the research messages about how children relate to one another and about how they learn to concentrate and control impulsive behaviour. This leads to a greater understanding of how children achieve their academic and social potential and assists staff in managing behaviour in the classroom.

The challenge of bad behaviour

It is quite normal for all pupils to exhibit bad behaviour from time to time. This is often manifest in pupils behaving less co-operatively or being less responsive than usual. Behaviour only becomes really problematic when it is either extreme and/or exceptional (e.g. completely unexpected and out of character) or when it is relatively low key but frequent in its occurrence (e.g. talking every time a teacher wishes to make a point).

Sometimes pupils' difficult behaviour can reach problematic proportions. Teachers will often find an individual pupil's behaviour will become particularly challenging in the following circumstances:

- when it inhibits his or her learning – resulting in underperformance;
- when it impacts on the learning of others – resulting in underachievement;
- when it irritates and annoys staff – upsetting a teacher's equilibrium;
- when it interrupts the delivery of a planned lesson – undermining a teacher's role, position and authority and spoiling the learning experience;
- when it invites a response (e.g. challenging behaviour). This is the most threatening to teachers and often makes them feel threatened and undermined. Teachers naturally tend to overreact to this last case more than to the first four, although exceptions abound. In this fifth case (challenging behaviour), it is often important to consult with colleagues or the head teacher for advice or reassurance.

It is extremely important that in a profession where teachers engage with a wide range of pupils (and parents and/or carers) they feel confident enough to discuss their concerns with colleagues. Failing to do so can often be problematic in itself and lead to unnecessary and protracted classroom conflict.

Teachers need to understand that there is often not one simple solution. A range of intervention strategies may be on offer. Selecting the best one for the occasion is often a task requiring skill and experience. This is where a colleague's advice can be helpful. Sometimes, your colleagues may be experiencing similar problems, even with the same pupil.

Generally, what enables teachers to be most effective is to understand the options, to select the right interaction or remedial strategy, and to implement it in as supportive a way as possible. Over time, as teachers gain more experience, the range of available strategies tends to increase, as do implementation confidence levels.

As a general rule, class teachers should always involve their head teacher (as a preliminary starting point) if they suspect any form of child abuse, bullying, substance misuse, victimisation, eating disorder, self-abuse or potentially serious emotional, social or behavioural disorder.

SEBDA

Many teachers and support professionals in the United Kingdom belong to the Society for the Education of Children with Social, Emotional and Behavioural Difficulties (SEBDA), which is a professional organisation for those who work with pupils who experience emotional, social or behavioural difficulties. SEBDA organises courses, training events and professional advice for its members. It also produces its own journal, *Emotional and Behavioural Difficulties*, which is published by Routledge several times a year. They also produce their own in-house magazine entitled *SEBDA News*, which also appears regularly several times a year.

The Children Act, 2004, and the Every Child Matters agenda

The focus of the Children Act, 2004, is upon improving every level of professional support for children perceived to be vulnerable and in need. The Act has led to the formation of Children's Services Departments within LAs in England and variations on this theme in Scotland and Wales. It is also leading to more integrated professional practice and closer liaison between health, education and social services. The theory is that once a professional refers a child or young person for help for a wide range of possible problems, a lead professional will take responsibility for co-ordinating the case work, assessment and longer-term practices. The reality is that the Children Act is operating more effectively in some parts of the UK and better within some LAs than others.

The main aim of the Children Act was to protect children from harm, abuse or neglect; particularly to ensure that some pupils do not fall between the boundaries of different LA services as recommended in the Laming Report (2003). The Laming Report recognised that all too often children experience difficulties at home or at school, but receive appropriate help and support much too late, sometimes after problems have reached crisis point.

The Children Act, 2004, therefore, sets out to ensure that all agencies involved in the universal framework of services that support children and young people to reach their full potential work together in a uniform and concerted way and follow the same core principles. These ideas and principles were originally established in the Green Paper Every Child Matters (2003). It has led to changes in how parents and carers are supported with, in theory at least, much earlier intervention, more accountability and integration between health, education and social services. Since the introduction of the new legislation some infant and primary schools have become all-the-year-round community centres with amended opening hours, particularly in order to meet the needs of disadvantaged youngsters and their families. Variations on how these children's centres operate abound, however. Moreover, there is a general professional feeling that some attendance and behavioural problems now receive too low a priority, often blighted by professional shortages within social service departments, high caseloads and local demands and preference being given to potentially or actually more serious cases.

Related interdisciplinary and multidisciplinary approaches

Figures 1.1 to 1.3 show diagrammatically how children services departments now jointly plan their intervention strategies for working with difficult and challenging pupils. The Children Act, 2004, was intended to make the interaction between local education, social service and health departments much easier and better co-ordinated, thereby avoiding duplication between agencies and providing more consistency and continuity of practice in providing support to vulnerable children and their families. Figure 1.2 shows the implementation of the Children and Young People's Plans and Partnerships at local authority level, while Figure 1.3

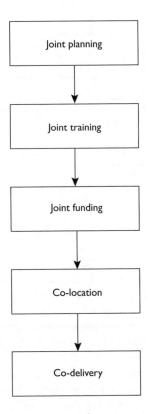

Figure 1.1 Securing effective inter-agency practice

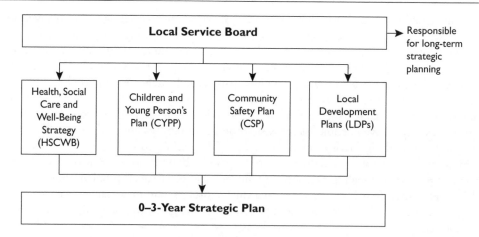

Figure 1.2 The implementation of the Children and Young People's Plans and Partnerships at local authority level

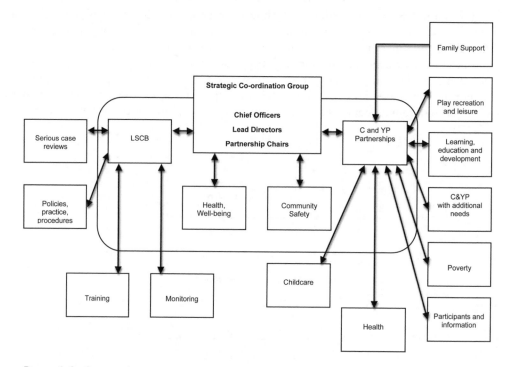

Figure 1.3 Community strategy

provides a local community strategy. It is important to appreciate that significant variations in practice exist between these functions, tasks and their organisation in England, Scotland, Northern Ireland and Wales, and therefore these diagrams are only illustrative.

The integrated team approach through children's services is intended to improve much earlier intervention and effective child protection by the following means:

• Improving information sharing between all local agencies to ensure each has the same list of children in need, of actions taken by the respective services, and of the correct contact details of the relevant professionals who work with the families and children. Information sharing is now supposedly the norm, with former professional barriers having been removed. Every child is given a unique, single identification number and single case file with, in principle, common data collection standards on the recording of information.

- Developing a common assessment framework (CAF) across all agencies and services for children. This covers a wide range of potential issues such as special educational needs, youth offending, child abuse, neglect, victimisation, as well as bullying, challenging behaviour and truancy.
- Ensuring, in theory at least, that a single named professional will be responsible for taking the lead on each case and for ensuring a coherent package of services to meet every child's needs. In practice, the high turnover of key staff, especially within social services, has bedevilled this core aim and blighted the continuity of the provision of services to some children and their families.
- Endeavouring to make sure that multidisciplinary teams are being encouraged to develop a one-stop, on-the-spot delivery of services. This is often based around or in schools or children's centres. The concept is to provide a rapid response to children's needs, especially those of young children.

Pupils' rights

The respect agenda and children and young people's rights are two of the fastest growing fields in educational policy and practice today. Their combined ideals as applied to primary school management are:

- to safeguard and protect the child through the considered management of behaviour, attendance and bullying;
- to provide all pupils with the right to a full-time, well-delivered education which meets their social, emotional and educational needs;
- to ensure social inclusion is at the centre of provision for children, with young people, parent(s) and carer(s) fully involved;
- to make sure behaviour, attendance and anti-bullying strategies are the responsibility of everyone who is engaged in the business of education;
- to ensure that child-centred and positive outcomes are of paramount importance in any educational and related activities;
- ideally, to ensure that managed interventions are prevention focused and made as soon as possible after an incident or episode;
- to ensure that these interventions are primarily curative, whilst at the same time recognising that some major interventions are necessary with deeply troubled pupils;
- to ensure that intervention techniques have a positive cost–benefit analysis;
- to make sure that equality of opportunity is applied to all children irrespective of race, colour or religious beliefs;
- to ensure everyone's rights are equally respected.

The four countries which comprise the United Kingdom are signed-up members of the United Nations Convention on the Rights of the Child. The UN's vision states that all children and young people should:

- have a comprehensive range of education and learning opportunities;
- enjoy the best possible health and be free from abuse, victimisation and exploitation;
- have access to play, leisure, sporting and cultural activities,
- be listened to, treated with respect, and have their race and cultural identity recognised;
- have a safe home and a community which supports physical and emotional well-being;
- not be disadvantaged by poverty.

Some countries, such as England and Wales, have their own Children's Commissioner, who has a team of officials to ensure that children and young people's rights are respected. Clearly, the areas of behaviour, bullying, victimisation and safety in schools fall well within this remit. Therefore, schools and their policy documents should comply with children and young people's rights. In creating these documents, it is sensible to take cognisance of pupils' voices either through the school council or in other ways. Later in the Handbook we will present some evidence on pupils' views on behaviour and attendance in relevant chapters.

Research into pupils' views

Since promoting pupils' rights and listening to pupils' voices became official policy, research in the field has started apace. Research and reports in Wales alone, for example, include the work of the Children and Young People's Consortium for Wales (2006), the Children and Young People's Commissioner's Report for Wales (2007), Funky Dragon Reports (2007a, 2007b), the Save the Children Report, Wales (2007) and the CAZBAH Report (2008). These latter findings and their implications can be found in two academic papers published in the journals *Education Studies* and *Educational Review* (Reid *et al.*, 2010a, 2010b). The CAZBAH study involved both primary and secondary age ranges, including significantly disadvantaged groups and out-of-school pupils. For the purposes of this Handbook only the primary findings on behaviour and attendance are now presented.

The findings on primary pupils' views on behaviour and attendance were ascertained from in-depth interviews with seventy-eight key stage 2 pupils aged between eight and eleven from eight primary schools located throughout and across Wales. Fifty-four per cent of the pupils were boys, the remainder girls; 87.2 per cent of the pupils were selected from mainstream schools and the remainder came from a specialist pupil referral unit (PRU); 12.8 per cent of those interviewed were from a range of ethnic minority groups.

Primary pupils' views on behaviour

The core findings were as follows:

1   There was a general respect for discipline as long as it was perceived to be 'fair'.
2   The children could be scathing about inconsistency in the way some teachers administered discipline, especially when staff acted upon a student's previous reputation without first checking the full facts.
3   The children felt that disciplinary measures (including codes of practice) should be made more explicit to them rather than simply being referred to in moments of crisis.
4   A small minority of pupils considered that some teachers are too weak when disciplining pupils. For example, some thought that teachers tended to be 'too lenient' and sometimes could be 'harsher' when applying punishments. This may have reflected the views of some pupils who were being 'turned off' by having their lessons interrupted or spoilt by the behaviour of some of their nonconformist peers.
5   The pupils felt that their classroom behaviour was influenced positively or negatively by specific classroom teachers. The teacher–pupil relationship was therefore crucial. The pupils particularly respected teachers who engaged them critically in the learning and teaching process.
6   The pupils were often especially critical about the use of supply teachers. Many saw supply teachers as 'fair game' and even admitted to changing their behaviour when their own classroom teachers were away from school.
7   The pupils were more likely to misbehave with teachers who were perceived to be 'robotic' (i.e. those that gave them too much 'copying up' or were perceived to be 'boring'). The pupils preferred more active, practical lessons which were 'stimulating'.

8   About half the pupils supported the use of mentoring or buddy systems to help develop good behaviour.

9   Some pupils disliked certain subjects more than others and, in some cases, behaved accordingly, even though these lessons were often taught by the same staff.

Primary pupils' views on attendance

The findings were as follows:

1   There was an almost universal understanding that missing school or choosing not to attend school regularly adversely affected pupils' long-term life chances. Pupils from every single primary school setting – including the PRU – understood the value of education and the consequences of missing out on it through non-attendance. By key stage 2, they could already begin to see a link between doing well at school and ending up with a good job/career and 'money'.

2   The pupils were especially concerned about bullying in their schools. Bullying was cited as the single most significant reason for not attending school by both boys and girls (Reid, 2008). Bullying was perceived to take several forms. This included physical and emotional bullying. It could occur within the community, on the way to or from school, as well as in school. Most pupils were aware of someone who was perceived to be being bullied.

3   Perhaps surprisingly, most of the key stage 2 pupils were already aware of the legal requirements of attending school as well as the consequences of not doing so. This was partly because both they and their parent(s) or carer(s) had been informed by their schools of the legal requirement for school attendance. They were mostly aware that truancy from school could lead to fines or a possible jail sentence for their parents or carers in extreme cases.

4   It was clear that attending school was seen as a social as well as an educational benefit, with friendships valued particularly highly. Amongst the benefits of going to school, 'making friends' and 'seeing my friends' came out close to the top in all group feedback sessions. An unexpected side-effect of this finding was an understanding that one of the consequences of non-attendance or bad behaviour might be them missing their friends or losing them altogether because their parents or carers would 'not let them play with me any longer'. Interestingly, 'not being allowed to see or play with friends' was feared by pupils more than other school-based sanctions such as 'being made to sit on your own', or 'being moved to an isolation unit'.

5   The quality of teaching was perceived to be a vital factor in pupils' decision-making about whether to attend school regularly or not. A classroom teacher the young person felt he or she had empathy with could provide support for him or her developing a positive pattern of school attendance. Conversely, a less empathetic teacher could enhance negative connotations regarding attendance. In extreme cases, a poor teacher–pupil relationship could be the prime reason for a pupil not going to school at all. This finding applied to both boys and girls and to pupils from mainstream settings as well as from PRUs.

6   As with behaviour, the use of supply teachers engendered keen criticism from some pupils. They were perceived as being 'powerless' and 'ineffective' – in some cases, an 'easy' target. Supply teachers were often perceived as being 'inconsistent' in their dealings with pupils and tended to single out some pupils 'unfairly'. This meant that some pupils disliked attending school when their regular classroom teacher was away.

7   Younger-age pupils seem to accept, enjoy and respond positively to school-based reward systems. The selective use of school trips, certificates and prizes seemed to work well. Most schools in the study used certificates or prizes for good attendance and this was appreciated by their pupils. Sports, recreational, aesthetic and other social activities were also cited as reasons for encouraging regular attendance. Some pupils felt that the more

incentives there were on offer, the better some pupils would respond to the attendance initiatives.

8   More pupils in the PRU group felt school tended to be 'boring and irrelevant' compared with their mainstream peers.

9   Individual tailor-made approaches (especially in one-to-one learning situations) which helped pupils to catch up on missed work/assignments were especially appreciated and the most successful in re-engaging those who were non-attenders or who had given up on school.

10 Some primary pupils felt they 'had a right' to miss school on the day of their birthday. This was perceived to be a 'treat'. Some schools even appeared to accept that pupils were becoming used to taking a day off on their birthdays. The exception to this was when some schools celebrated the young person's birthday in class. Some schools even provide birthday cakes and/or 'fizzy' drinks for the occasion.

11 The specific reasons given by the key stage 2 pupils for missing school in this study were: 'being ill', 'too tired', 'school being boring', 'being bullied', 'it's my birthday', 'being on holiday with parents', 'being accused of doing something wrong all the time', 'because teachers pick on you', 'having transport problems', 'parents or carers being ill', 'not doing homework' and 'feeling fed up'.

How to elicit pupils' views: a practical approach

Young pupils at key stage 1 or 2 may not respond particularly well to the use of questionnaires. If you wish to try to discover the views of young pupils in school why not try this approach.

Place the pupils in small focus groups, perhaps three or five per group. Then, voice record all answers to questions. Utilise written notes, flipcharts and Post-it notes for pupils and their groups to record their ideas.

Select an introductory theme – an icebreaking task to make the pupils feel comfortable and to start them on a focused task. Good icebreaker tasks will generate fun and empathy. Then, move on to a circle time activity. Select an appropriate theme to use. At stage three, involve visual questions, with voting taking place on the answers. At stage four, utilise a flipchart and Post-it notes, perhaps on the theme of 'feedback' and 'consequences' or similar tasks. At stage five, use a graffiti board. For the session on 'attendance', CAZBAH (2008) used the theme of 'rewards and sanctions'.

Flipcharts can be used for any two or more pupils, or with groups or for whole-class situations. Give each pairing or group questions at the top of the flipchart to discuss. These could be the same or different for each group.

The use of graffiti boards provides a chance for those who may have been reluctant to discuss their views openly in the class or group sessions to give their opinions. It is always important to ensure that all pupils participate in the feedback and that these sessions are not dominated by a few individuals.

The use of Post-it notes with a pen can provide encouragement for everyone to write their own ideas down. Then, get the pupils to stick their Post-it notes onto the flipchart. This can be done anonymously or openly.

Time each activity. Usually make the feedback session last no more than one hour. Allow no more than ten or fifteen minutes for each task.

After the feedback and information-gathering sessions are over, the data should be collated. Afterwards, feed back the results to the whole class and then ascertain and discuss their reactions to the findings. Add to or change the feedback results based on their whole-class responses.

Make sure during the feedback sessions that:

●   all pupils participate;
●   all pupils' views are treated with equal respect;

- the results are forwarded to the school council for further information and/or discussion.

Inclusivity, equal opportunities and diversity

In managing inclusivity, equal opportunities and diversity, it is important not to focus solely upon quotas, targets and statistics, although these all need to be taken into account, but instead:

- to examine all the pupils' requirements in terms of their attendance, behavioural and anti-bullying needs, as well as in the context of:
  - their special or additional learning needs;
  - their disabilities or special requirements;
  - any psychological, emotional or familial handicaps;
- to be consistent with pupils and their parents or carers in how the behavioural policies are applied;
- to ensure there is no discrimination in terms of gender, race or religion.

A useful definition of inclusivity is set out in the NBAR Report, which states:

> Inclusive education is an ongoing process concerned with ensuring equality of educational opportunity by accounting for and addressing the diversity present in schools. It requires the commitment of schools and LAs to develop policies and practices that ensure equality of educational opportunity and access; safeguard vulnerable pupils; and focus on raising the achievement of all learners and increasing their participation in their schools and local communities.
>
> (NBAR, 2008: 15)

A key concept within this definition is that of additional learning needs (ALN), which can be defined as follows:

> The term 'additional learning needs' includes those learners who require additional support either due to their circumstances or because they have a longer-term disorder or condition. In many cases, for example through sickness or where a family is experiencing temporary difficulties, children and young people may have additional learning needs for a short period only.
>
> (NBAR, 2008: 15)

The school council

It was envisaged that the establishment of effective, well-organised school councils would lead to better teacher–pupil relationships and to pupils' voices gaining more respect and consideration. The Children Act agenda anticipated pupils gaining in confidence, developing greater feelings of participation and ownership for the school and even having a say in the organisation and running of the school at the governing body level, including in the making of teacher and head teacher appointments. There is little doubt that some school councils currently operate more effectively than others and that some are taken more seriously and have more of an influence than others. The range in the type of school councils which are presently operating extends from those which are merely given lip-service by staff and are often teacher dominated and/or controlled to those which are fully participatory and well respected, well managed and run smoothly (Estyn, 2008).

Some schools utilise school council websites and e-mail and internet communication strategies. Others remain organised along old-fashioned and traditional lines. In some schools, the impact of school councils appears to be limited to influencing decisions about practical arrangements, such as matters about school uniform, toilet facilities and meal options. In the best they are involved in school-based surveys, policy-making and decision-making, in financial issues, assessment matters, appointments and drafting documents which lead to attendance, behavioural and anti-bullying policy documents and their subsequent reviews. Increasingly, too, school councils are becoming involved in school inspections and internal school review procedures.

At a national level, policies currently differ. The Welsh Assembly, for example, has created a Children and Young People's Assembly for Wales. This is attended by school council representatives from across Wales.

Using the school council

Below are some common tips to help run a school council effectively.

TIPS: How to make your school council effective

- Find out about the interest of the pupils through surveys and make a list of activities in which they have expressed an interest.
- Make sure there is a good selection of council members to ensure its success. It is important that members of the council are enthusiastic, proactive and vigilant, co-operate with peers and have leadership qualities.
- Organise group meetings at regular intervals throughout the term in order to discuss the relevant agenda as well as other interesting topics. These might include a range of school policies, including behaviour, attendance, bullying, school uniform, out-of-school activities, etc.
- The school council is ultimately for the benefit of the pupils so ensure they assume ownership and are actively involved. Use assembly and suggestion boxes to encourage ideas for inclusion on the agenda. Schools should endeavour to avoid all-teacher-dominated agenda items as pupils may soon lose interest. One positive idea is to encourage pupils to take surveys on specific ideas discussed at meetings to provide meaningful evidence.

The role of governors

Increasingly, the role of governors is getting heavier, broader and more time consuming. Nevertheless, it is extremely important that the Board of Governors consider on an annual basis at least the following:

- The school attendance data, including unauthorised absences, court prosecutions of parent(s) of pupils from their schools and the outcomes, and whether to amend or update the school attendance strategy and policy document.
- The data on behaviour, including the number of fixed-term and permanent exclusions, the effectiveness of the anti-bullying policy or otherwise.
- The school's well-being and respect and relationships policy document and its effectiveness.
- The views of pupils and the school council on the above issues and any specific concerns from amongst the student body.
- The governors include in the annual performance review of the head teacher issues concerned with behaviour, bullying, school attendance and exclusions, and listen to any of her concerns on these issues.

The use of nurture groups

Nurture groups

Nurture groups provide effective learning environments for children with social, emotional and behavioural difficulties derived from attachment issues. Depending on the child's background and experiences (disruptive relationships and/or limited early learning experiences) they can either display high emotions or be very withdrawn.

Nurture groups have been shown to be an effective short-term intervention, therefore children remain in the nurture group for no more than four school terms; except in exceptional circumstances, the child is then reintegrated back into their mainstream class. The nurture group staff work closely with the child's class teacher to start on the reintegration process as soon as the child re-enters the group.

Background

In 1969, Marjorie Boxall, an educational psychologist for Inner London Education Authority, started nurture groups for children from stressful or disrupted backgrounds. She realised that most of these children were unable to make trusting relationships with adults or engage appropriately with other children because of inadequate early nurturing. By providing a safe place in school she was able to create the right environment where these children could develop and grow.

Research

There has been a lot of evidence to support nurture groups since they started in 1969. The main emphasis is based on Bowlby's attachment theory, the relationship between the child and the adult. This theory identifies the way that high-quality and positive early experiences in a child's development interact and affect behaviour. The therapy which nurture groups provide helps to reverse the damage caused through neglect or abuse.

The effectiveness of nurture groups was researched by Iszatt and Wasilewska (1997). They looked at two sets of children with emotional and behavioural difficulties. One set of children were placed in a nurture group and one set in a mainstream school. The group who had not received the support of a nurture group were three times more likely to require formal assessments than those in the nurture group and seven times more likely to require special school provision.

How nurture groups work

Within a nurture group there will be between six and twelve children, with one teacher and one teaching assistant. Before a child is accepted into a nurture group assessments are made and a series of observations carried out. The parent(s)/carer(s) are encouraged to support the programme and consent is always obtained before the child starts the group.

The nurture group environment is a crucial factor in its success. It is designed to help the child feel cared for and safe. Children are encouraged and supported to help develop a trusting relationship with an adult. Over time the child's self-esteem, self-respect and a sense of well-being are increased, resulting in them feeling happier, more confident and more motivated to learn. The children also begin to learn to use effective social skills and adopt alternative strategies to use in difficult situations.

The nurturing atmosphere in the room is created by including a sofa and a cooking area. The cooking area is a fundamental part of the room as this is where the children eat their breakfast and snacks and they are encouraged to share through communication anything of interest or concern, which provides an excellent opportunity for social learning.

Typically, the children register with their mainstream class and are collected and taken to the nurture group. The children are reintegrated with the rest of the school during lunch and breaks.

A nurture group:

- develops well-being through relationship building;
- values individuals' achievements;
- promotes the personal, social and emotional well-being of everyone involved;
- understands that how we feel can affect the way we learn and interact;
- creates a safe environment within the classroom ensuring rules, routines and positive reinforcements are in place;
- understands developmentally the learning of children – staff address the children's emotional and developmental needs, which encourages them to develop further;
- develops positive relationships to improve children's self-esteem and to make them feel they are valued individuals;
- communicates and prepares children for changes in their daily routine, for example going to lunch early, a class trip, visitors, a supply teacher.

Staff understand that changes such as these can be overwhelming and unsettling for some children, and staff are helped to understand the child's behaviour and provide them with proactive and reactive strategies to help defuse situations in a calm way. The Boxall Profile can be used to help with this process. (The Boxall Profile is a two-part checklist which provides an assessment framework for the child and an intervention plan for staff. The Boxall Profile is completed by staff who know the child.)

A typical day in a nurture group

A typical day in a nurture group should be 'equivalent to the first three years at home' (Boxall, 2002). This is achieved by keeping to the same routine, including the same people, place and times, which helps to develop the child's trust and self-esteem. Below is an example of a typical day in a nurture group, which is intended as guidance only. It has been adapted from the book *Running a Nurture Group* by Simon Bishop (2008).

TIPS: A typical day in a nurture group

9.00–9.40	Register
	Showing
	What are we doing today?
	Action songs
	Preparing for breakfast
9.40–10.10	Breakfast
10.15–10.30	Assembly
10.30–10.45	Playtime
10.45–12.15	Free-choice activities
	Literacy
	Maths
12.15–1.15	Lunch
1.15–1.30	Reading
1.30–2.30	Monday: games outside
	Tuesday: art activities
	Wednesday: trip to shops for ingredients

2.30–3.15	Thursday: cooking Friday: in classes Key stage 1: children out to play and back to class Key stage 2: children return to class at 2.45

Characteristics of nurture groups

The Nurture Groups Research Project, in consultation with members of the Nurture Group Network and staff working in nurture groups, devised the following list of characteristics which should be evident in nurture groups (Boxall, 2002):

TIPS: Characteristics of a nurture group

A nurture group should:

- be located clearly within the policies and structures of a local authority or school continuum of special educational needs provision, either as an integral part of an individual school or as a resource for a cluster of schools;
- ensure that children attending the nurture group remain members of a mainstream class where they register daily and attend selected activities;
- have a pattern of attendance whereby children spend part of each day in the nurture group or attend for regular sessions during the week;
- be staffed by two adults working together modelling good adult relationships in a structured and predictable environment, which encourages children to begin to trust adults and to learn;
- offer support for children's positive emotional and social growth and cognitive development at whatever level of need the children show by responding to them in a developmentally appropriate way;
- supply a setting and relationships for children in which missing or insufficiently internalised essential early learning experiences are provided;
- ensure that relevant National Curriculum guidelines are followed for all children;
- be taken full account of in school policies, participate fully, and be fully considered in the development and review of policies;
- offer short- or medium-term placements, usually for between two and four terms, depending on the child's specific needs;
- ensure placement in the group is determined on the basis of systematic assessment in which appropriate diagnostic and evaluative instruments have been used, with the aim always being to return the child to full-time mainstream provision;
- place an emphasis on communication and language development through intensive interaction with an adult and with other children;
- provide opportunities for social learning through co-operation and play with others in a group with an appropriate mix of children;
- monitor and evaluate its effectiveness in promoting the positive social, emotional and educational development of each child;
- recognise the importance of quality play experiences in the development of children's learning.

Summary

In this chapter we have begun to set the scene for the remainder of this book. We have considered issues ranging from the role of the head teacher and senior and behaviour management teams to the new Children Act agenda, pupils' rights, the school council and the use of nurture groups, as well as the interdisciplinary and multidisciplinary context in which managing pupils' behaviour within primary schools now takes place. In Chapter 2, we will begin by considering the five levels at which to address behaviour, from the role of the national government and its administrative departments to the role of the local authority, school and teachers at a variety of levels.

New approaches 2
The five levels at which to address behaviour

In this chapter we will continue the theme established in Chapter 1 by considering the five levels at which to address behaviour, from the national strategic level down through to the individual pupil level. In Chapter 3 we will develop some of these themes through a consideration of respect and relationship and well-being policy documents, the various categories of pupils' behaviour and the role of the primary behaviour support team.

Five levels at which to address behaviour

Figure 2.1 shows the five levels at which to address behaviour. These are:

- the national government level;
- the LA and other service levels;
- the school level;
- the classroom level;
- the individual level.

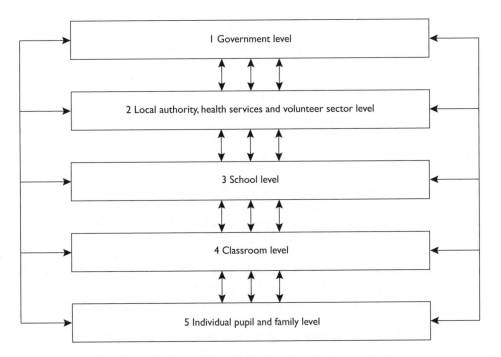

Figure 2.1 Five levels at which to address behaviour

We will now consider each of these five levels in turn.

1. THE NATIONAL LEVEL

National governments drive the behavioural management agenda. They create policies for teachers, schools, LAs and other support agencies to follow. They provide guidance and the regulatory frameworks for the sector to follow. Their actions are driven by the legislative requirements of national Parliaments or Assemblies. Therefore, following the passing of the Anti-Social Behaviour Act in 2003 a whole raft of new policy and guidance notes were issued for LAs, the police and schools, amongst others, to follow. For example, the kind of work and tasks being carried out at a strategic level by these national governments currently includes some of the ideas below, although these are constantly changing and being updated and new policies are being formed, created and implemented as new legislation is passed.

Figure 2.2 presents a possible national strategy for all schools which are facing issues in managing behaviour and we will develop some of these themes as we continue this chapter.

National governments and their supporting civil service departments are responsible for the following:

1 Developing a national strategy for improving pupils' behaviour and attendance and constantly reviewing these frameworks, regulations and policies.
2 Establishing and constantly improving the framework for better and more effective inter-agency practice in responding to pupils with social, emotional and behavioural difficulties (SEBD).
3 Devising common standards for all systems that encourage strategic managers to measure success by the extent to which frontline practitioners engage in effective, complementary practice in responding to the needs of children and young people with SEBD.
4 Devising standards for agency practice in meeting the needs of children and young people with SEBD. These standards include:
   • how to ensure that all school staff have an appropriate level of training in behaviour management;
   • how to minimise the use of exclusions as a means of coping with unwanted behaviours;
   • how to ensure excluded pupils receive their statutory rights to full-time equivalent learning;
   • how to make sure that SEBD pupils have their needs statutorily assessed and met under national Special Needs Codes of Practice;
   • how to support pupils with SEBD in mainstream schools.

At a national and strategic level, government departments (e.g. the Department for Education (DfES)) also have to establish how to meet and manage such important issues as the following:

• how best to interact with parents and voluntary and caring agencies involved in supporting SEBD children;
• promoting better common standards and increased collaboration between LAs and other agencies in meeting pupils' SEBD needs, across a wide spectrum of activity but particularly in the area of meeting the needs of the most vulnerable and challenging children;
• developing detailed practical guidance on a range of key issues that includes examples of excellent practice – the fields where this information is required include:
   – dealing with and meeting the needs of pupils who are being bullied, including sexual and cyber bullying;
   – dealing with and meeting the needs of looked after children;
   – physical intervention strategies to make pupils safe;
   – alcohol misuse;

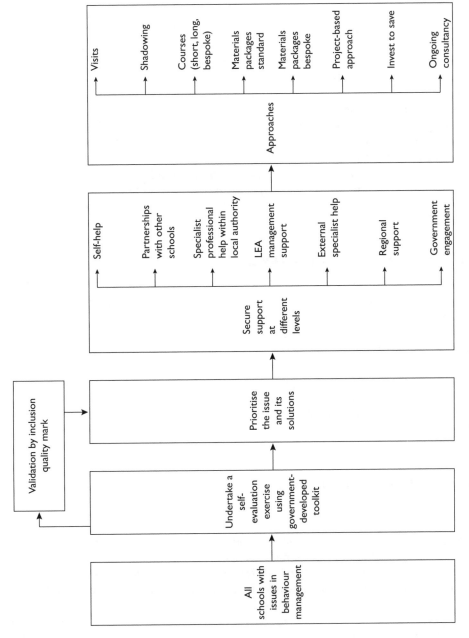

Figure 2.2 A national strategy for all schools facing issues in managing behaviour

- drug misuse and abuse;
- attention deficit hyperactivity disorder (ADHD) and medication for behavioural problems;
- attention deficit disorder (ADD), autistic spectrum disorders (ASD), etc.;
- weapons in schools;
- engaging parental support and parental group organisations;
- developing literacy and numeracy strategies.

It is especially important to develop clear guidance on the effective use of physical intervention to make all pupils and teachers feel safe during their time in school.

At the enabling level, national governments can create and provide useful and good practice guidelines on dedicated websites, through appropriate publications in specific fields (e.g. on managing autism in mainstream schools); through the provision and funding of relevant and up-to-date training and development programmes; by undertaking and sponsoring research; by promoting developmental projects and funding in difficult or emerging areas; by analysing and evaluating local and national data and writing related reports; by driving re-inclusion and reintegration strategies; by amending and updating policy directives and guidelines; and by establishing, where or as necessary, specific task and finish or review groups, working parties, steering groups or projects or, as and when things go badly wrong or require further investigation, by establishing major committees of enquiry such as occurred with the Laming Report (2003).

2. THE LOCAL AUTHORITY LEVEL

In terms of the management of behaviour in schools, the LA, with its partner organisations, provides the policy framework and support system in which schools can thrive and flourish. LAs have a direct and distinct role in supporting schools through their policies, procedures and practices. The framework partnership through a collegiate approach with other agencies should provide consistency and coherence across their area to encompass all bodies that are involved with children and young people. Since the Children Act, 2004, the innovation of the single Children and Young People's Plan (referred to differently in different regions of the UK) seems to be contributing towards an enhanced dialogue between education, health, social care, police, youth offending services and the voluntary sector about improving their joint approach to their work with children and young people, as indicated in Figure 1.2 (p. 12).

The role of the local authority

Prevention

Local authorities work closely with schools, other providers and support agencies, national and regional organisations to reduce the likelihood of behavioural difficulties in school and amongst difficult and disaffected pupils. Effective teaching and learning is a key factor in keeping the level of behavioural difficulties to a minimum, along with the sound leadership and management of schools. Evidence suggests that well-prepared, interesting and well-differentiated lessons are less likely to be disrupted by difficult pupil behaviour. Local authorities, through their school improvement strategies, have a clear responsibility to monitor and enhance the quality of teaching and learning across all our schools.

As a critical friend

LAs gather both qualitative and quantitative data on a wide range of performance issues in schools. In terms of behaviour, some of these benchmark indicators are:

- the level of attendance, by school, within schools, by area, by phase and type of school, by gender, etc.;
- the level of parental participation in parents' evenings;
- the number of fixed-term and permanent exclusions, including individual school statistics;
- the number of managed transfers or managed moves;
- the number of pupils with special or additional learning needs, behavioural difficulties, or those falling below key stage 1 or 2 benchmark targets and having reading, literacy and numeracy difficulties, amongst others.

Sometimes the aggregation or individual results of these benchmarks may provide a clue to and even be a good measure of an individual primary school's difficulties and provide a guide to how a school is managing its pupils' behaviour. One of the roles of the LA as a critical friend is to enable a school to assess and consider its own data, to analyse their significance for the school's practice and to address any issues arising.

Of course, to be truly effective this role needs to be implemented alongside a similar investment in parenting education. In this way, both children and young people and parents and carers receive a consistent message about acceptable behaviour and how to achieve it.

As a provider of services

LAs provide schools with a range of professional support services. In terms of behaviour, these include the education psychology service, education welfare service, school improvement, advisory and advisory teacher service, special/additional learning needs and support, governors' support, equal opportunities, disability and ethnicity support, amongst a range of other potential roles. The precise nature of the organisation, roles and responsibilities of individual LAs varies from LA to LA depending upon such factors as location, size, country, need and local or regional culture and history.

For example, at one end of the spectrum, visiting specialist behaviour teachers might:

- observe and assess pupils;
- provide advice or guidance to class teachers, LSMs or classroom assistants;
- engage directly with a pupil;
- engage with a pupil(s) and parents/carers together or separately.

Such work might be supported by the work of the educational psychologist and, ideally, be reinforced by an educational psychologist who specialises in managing and changing pupil behaviour.

At the more challenging end of this continuum the LA might provide the services of specialised centres, such as pupil referral units, alternative curriculum centres, personalised learning, home tuition or specialist mental health support groups/centres, special educational needs schools or specialist units (e.g. an autistic centre), amongst other possibilities.

In participating in inter-agency and multi-agency practice

One of the major problems facing parents/carers, teachers and schools is the complexity of the number and different types of services which are currently available to help pupils with behavioural difficulties, special educational needs or disabilities, amongst others. Some parents and teachers, for example, are unaware of what different services can and cannot do (NBAR, 2008: 117–120). Some parents and teachers may hold unreal expectations from some services. Others fail to understand the constraints of working with high caseloads with limited numbers of staff. Many have very little understanding of how to access grants, make referrals or cross-referrals or gain access to specialist advice (e.g. a clinical psychologist). Since the advent of the Children Act, 2004, these aspects of LA services may have begun to improve. However, all good LAs should now provide a communications directory which sets out the names, departments and responsibilities of key staff, a central or specialist helpline number(s) and other fundamental information about the role and support provided by the authority.

The policy of local authorities on behaviour management

Sound behaviour resource packs created by local authorities will also provide information on the structure and management of the services available from the local authority. Therefore, they will show the internal management of responsibilities from the Children's Director or Director of Children's Services through to the Director of Education, Head of Inclusion, Behaviour Support, Education Psychology, Welfare, Special Needs and Education Otherwise, amongst others.

Presently, local authorities in the UK are concentrating on establishing good practice at a variety of levels. These are as follows:

- *Policy level*: local authorities are endeavouring to promote inclusive practice, provide training and professional development for mainstream teachers in the skills of behaviour management, refining and reinforcing their approach and supporting schools in their interventions with individuals and groups of pupils.
- *Out-of-school provision*: developing provision to meet the needs of those pupils who, for whatever reason, have lost their place in mainstream schools. Therefore, they are fast developing their on-site provision, robust off-site provision, as well as developing alternative and wider curriculum approaches particularly for pupils in challenging circumstances. Unfortunately, the extent of on-site and off-site and alternative curriculum provision varies throughout the UK in terms of availability, type and utility.

  Ideally, good local authorities will encourage schools to manage their own behavioural-problem pupils as much as possible by improving their own capacities to do so.
- *Whole-school and whole-authority approaches*: irrespective of the support systems developed by the local authority, the individual primary teacher's capacity to manage behaviour effectively is much more likely to be influenced by the context of the school in which she works.

  The management of behaviour by an individual teacher will be affected by a school's own policy document. This may include the school's vision: the ambition that the whole school community shares as to the kind of school everyone is striving to build. It will also be affected by a school's aims and objectives. This may include ways in which the school will develop in the medium and longer term and the steps that the school will take to achieve these goals.

  Whilst aims and objectives can be tangible and practical, developing an ethos based on shared core values can sometimes seem an elusive goal. After all, staff views can fundamentally differ, as can personalities. These potential difficulties should never be allowed to impede a school's consistent use of its school policy document on behaviour. A school is only as good as all the bricks in its wall. This means the management of behaviour is always a team game.

  This team game ethos affects a school's 'climate' and can be sensed by astute pupils within classrooms, corridors and playgrounds and in its communication with its community, parents and external agencies.
- *Sharing culture*: therefore, the best local authorities and schools strive to develop a shared culture. This can be the most challenging element. It means turning ideals and aims and objectives into day-to-day practice. When schools, staff, pupils and parents and the wider community share a common culture then it becomes much simpler to implement consistent responses to behaviour. In such a scenario, the confidence levels of all engaged in the enterprise, including parents and pupils, are raised significantly.

- *Best practice*: in the best-case scenario, interactions between key local authority staff and schools are seamless daily or regular events. Consultation between the two organisations is best when it is advisory and empathetic and helps to reduce and manage conflicts (e.g. exclusions).

Local authorities can help schools to organise and manage case reviews, conferences, in-service training events, disciplinary hearings and, in particularly serious cases (e.g. child abuse), the legal issues.

A sound local authority resource pack or behaviour pack will cover all these practical issues and facilitate hearings which involve members of governing bodies (e.g. appeals against permanent or fixed-term exclusions). The local authority resource pack should be intended to provide schools with a helpful, practical resource which means that teachers can focus their main attention on pupils' learning, knowing that the 'behaviour bible' is always available for their use.

The resource pack

Local authority resource packs on behaviour management for schools and teachers vary considerably in both size and content. Some are more freely available than others. This is wrong and bad practice. A copy of each local authority resource pack on behaviour management should be made available to every school and every support professional. Ideally, they should also be available as a reference point for parents. It is useful to lodge a copy in county-wide libraries for public use. Resource packs should be regularly updated as and when necessary.

The content of these resource packs currently differs throughout the UK. Ideally, there should be broad agreement on issues to be included. Therefore, the utility of these packs is inclined to vary between local authorities, making some of more use to schools than others. It is particularly regrettable when local authority resource packs are retained solely for the use of support officers and not for the use of teachers and schools.

A good LA behaviour management handbook should provide important information on such issues as, for example: an introduction to behaviour covering fields like the behaviour and inclusion strategy, definitions, professional development, initial teacher education, case studies and useful tools for teachers to use in school. This is followed by a reflective section on understanding behaviour, including theoretical and practical approaches.

The third section may be on prevention. This includes sections on natural and local policies, whole-school approaches, developing a county-wide school behaviour policy, managing space, setting up to succeed, the use of sanctions, and lesson preparation and planning.

Section four might cover all aspects of effective classroom management and is a vital section for teachers and all caring practitioners to read.

Section five could discuss using resources effectively for troubled children. This could be followed by a discussion on securing support within schools and understanding incidents and incident management. The latter section is particularly significant and should be read and understood by all head teachers and teachers in primary schools. A similar section needs to be included in many other existing local authority resource packs as it often appears to be omitted.

Section six could be on how best to engage with children and young people and should be full of sound practical advice. The following sections could include for example working for change with pupils and some of these ideas could be similar to those replicated in later sections in this Handbook.

The final two sections are essential and equally important. The penultimate section could/ should be about working with pupils with disabilities and challenging behaviour. The final section, then, is vital. It is about working with and understanding parents and carers. Some

LAs now provide a separate second resource pack on implementing sound whole-school policies, which are often of a very high standard. As mentioned earlier, one of the failings of some LA resource packs in the UK is that they do not provide a name and contact directory for schools and for parents to access. This is vital, especially in emergency or serious 'incident' referrals. Local authorities should include in this contact directory the names of all their head teachers, key LA staff and other possible external agency staff, including the names of core social services and health and voluntary sector personnel. These lists should be updated regularly and at least annually. This name and contact directory is often the first point of access for head teachers, teachers and parents to use. The absence of such a list can lead to both delays and misunderstandings, as well as, on occasions, frustration and unnecessary duplication.

The future

At the time of writing, local authorities in the UK are changing the emphasis of some parts of their older and more traditional approaches to behaviour management to incorporate the new policy ideals which we have outlined in Chapters 1 and 3 and which are beginning to be followed by their respective national governments and which are having a potentially huge impact upon primary schools.

These developments include:

- new curricular approaches, especially the introduction of the revised early years curriculum;
- the drive for more child-centred and child-friendly approaches;
- the move to more national-orientated educational policies;
- the remodelling of the workforce agreement;
- the implementation of the school improvement/effectiveness strategies and national and local behavioural management frameworks;
- ensuring that all schools are fit for the twenty-first century;
- the Social Inclusion Strategy;
- the drive to raise standards, including improving achievement levels, behaviour and attendance;
- providing parents with the opportunity to make their preference for a mainstream placement for a child with additional learning needs a well-supported reality;
- the development of an integrated education and children's service aiming to provide a seamless service in effective teaching and learning for all, meeting children and young people's needs and, most importantly, protecting them from harm.

Achieving these new policy aims will prove a considerable challenge to schools and local authorities in the foreseeable future. Currently, local authorities throughout the UK are striving to achieve fully integrated children's services departments with better links between education, social services and health (although the methodology and practice vary considerably between England, Scotland, Northern Ireland and Wales).

3. THE SCHOOL LEVEL

Whilst behaviour is an ongoing concern, most primary schools manage their behaviour well. There is often a media frenzy when serious acts of misbehaviour, anti-social behaviour and even violent crimes erupt in certain parts of the UK. The overwhelming majority of serious incidents of challenging behaviour take place in or around secondary schools, but in some parts of the UK police and other forms of external interventions do take place in primary schools from time to time. One of the difficulties has been the poor attitude of some parents or carers towards schools and education (Dalziel and Henthorne, 2005). Another has been the growth of gangs and gang-related cultures, knife crime, drugs, alcohol and substance abuse in some communities, the rise of disaffected behaviour, cyber bullying, amongst other issues. Fortunately, most primary school head teachers, and their SMT and BMTs, manage difficult pupils' misbehaviour and poor parental attitudes extremely well, although it is often more of a challenge for newer, younger staff and for some classroom assistants (CAs), learning school mentors (LSMs) and playground assistants.

Leadership styles

Evidence from studies into school leadership and leadership styles suggest that remaining focused and being positive and optimistic are good qualities to possess. It is important for school leaders to have a clear vision for how the school can be taken forward and how to work within the rest of the educational and professional community to achieve this goal. Sustaining a positive school ethos is equally vital. Such head teachers are likely to work inside schools which manage the behaviour of all their pupils well and effectively.

Schools are complex learning and social systems and head teachers need to develop distributed leadership across the school to create a positive climate in the school and a coherent approach to managing behaviour. Distributed leadership involves giving responsibility to key members of the team, making clear the expectations that come with such responsibility, providing development and support to fulfil these expectations and holding the individuals to account for their delivery. Establishing high expectations of pupils and staff is important, but holding pupils, parents and staff accountable for these is essential.

Evidence from research suggests that in managing pupils' behaviour successful head teachers:

- have a clear sense of the values they wish to encourage;
- consult pupils and involve the wider community in considering these values;
- recognise that pupils' social responsibilities develop best when their classroom learning reflects the values that are present in all other aspects of school life.

Another finding from research is that in these kinds of primary schools standards, attendance and behaviour often change for the better.

Governance

In well-managed and competent schools the governing body should be actively engaged in the development of the school's behaviour policy. The governing body is often comprised of a number of well-respected voices from within the local community. The governors support the SMT and BMT in their leadership style and expectations as to both the school's goals academically as well as what it contributes to the overall development of its pupils. The governing body (including the pupil governor) should be actively involved not only in the development of the school's behaviour policy but also in its formal reviews and supporting data analysis. The latter would include statistical data on the use of correctives, reports on incidents of bullying, reasons for visits from police, numbers of fixed and permanent exclusions and related information.

Governors need to be assured of and agree to the behavioural policies outlined in the document as well as the expectations it sets for its pupils, parents and staff. They should ensure the policy is written in plain language and is free of jargon. The policy should be accessible for everybody to read. Therefore, copies should be available in the school library.

Whilst governors in many schools are aware of their school's expectations of pupils and understand the use of rewards and sanctions used by the school, they also need to know and understand the following:

- the reasons why some pupils struggle to manage their behaviour;
- the methods by which schools can achieve change in their pupils' behaviour by using their own resources;
- the ways in which schools can achieve change in their pupils' behaviour through the involvement of a range of other external agencies.

It is often useful to provide the governors with a formal presentation of the school's behavioural policy and the issues outlined above from time to time. It is important to have all the governors on board on all matters associated with behaviour. Some successful schools actively prepare a brief and highly informative guide on behaviour for their governors.

The school behaviour policy

Later in this Handbook we will provide a specific example of a practical school behaviour policy (pp. 47–63). In Chapter 3, we will illustrate how behaviour is linked to emerging respect and relationships policies and to well-being.

As mentioned earlier, and as we now reinforce, the key issue for schools is managing pupils' learning and teaching. When teachers are enthusiastic, creative and deliver well-prepared and well-differentiated lessons, the potential for misbehaviour is markedly reduced. Often, badly prepared lessons lead to noisier, sometimes rowdy classrooms. When disruptive conduct is apparent in classrooms it is often a sign that all is not well with the quality of the teaching.

Whole-school behaviour policies should be collectively developed through the active involvement of pupils, parents, ancillary and support staff, CAs, LSMs, teachers and governors. Advice on how best to create a competent policy document can normally be given by an LA's behaviour support team. The most effective policy documents are couched in a positive framework using positive language, emphasising positive expectations and providing recognition and/or the use of rewards for positive behaviour and positive achievements. You will have noticed the use of the five 'positives' in the same sentence.

Whilst the development of the policy is really important, it is its implementation which is crucial. There is considerable evidence (NBAR, 2008: 122) that some pupils and parents find the inconsistent use and application of a school's behaviour policy to be both confusing and unfair. All pupils, parents, carers and staff need to know and understand what the policy means for them in practice. It is often the effective dissemination, implementation and monitoring of the policy that is so important.

The significance of parents

Research has consistently shown (Desforges and Abouchaar, 2003) that parents/carers have a major influence upon their children's success in school, both academically and behaviourally. Crucially, their support of reading and speech development in the early years is profoundly important. This is one of the reasons why all schools should endeavour to engage positively with parents/carers at all times. This process begins with parents before the children enter the school. It is essential to start to get to know parents/carers from the onset and to start to develop a positive relationship. This developing bond is reinforced via sustained positive contact through parents' afternoons/evenings, children's progress reports, school and/or home visits or meetings which indirectly or directly feed back on their children's efforts, progress, academic achievement, attendance and behaviour. Such positive feedback draws parents to support and like their children's school. Negative feedback, especially constant negative feedback, has, of course, the opposite effect. If in the early years a bond is developed between parents and the school, it helps to make it easier when the head teacher has to discuss children's social, emotional and behavioural difficulties.

Since some parents have poor and negative attitudes towards schooling (often borne of their own experiences) and towards authority figures in general (Dalziel and Henthorne,

2005), perhaps because of their own poor achievements, communication skills or anxieties, this is even more reason to help newer parents during the early years so as to foster and promote a positive school–parent relationship.

Sometimes, however, it does become necessary to deploy a range of strategies to secure the involvement of parents, especially those who fail to attend school meetings or distance themselves from the school. As increasingly both parents or single mothers now work, getting to know the children's grandparents or their school transport providers is another part of this complex process. A remark from an experienced primary head teacher of a large and successful school during the data gathering for a report one of us was writing for Sefton LA has remained uppermost in our minds. He said that whilst he could guarantee the attendance of his pupils after arrival at school, he often did not know from which direction they might be arriving; a distressing sign of these times. He indicated that some of his pupils lived in different houses with different parents or even grandparents on different days of the week.

Partnerships with parents of SEBD pupils

When a school has developed positive relationships with all its parents as a whole and as individuals, it is in a position to engage in a better partnership with the parents/carers of those children who develop social, emotional or behavioural difficulties or those who have special or additional learning needs. Then, for example, a school can begin to deal more confidently with parents whose children are being repeatedly sanctioned for their misbehaviour. In these circumstances, it becomes easier to explore with parents how to change the inappropriate conduct, what is causing it and how the school and parent(s) can work together on the issues. Explicitly, does the pupil lack the skills to access the curriculum, have literacy or numeracy difficulties or have serious concerns about what is going on in his/her life at home or in the community?

This is a skilled, often delicate and confidential task. It is one reason why appropriate training in behaviour management is so important for all staff. A bungled meeting or home visit with a parent can destroy a good home–school relationship in a flash and it may never recover. Equally important is the need for such discussions to take place in a quiet and private room. As well as equipping staff to develop the skills required for relating well with parents, head teachers also need to find and create the time and space for parent–school interactions to take place. Such work cannot and should not be undertaken in corridors and classrooms, where there is a risk of constant interruption and little chance of confidentiality. Breaking parental confidentiality is one of the prime causes of failed home–school relationships.

Schools and inter-agency engagement

One of the major issues which emerged during the evidence-gathering for the National Behaviour and Attendance Review Report (2008) was the significant level of concern from parents about the failure to provide them with sufficient and effective information about their children's progress. This often left them feeling frustrated and exasperated.

Another prime concern amongst support and caring professionals is that referrals to them were made much too late and often pre-empted early intervention strategies. Some head teachers and teaching staff voiced their own concerns that after making referrals to external agencies some failed to respond or responded too slowly or too late and, in so doing, sometimes made a situation worse. We came across examples where in particular situations, as no action by an agency had been taken, schools had felt it necessary to call in the police. This should, in theory, never happen. However, high caseloads and inter-service communication difficulties are the major impediment in applying appropriate, inter-agency practice within children's services, and this is made worse by constant staff turnover in some fields in some parts of the country.

These are complex professional matters. The NBAR Report (2008: 126) team found that in some instances schools:

- had too little knowledge of the range of support available in their localities both from statutory agencies and from the voluntary sector;
- had too little understanding of the capacity of local services and their need to prioritise their casework;
- made too many inappropriate referrals that:
  - showed too little evidence of the work already done by the school;
  - failed to secure the pupil's or parent's consent;
  - lay outside an agency's remit.

These issues can be addressed through better inter-agency signposting, referral pathways and the production of the LA service directory which we referred to on pp. 28–30. Even when schools are successful in referring pupils to other agencies and in drawing them into work in school, there is a need for schools to learn how to work effectively and collaboratively with the visiting professionals and to understand the constraints of their roles. It is one of our constant themes in the training we give to schools and LA staff that there needs to be a consistent policy on and approach to when and how to make referrals and that each referral must be properly logged in a designated log book, including the date and time of referral, the name of the agency and person to whom the referral was made, and the name of the person and agency providing the feedback, along with a date and time. If no feedback is received or feedback is inadequate, head teachers and/or governors may sometimes need to take appropriate follow-up action, which sometimes can be urgent. This may include involving their key LA support professionals or engaging with the SMT of the LA.

Risk assessment and incident management

Risk assessment and incident management play an important part in how well a school manages behaviour and records the difficult misbehaviour which takes place. In principle and in practice, when a school has clear, coherent practices and policies, which are adopted and made explicit to parents, pupils and staff, the basic management of behavioural incidents is placed on a firm foundation. These practices should be incorporated into a school's behavioural policy and followed up during staff training events.

It is equally essential that a strategic behaviour policy for a whole LA area is agreed at the appropriate children's services framework partnership meetings. This is needed to underpin the whole of the LA's work, especially its responsibility for children's safety and the prevention of child abuse. These supporting LA agencies include youth offending teams, community safety teams/groups, schools, social work, health, voluntary groups and other local organisations which may differ between LA areas. All of these agencies should be consulted about risk assessment strategies and incident management. Ideally, this co-ordinated and concerted effort outside the school environment will have a beneficial effect upon teachers, pupils and staff within every education/school setting. Hopefully, it should also help to reduce local risk, prevent major incidents occurring and lead to better inter-agency teamwork.

4. THE CLASSROOM LEVEL

It is clear that classroom teachers and CAs and LSMs manage the bulk of pupils' social, emotional and behavioural difficulties in the primary school. Therefore it is vital that proper time and effort is spent on their preparation and training at every level, including initial teacher training (ITT), induction, in-service and continuous professional development (CPD). There is little doubt that continuous investment in the enhancement of classroom teachers (CTs), CAs and LSMs will be necessary for the foreseeable future. Presently, too many primary staff feel inappropriately prepared by their initial training to manage the pupils that they encounter in their first posts and early years of professional practice. Some feel that they have had no or very little training on behaviour management or that the type of training they received was inadequate, even woeful. Furthermore, many of them have had few, if any, opportunities to undertake relevant behaviour management training and to be coached in the best techniques and the most effective ways of responding to troubled behaviour within the school or at the classroom level.

The reality is that far too many teachers have developed their own survival skills in the classroom. What do we mean? Answer: they have learnt their survival skills as best they can whilst on the job or, as the jargon puts it, on task! Perhaps, to an extent, even from the 'tips' given by their head teachers, colleagues and peers. Perhaps staff have learnt from specific situations. One of us can remember in his first week as a teacher having to deal with a pupil who suddenly collapsed on the floor having had a fit. No one had ever mentioned the word 'fit' before, nor had one ever been witnessed. The writer acted instinctively. Fortunately, no blunders were made. But you know what it's all about afterwards.

So, one way or another, many teachers piece together skills that enable them to manage the pupils they teach. Whilst we applaud those who survive, and their commitment to the teaching profession, we also regret the loss of colleagues, often unnecessarily, who qualified but then quit because they found it a struggle to deal with pupils' behaviour in the classroom and around the wider school. How did you react the first time a pupil swore at you?

Preventing behavioural difficulties in the classroom

It is our personal view that all primary staff should be given the right to improve or update their behavioural skills at least once every five years. Why? Behavioural management is a very wide field. Staff get promoted, move on or change schools or roles. New skills need to be developed. How many head teachers are trained to cope with cyber bullying or abuse on the internet or their staff on the internet? We respectfully suggest that such an entitlement would not only strengthen the profession but give teachers, CAs and LSMs a much wider range of skills. It would make them better able to respond to incidents of pupil misbehaviour. Furthermore, on a professional basis, staff would feel more confident in their capacity to manage both classroom and within-school behaviour. Consequently, professionals would be much more likely to engage in appropriate dialogue with pupils, parents and colleagues.

There is no single, standard way to teach behaviour management. We believe that if you follow the outline in this Handbook you will not go too far astray. Figure 2.3 presents some ideas relating to the areas which primary classroom teachers' courses might follow.

1	Understanding behaviour
2	Organising the classroom to support effective learning
3	Understanding the effective use of rules and routines in the classroom
4	Developing pupils' responsibility for their own learning and behaviour
5	Creating a rewarding classroom
6	Adapting the curriculum to meet the preferred learning style of pupils
7	Effective lesson planning to match pupils' capability and needs
8	Differentiating and personalising learning for pupils with attention difficulties
9	Involving children and young people

Figure 2.3 Preventing behavioural difficulties in the classroom

Effective classroom management

This programme might be complemented by a second programme which covers issues in effective classroom management. These ideas are shown in Figure 2.4.

Effective responses to troubled behaviour

The next element of a progressive course might examine the range of skills and techniques which teachers can use in the classroom in response to a pupil or pupils beginning to misbehave or move off task. These skills are presented in Figure 2.5. The list is not exhaustive, otherwise it would be too long. Therefore, treat the items in the list as exemplars. Add your own additional skill needs to suit particular circumstances.

Understanding incidents and incident management

An often under-applied but extremely important area is in the field of understanding behavioural incidents, how they develop and how to manage them effectively. These aspects are presented in Figure 2.6.

Participation in a programme like the one shown in Figure 2.6 would help classroom staff to anticipate, prepare and plan for the confident management of an incident with a pupil or pupils in the classroom. Many teachers may be naturally fortunate enough not to need such insight, understanding and skills. Perhaps they are 'naturals'. But, for many, who suddenly stumble across serious incidents in their classroom or for whom these occur regularly in their

1	Controlling entry to class
2	Using seating plans
3	Effective teacher positioning in class
4	Setting the tone for the lesson
5	Lesson delivery
6	Providing explanations
7	Giving timely support
8	Managing transitions between activities
9	Offering praise and recognition
10	Positive lesson ending
11	Self-management
12	Effective impression management
13	Modelling desirable behaviour
14	Using inclusive language
15	Movement – the use of space and teacher authority
16	Screening for difficulty
17	Using positive prompts for behaviour
18	Ensuring children and young people's participation

Figure 2.4 Effective classroom management

1	Giving recognition for effort
2	Rewarding positive behaviour
3	Catching pupils 'being good'
4	Using low-key confident responses
5	Recalling past good performance
6	Catching others being good
7	Reinforcing what is required
8	Giving notice of a question
9	Acknowledging difficulties
10	Offering choices
11	Using deferred injunctions
12	Seeking better for both solutions
13	Moving pupils
14	Removing the audience
15	Following up and following through

Figure 2.5 Effective responses to troubled behaviour

1	Understanding the potential for an incident to occur
2	Risk assessment in the classroom
3	Risk mitigation and management
4	A five-stage model for understanding an incident
5	Ways to respond effectively at each stage of an incident
6	Post-incident management
7	Notifying parents and carers
8	Reporting an incident
9	Record keeping

Figure 2.6 Understanding incidents and incident management

day-to-day work, participation in such a programme would help considerably; not least to cope with the stress of such events.

In an ideal world, teachers' CPD for behaviour management would also include:

- observation of peers;
- observation of best practice;
- shadowing;
- role exchange;
- participation in an action learning set.

The emphasis of such programmes should always be on the applied. It is useful to create case studies or role-play incidents during the training in order to learn how to apply the skills. This helps breed confidence. Confident, ably skilled teachers are less likely to be challenged by pupils. In fact, this simple rationale forms the whole basis for the effective management of behaviour in primary schools today.

Confident, skilled teachers are much more likely to be relaxed in the classroom. For example, they are more likely to scan the room, recognise changes in appearance or body language amongst pupils in their stance, posture, attitude, language and behaviour. The simple fact is (and too many caring professionals fail to grasp this point and its significance) that classroom teachers and/or their assistants are likely to be the frontline people who identify a pupil in trouble or difficulty. Sometimes these warning signs are relatively simple (e.g. tears or tantrums). Sometimes they are more subtle and require closer observation, such as a deterioration in the quality of work, interest or endeavour. Teachers, too, are often the only people outside the home who are in a position to witness a change in the pupil's normal demeanour or a significant change in home circumstances. When the problems are caused by changes in a pupil's home circumstances, the class teacher may become the key link in enabling the child to access appropriate support from inside or outside the school. Therefore, teachers should have a basic understanding of key aspects of the law, such as the principles of family law. Teachers can be the first to spot and prevent abuse, depression, self-harm or other potentially major problems like dyslexia or anorexia.

Classroom teachers can only really learn and develop all these skills in the following cases:

- when head teachers, deputy heads and senior staff in schools have themselves learnt the necessary skills to address the needs of pupils referred to them;
- when head teachers, deputies and senior staff have the understanding, awareness and knowledge necessary to help the pupil with a particular difficulty;
- when head teachers, deputies and senior managers have the confidence, knowledge and capacity to secure the right support for the child from the agency best placed to support him or her.

5. THE INDIVIDUAL LEVEL

The fifth level is the individual child and family. The key principles at this level are as follows:

- Safeguarding and protecting the individual child through the considered management of pupils' behaviour and attendance is paramount.
- All children have a right to full-time education, meeting their social, emotional, behavioural and learning needs.
- Child-centred outcomes should be the paramount consideration in any activity.

Therefore the individual child has the right to feel welcomed, safe and able to learn properly in school. Equally, children need to receive a clear message of what is expected of them in school. It is a two-way relationship. Most importantly, the individual pupil needs to know who to turn to for help and support with confidence. Consistency in response by a teacher, whether applied to learning or behaviour, is most important in establishing this relationship. Sudden mood swings by teachers, shouting or making unfair comments can all hinder the development of these relationships or, in serious cases, ruin them.

Children also, as we indicated earlier, need the support, encouragement and help of their parents or carers from their earliest formative years and throughout their time at school. Those pupils who lack appropriate support from parents are already placed at a massive disadvantage in terms of their capacity to thrive and progress at school. As we will discover in Chapter 13, pupils with difficult home backgrounds are more likely to become absentees or truants, or bullies, or to misbehave and be excluded.

1   An individual pupil exhibits behavioural difficulties in lessons.

2   School determines whether s/he has any learning difficulties that may be inhibiting his/her capacity to learn.

3   If so, school assesses and identifies his/her needs and plans to meet them under the Code of Practice for Special Educational Needs.

4   If not, school explores his/her:
    • understanding of his/her behaviour;
    • awareness of its impact on others;
    • knowledge of how to behave differently;
    • skills and capability to behave in a different and more positive way.

5   Depending upon the outcome, school may need to:
    • talk through with him/her the behaviour that is unacceptable;
    • provide the opportunity to understand the impact of his/her behaviour upon others;
    • describe and if necessary model the desirable behaviours;
    • coach him/her in these new behaviours;
    • ensure all those who engage with him/her recognise and encourage his/her attempts to behave differently;
    • provide him/her with a buddy, mentor or ongoing coach.

6   When the unwanted behaviour either:
    • occurs in school, at home and in the wider community; or
    • seems resistant to change in school,
    the school involves the parents/carers in working for change with the child.

7   Involving parents may require:
    • exploring the problems they are experiencing with their child;
    • enquiring about what they have done to deal with this to date and how they have done it;
    • testing their understanding of the impact of their child's behaviour on the learning and behaviour of other pupils;
    • acknowledging that they cannot be happy with this situation;
    • inviting them to work in partnership to change their child's behaviour;
    • developing a pastoral support programme and/or a behavioural contract about how the school, the parents and the pupil will work together to secure a lasting change in behaviour;
    • providing them with parenting courses to modify or change their response to unwanted behaviour.

8   Should this not succeed, school may:
    • secure a parent's agreement to the involvement of appropriate other agencies in striving to enable the child or young person to change;
    • issue a behavioural contract about how the school, the parents and the pupil will work together to secure a lasting change in behaviour.

9   Should this also fail and the unwanted and undesirable behaviours continue unchanged, then the school has a legitimate concern that the long-term adverse effect of the individual's behaviour on the rest of the class is too severe to continue. At this point, short-term placement in a behaviour setting or a managed transfer to a longer-term placement may be the only reasonable option. Ideally, however, a placement in a school's own 'learning unit' should be tried first if one is available.

Figure 2.7 Example of a stepwise approach to addressing an individual pupil's needs

One of the constant difficulties for teachers is to reconcile the needs of the majority in the class/school to learn in a calm, stimulating way with, say, the attention-seeking demands of a very needy pupil who is ill prepared for school and lacks support at home. Do we protect the learning of the majority? Or do we jump to the aid of or reject the troubled pupil? Even worse, do we compound the difficulties of the troubled child further by exposing him/her to even further rejection, perhaps through ridicule?

The well-resourced, caring, good school might attempt to meet a troubled pupil's needs by following the approach, step-by-step, outlined in Figure 2.7. We believe that by following this step-by-step approach, you will clarify your thinking and actions. It should prove helpful.

The dilemma

The real dilemma for teachers and schools at present is that too few whole-school staff teams have had the opportunity to acquire the skills to be able to work with and apply them with their troubled pupils. Consequently, ill-conceived interventions can frequently make things worse rather than better. This lowers teachers' morale and confidence levels and often increases stress.

We support the notion that it is both cost-effective and professionally desirable to ensure that securing positive changes in pupils' behaviour through successful interventions is a wise and sensible policy worth following and implementing. It can lead to more successful early interventions (Allen and Smith, 2008). It enhances school improvement strategies. It reduces the reliance on external agencies and out-of-school provision.

Even in this ideal template, there may be a few pupils whose life circumstances are so adverse that they simply cannot change as they have little trust in adults and cannot commit to changing their behaviour. For some of these needy children, poor behaviour is a defence mechanism brought about by often dreadful home conditions (e.g. parental bullying or victimisation). Sometimes, their poor in-school behaviour is nothing less than a plea for help.

Summary

In this chapter we have considered the five stages at which to address behaviour. These are at the national, LA, school, classroom, and individual pupil and family levels. We have tried to provide you with relevant information and practical ideas at each of these stages. In Chapter 3, we will begin by considering respect and relationship and well-being policies, examine different types of pupils' behaviour and the role of the primary behaviour support team (PBST), before in Chapter 4 discussing a wide range of different issues which should help you to understand further the contextual framework for primary school behaviour management.

New approaches 3
Respect and relationships and well-being policies

About this chapter

It is becoming common practice for many schools and LAs to develop either respect and relationships or well-being policy documents which incorporate behaviour. In this chapter, we will begin by presenting and drafting a respect and relationships template which can be added to, altered or amended by individual schools or LAs depending upon individual preferences or needs. We will then present an example of a school's well-being policy document. Finally, we will present a contextual analysis of the ways in which pupils' behaviour can be analysed and a brief outline of the role of the primary support team. We will consider these issues in the following order:

- respect and relationships policy: an outline;
- well-being policy: a policy document exemplar;
- a primary school behaviour policy document;
- pupils' behaviour:
  - all children and young people in school;
  - children who display low-level misbehaviour/disruption;
  - children who display challenging behaviour;
  - children and young people at risk of exclusion;
  - children and young people educated outside school;
- the role of the primary behaviour support team (PBST).

A. RESPECT AND RELATIONSHIPS POLICY: A DRAFT OUTLINE

Respect and relationships policies (RRPs) are being used increasingly by both LAs and schools and often incorporate standard behavioural policy documents. Some RRPs only involve individual schools. Some are county-wide. RRP documents are now more commonly designed to operate between clusters or federations of primary schools. Some clusters/federations involve both secondary schools and feeder primaries. It is in this latter connection that we will suggest a template for a draft RRP document. We will now outline a possible draft RRP document with gaps in some sections for staff to insert their own ideas should you wish to do so.

Introduction

This policy document is a result of collaboration between schools A to J in the Adfast cluster/federation and the LA's achievement/schools improvement service. It is based on the views of pupils and staff from all schools, gathered through pupil focus groups and staff questionnaires. The policy is based also on ideas of good practice gathered from and shared between staff across the cluster.

The policy sets out expectations and processes in respect of behaviour and well-being which are shared by all members of the local community. The policy is supported by shared resources which have been developed by a working group, comprised of nominees from each school across the cluster. For the purposes of this policy, the term 'school community' is defined 'as all people who are part of or contribute to school life'. This includes pupils, staff, families, governors and all visitors to the school.

The policy is based on a recognition that pupils learn best when they feel safe and supported. The policy is intended to facilitate the emotional well-being of all members of our community. This policy should be considered alongside several other relevant policies, including the attendance policy, anti-bullying policy, SEN policy, the equalities scheme and the accessibility policy.

Ethos and culture

To maximise their potential, all members of a school community need to feel secure, happy and valued. Therefore, our aim is to create an ethos which is consistent, co-operative, clear, humanitarian, open and safe. We wish every member of the school community to feel proud of the school and to feel an important and valued member of that community, which should help to develop individuals' confidence and positive self-image. In turn, this should help promote positive behaviour and increased opportunities for effective teaching and learning.

Insert a paragraph here specific to the cluster's/federation's objectives. Points to be made might include issues, objectives and mission statements on the following:

- supporting the nurturing environment;
- effective communication;
- facilitating literacy and numeracy and early intervention strategies;
- emotional and physical health and well-being;
- equal opportunities, inclusivity, disabilities.

The five Rs

The cluster has adopted the five Rs as a behaviour framework which will support pupils in making good choices about their behaviour. The five Rs are:

- rewards and sanctions;
- routines;
- rules;
- responsibilities;
- rights.

Rights and responsibilities

All members of the community need to understand that they have rights and responsibilities and this is at the heart of the school ethos. All members of the community have a responsibility to consider the rights of others as well as their own.

Every member of the school community:

- has the right to feel safe and valued and has a responsibility to allow others to feel safe and valued;
- should respect all other members of that community;
- should use and promote effective and clear communication with others.

1   Pupils should:
  - endeavour to make the best progress across all aspects of their academic and emotional development;
  - be respectful of others and their learning needs.

2   Staff should:
  - ensure that pupils are aware of their rights and have their rights upheld;
  - ensure that pupils are supported in meeting their responsibilities;
  - offer leadership within the school by modelling appropriate behaviour and displaying genuine concern and emotional warmth towards others;
  - encourage all pupils by offering attractive learning experiences which are suitably challenging;
  - apply consistently the school's positive behaviour management framework, including the consistent use of rewards and sanctions;
  - communicate expectations clearly to pupils, parents/carers and colleagues.

3   Parents and carers should:
  - be familiar with and supportive of the cluster's respect and relationships policy and its rewards and sanctions;
  - provide a home environment which complements the school ethos;
  - be active partners in their children's learning.

4   The school's governing body should:
  - support the school community in actively promoting and maintaining a school ethos that encourages respect and positive relationships;
  - monitor and support the implementation, monitoring and evaluation of the cluster's respect and relationships policy.

Routines

Routines help the school run smoothly and relate to organisation, communication and transitions during the school day. Routines are necessary to ensure that expectations are clear and they consolidate rights and responsibilities. Routines are established at the start of each academic year. They are subsequently rehearsed and reviewed at the start of each term and reinforced through ongoing positive interaction.

Why not undertake a staff exercise to determine a school's/cluster's routines and possibly append these to the policy?

Rules

School rules make clear expectations of behaviour. They help to promote positive relationships and increased opportunities for effective teaching and learning. Together with routines, rules support the rights and responsibilities of all community members. The cluster's rules are implemented consistently and regularly reinforced through a system of clear rewards and sanctions. There are general school rules which all members of the school's community are expected to follow and specific classroom, playground and dining-area rules for pupils which comply with commonsense expectations and health and safety regulations. Both pupils and parents/carers have participated in and agreed to all these rules. Generally, these rules are agreed at the start of each year and revisited regularly.

Examples of classroom rules might include the following:

- Only leave the classroom with permission.
- Raise your hand to ask for help.

Why not undertake an exercise on agreeing and implementing the cluster's rules and append them to the back of the policy document? Ideally, rules should be kept to a bare minimum, and be reasonable, fair and enforceable.

Rewards

Rewards help to enhance self-image and build and maintain positive relationships. Positive consequences are the key to the promotion of effective classroom behaviour. Rewards are likely to encourage pupils to repeat a desired behaviour. The cluster will use reward systems that emphasise praise in order to support pupils to make positive choices. For many of our pupils, the reward may simply be receiving positive adult attention or praise.

Rewards should be given immediately so that pupils will see the link between the conduct and the reward. They will be used consistently by all staff and distributed fairly. They should not be used as an inducement. Rewards and sanctions used by cluster schools will be appropriate to pupils' developmental needs.

The cluster will utilise the 4-Step Reward Scheme, which consists of the following steps:

- Step 1: informal recognition/reward;
- Step 2: verbal praise;
- Step 3: tangible rewards;
- Step 4: school-based rewards.

The cluster's awards include both informal and tangible rewards. Informal rewards may include smiling, verbal praise, tone of voice, showing trust and the use of thumbs-up signals. Tangible rewards may include stickers, certificates, the use of a points system, 'golden time', praise assemblies, positive postcards sent home, prizes, lottery draws, Friday afternoon fun clubs, etc.

Sanctions

Sanctions will only be used where effective rules, rights, responsibilities, routines and rewards have been applied consistently and in conjunction with a range of classroom strategies and rewards. The sanctions used will always be:

- fair and reasonable;
- known and understood by all pupils, parents, carers and staff;
- applied consistently;
- logical and proportionate to the behaviour;
- applied at the lowest possible level to achieve a result.

Ideally, teachers should use positive behaviour management strategies to avoid unnecessary escalation through the stages or to avoid the use of sanctions. The following are amongst the list of possible classroom strategies: praise, distraction, diversion, proximal praise (praising children close by for good behaviour), presenting a range of different choices, modifying curricular tasks, change of curricular tasks, working in silence.

As with the application of rules, the cluster uses a 4 Steps to Sanctions approach. These are:

- Step 1: verbal warning or redirection and rule reminder;
- Step 2: second warning/further redirection and consequences reminder;
- Step 3: the use of in-class sanctions;
- Step 4: the loss of privilege(s) and/or referral to senior member of staff or the head teacher.

At this point, it is necessary to state that when, exceptionally, serious incidents of misbehaviour occur (e.g. actual or threatened violence, serious verbal abuse or assault, supply or use of an illegal drug and use or threatened use of an offensive weapon) pupils may be fast-tracked through these stages and, if necessary, into possible exclusion processes.

A graduated response to inappropriate behaviour

Of course, even when staff use some of the most effective classroom management and communication skills and focus upon prevention and early intervention, incidents may still occur. Therefore it is sensible for staff to follow the agreed and graduated response to unwanted behaviour. This response will be partially dependent upon the age and stage of development of the pupils.

Stage 1

When a pupil's behaviour is unacceptable and the pupil does not respond to the usual intervention strategies, the staff will work with the child in a focused way to assist him or her to modify the inappropriate behaviour and to change and/or develop relationships. The pupil may be given individual goals, with staff support to help them achieve them. The pupil's progress will then be modified over a period of time.

Stage 2

When inappropriate behaviour persists or is repeated through, for example, repeated episodes of bad behaviour or an occurrence of a number of incidents, parent(s) or carer(s) will be invited into the school to discuss concerns and agree a mutual plan going forward. This may necessitate a review as to whether the pupil has special (SEN) or additional educational needs (ADELN) or should be referred under the terms of the Children Act, 2004. If the pupil is identified as having either SEN or ADELN this may require the formulation and use of an Individual Behaviour Plan (IBP), which will include targets for change which will be identified, agreed and regularly reviewed and monitored.

Sometimes this in-school work may require more substantial and sustained support from an LA's specialist support services, which might, for example, involve access to an educational psychologist, behaviour or SEN support.

Stage 3

Interventions occur following a serious or significant incident. This may necessitate the use of fixed-term or permanent exclusion or, in extreme circumstances, physical intervention. When an incident is deemed to be serious or significant, a written record will be kept by staff and pupils concerned and logged in the Serious Incident Book/Data Base. Parents/carers will be notified by phone, by post or through a home or school visit (depending upon the circumstances). Similarly, as and when necessary, the relevant authorities (such as the LA, police, health, social care or children's services) will be informed and their advice sought and implemented.

Use of exclusions

Exclusions should only be considered as a last resort and only after all other possible avenues have been exhausted. This means that all the aforementioned rules, rights, responsibilities, routines and rewards have been followed consistently and applied properly. Normally, the decision to exclude will only be taken in the following circumstances:

- in response to serious breaches of the cluster's behaviour policy; and
- if allowing the pupil to remain in school would seriously harm the education or the welfare of the pupil or others in the school.

The relevant national guidance on following exclusions policy and practice issued by the English, Scottish, Irish, Welsh or other government agencies should be rigorously adhered to at all times.

Safe and effective intervention

All school members have a legal right to use reasonable force to prevent pupils committing a criminal offence, injuring themselves or others, or damaging property; and to maintain good order and discipline amongst pupils. This reasonable force, however, should be used only in the most exceptional circumstances. Paramount in considering or taking such action is the safety of other pupils and/or staff. It should be remembered that every member of staff and pupil has the right to feel safe in school.

Technically, if used at all, restraint should be used as a last resort and in the context of being a further positive action guided by care and concern for the pupil. In fact, restraint is often referred to by professionals as 'positive handling'. As part of best practice, restraint policies should be considered alongside other relevant cluster policies, particularly health and safety and child protection.

All incidents of restraint or positive handling will be recorded on the appropriate form in the cluster's bound Serious Incident Book. Parents and/or carers will be informed as soon as possible after the incident. When incidents are deemed likely to recur, advice should be sought from the Behaviour Support Service and a Positive Handling Plan created and an appropriate risk assessment undertaken.

Transition between phases

The transition between phases (whether pre-school to nursery/infants/primary, infants to juniors or primary to secondary school) can be amongst the most challenging educational periods for parents/carers and children alike. The cluster will ensure at all times that healthy relationships are forged and maintained with parents/carers and pupils in order to ensure their well-being through, for example, good cluster transition meetings, the sharing of good practice across the cluster and shared reflection on this RRP.

The cluster will ensure that pre-school providers are aware of this RRP so there is an opportunity to begin to familiarise pupils with their rights and responsibilities, routines, rules and choices prior to school entry. The cluster will aim to ensure that consistent messages regarding relationships and respect are shared within and across the schools' communities and across phases. Nevertheless, each cluster school is unique.

The cluster will, especially, endeavour to ensure that pupils transferring from key stage 2 to key stage 3 are given opportunities to become familiar with the rules and routines of their new school. The rights of pupils at their new secondary school will be introduced to them and revisited regularly.

This RRP will be shared with all potential new parents and carers prior to pupils entering their specific school. Clear communication about the RRP will enable parents and carers to help their children to follow the rules and make good choices.

Monitoring

Following implementation of this policy, a nominated member of each school's staff will meet regularly with other cluster-school nominees to monitor and evaluate its effectiveness. Responsibility for the overall monitoring of this RRP rests with each school's governing body and with the LA's School Improvement Service (SIS), the Standards Unit, the Behaviour Support Team or the Achievement advisory service. (NB Local terms change depending upon the LA's practice, location and size.) Monitoring documents should include the following sections for completion:

- compiled by;
- to be revised on;
- date of approval by cluster;
- date of approval by governing body.

B. WELL-BEING: A POLICY DOCUMENT EXEMPLAR

Whilst some schools, clusters and LAs have been focusing upon respect and relationships policy documents, others have been concentrating on promoting or implementing well-being policies or utilising both. Some of these incorporate behaviour policies; others have a different school(s), and often a more traditional, behaviour policy document. We will present an example of one of these documents later in the book (pp. 51–63).

We will now present a typical primary school well-being policy document. It is not presented as one of the best examples of its kind but rather to illustrate everyday practice in a British primary school. This particular school also incorporates its emotional health policy into its well-being strategy, which is entirely normal. As with respect and relationships policies and behaviour policy documents, both the content and structure of well-being policy documents vary considerably between schools and LAs.

Case study: St Jude's Primary School well-being policy document

A healthy school ensures that when pupils are unhappy, anxious, disturbed or depressed there are open channels for them to seek or be offered support, without stigma and with appropriate confidentiality. A healthy school actively seeks to promote emotional health and well-being and helps pupils to understand their feelings.

At St Jude's we work towards positive emotional health and well-being in the whole of our school community for adults as well as children.

Context and rationale

Emotional health and well-being promote school success and improvement by:

- contributing positively to priorities such as enhancing teaching and learning, raising standards, promoting social inclusion and improving behaviour and attendance;
- involving pupils more fully in the operation of the school;
- helping pupils and staff feel happier, more confident and more motivated;
- helping to meet legal, ethical and curricular obligations.

Emotional health and well-being are central to the *Every Child Matters* (2003) strategy.

Aims

The general aims are:

- happier and more motivated pupils and staff who get more out of life teaching and learning;
- pupils who are more engaged in the learning process;
- pupils who can concentrate and learn better;
- striving for improved standards in all subjects, including literacy and numeracy;
- improved attainment;
- more effective teaching;
- parents and carers becoming more involved in school life and learning.

The aims in terms of behaviour and attendance are:

- pupils with high self-esteem and confidence;
- pupils who have a say in what happens at school;
- fewer disaffected pupils and those disengaged from learning;
- improved behaviour and attendance;
- less bullying;
- lower rates of truancy.

Staff confidence and development aims are:

- improved morale;
- lower absenteeism;
- better recruitment levels;
- positive and effective relationships with pupils.

Ways of establishing emotional health and well-being

The school promotes and provides a range of services to pupils:

- hygienic toilets which ensure privacy and safety;
- members of the school council acting as mentors;
- a pastoral base staffed with non-teaching pastoral assistants and a qualified first aider;
- co-ordinated support from a range of external organisations;
- welcome days and transition events.

The school promotes an anti-bullying culture through:

- a strong school ethos which empowers tolerance and respect, including respect for difference and diversity;
- a high profile for anti-bullying procedures and policy through corporate posters, assemblies and events such as national anti-bullying week and using SEAL materials;
- active listeners, including assistants and adults other than school staff to whom the victim may turn.

The school promotes and strengthens the pupil voice through:

- a democratic process for the election of school council representatives;
- timetabled meeting time for members of the school council;
- involving pupils in interviews for members of staff;
- consulting pupils about change and policy development;
- allocating a school council budget;
- pupil-led assemblies.

The school promotes the involvement of parents and carers in the life and learning of the school through:

- parent questionnaires;
- regular consultation about change and development through questionnaires and special meetings;
- Subject Focus evenings, Sports and Theme Weeks and concerts/music events;
- involvement in school trips and extracurricular activities;
- regular communication about and involvement in pupil progress, behaviour and pastoral issues.

The school facilitates a context for learning by:

- enhancing school and classroom layout, facilities and resources;
- recognising the background of individual pupils and their physical, social and emotional needs;
- establishing clear rules, routines and expectations about behaviour for learning and social cohesion;
- encouraging positive, caring and constructive relationships.

The school enhances pupil motivation and learning through:

- consistent support for vulnerable children and those with SEN from trained teams of pastoral, learning support, teaching assistants and other agencies where appropriate;
- a range of challenging opportunities for gifted and talented pupils;
- an exciting and varied range of extracurricular events and trips;
- a balanced curriculum with opportunities for intellectual, physical and expressive development;
- recognising a range of learning styles;
- encouraging independence in learning;
- using a range of teaching styles such as circle time appropriate to pupils' age, ability and level of maturity;
- using the SEAL materials to raise self-esteem and confidence levels.

The school enhances pupils' self-esteem and personal development through:

- the Personal Development Curriculum, which includes Citizenship and PSHE (personal, social, health and economic education);
- information, advice and guidance on sex and relationships and drugs;

- careers advice;
- opportunities for pupil leadership through school council, library mentorship and a student receptionist;
- an emphasis on praise and reward;
- opportunities for reflection and spiritual development through art, literature and the RE (religious education) curriculum.

The school enhances staff motivation, learning and professional development through:

- curricular planning time within the school week;
- whole-school training events, including safeguarding;
- access to appropriate external training;
- involving all staff in decision-making and proposed change, e.g. timing of the school day, frequency of reporting to parents and so on;
- provision of non-contact time to allow for planning, delivery and evaluation of healthy school activities;
- consultation on training and support needs through regular review.

Roles and responsibilities

Staff roles and responsibilities are as follows:

- the promotion of emotional health and social well-being and raising the achievement of all pupils are the responsibility of the whole school staff and governors;
- the head teacher and Senior Leadership Team will demonstrate through their personal leadership the importance of this scheme, ensure all staff are aware of it and understand their role and responsibility in relation to it;
- governors – the governing body has adopted this scheme and will assess and monitor its impact annually;
- staff – staff will be expected to know what their responsibilities are in ensuring the scheme is implemented – they will be aware of the implications of it for their planning, teaching and learning strategies, management of activities, as well as behavioural issues;
- pupils – pupils will be made aware of how the emotional and social well-being policy applies to them as part of the school's aims and values and in the curriculum;
- parents/carers – parents and carers will be encouraged to participate fully in implementing it in partnership with the school.

Monitoring/review

The governors are committed to reviewing the impact of the emotional health and well-being policy as part of the rolling programme, taking into account the following aspects:

- motivation;
- self-esteem;
- behaviour;
- anti-bullying;

- anti-racism;
- anti-hate;
- anti-sexism;
- anti-homophobia;
- attendance;
- attainment;
- teaching.

Regular monitoring reports will be presented to governing body meetings at least annually.

C. A PRIMARY SCHOOL BEHAVIOUR POLICY DOCUMENT

Although respect and relationship and well-being policy documents are increasingly used, many schools continue to use more conventional primary school policy documents. We therefore include one of these based upon the policy document of Coed Eva Primary School, Cwmbran. These policy documents vary from school to school and local authority to local authority in terms of content, length and style.

Case study: Coed Eva Primary School Positive Behaviour Policy

Policies related to this: Anti-bullying Policy/Home–School Agreement/Attendance Strategy.

Aim

To provide a caring, stimulating, secure and happy environment in which each child can enjoy his/her work and is given every opportunity to achieve his/her potential.

Rationale

Behaviour is a key feature of school life about which there should be a clear, shared understanding between head teacher, staff, governors, parents and children.
   The behaviour policy has been developed as a response to:

- an awareness that more precise support should be given to both staff and pupils in respect of their desired behaviour;
- recent training in the use of Assertive Discipline;
- research/reports written on this topic e.g. NBAR Report, Elton Report, etc.

Objectives

- to develop pupils' self-discipline and self-control;
- to enable pupils to be on task with their learning;
- to encourage the individual child to recognise the rights of others;
- to promote the values of honesty, fairness and respect for others.

Good behaviour is necessary for effective learning and teaching to take place. We need a code of conduct and rules which the entire school community abides by. This code must be explicit and clearly communicated to all teachers, CAs, LSMs, pupils and parents or carers. Children should be encouraged to take responsibility for their own behaviour.

School expectations of good behaviour

Children are expected to behave in a way that makes it possible for everyone to learn and the teacher to teach. This means following the school rules which form part of our Positive Behaviour Plan.

The infant rules are as follows:

- Follow instructions.
- Keep hands, feet and objects to ourselves.
- Treat everything and everyone kindly.

The junior rules are as follows:

- Follow instructions first time.
- Keep hands, feet, objects and unkind words to ourselves.
- Respect one another and our surroundings.
- Be ready when an adult signals for attention.
- Use correct voice level.

Playtimes/lunchtimes

To aid consistency and in order to promote the importance of good behaviour during these times the expectations detailed above are promoted by midday supervisors in line with the Positive Behaviour Plan of the school.

Promoting good behaviour and discipline

- At Coed Eva Primary School we seek to foster good-quality relationships between all children, all school staff and parents. We are particularly sensitive to the needs and feelings of all disabled people.
- At the beginning of the school year, a home–school agreement is sent to parents by individual teachers outlining the school rules, positive rewards and correctives for both appropriate and inappropriate behaviour.
- The school works collaboratively with parents, so children receive consistent messages about how to behave at home and at school.
- The school's Positive Behaviour Plan will be taught to every pupil and clearly displayed throughout the school.
- Staff will expect good behaviour. They will demand and expect positive outcomes.
- We will provide a broad-based, relevant quality school curriculum.
- The school will do all it can to encourage and promote a variety of individual achievements, thus promoting pupil self-esteem.

- Rewards and correctives will be consistently applied by all staff.
- We will use support services, i.e. Educational Psychologist, Social Services, Medical Support and Educational Welfare as appropriate.

Rewards

Children need rewards to reinforce good behaviour and promote self-esteem. This leads to success at school. The emphasis of this policy is based on a positive approach to behaviour. The rewards that children will *receive* for keeping the school rules are clearly laid out in the school's Positive Behaviour Plan and are as follows:

- values – award points are given out to pupils who demonstrate positive behaviour which meets the school's values which are being promoted by staff for the month (e.g. politeness, courtesy, etc.);
- children will receive regular verbal praise for good work and behaviour (i.e. in personal, group or whole-class situations);
- children will receive regular stars and stickers;
- teachers will provide positive feedback to parents in the form of written and/or verbal communication in, for example, a weekly celebration assembly.

Lunchtime supervisors also follow the school's Positive Behaviour Plan and award their own rewards. Teachers also award prizes to children in class in termly celebration gatherings.

Correctives

There is a need to register disapproval and ensure that effective teaching and learning can take place. This is essential for the stability, security and success of the school. *Unacceptable behaviour cannot be ignored.*

It is of the utmost importance that children understand fully that it is the behaviour which is unacceptable. Therefore teachers need to choose their words carefully when reprimanding pupils so as not to personalise their remarks.

If a child chooses not to follow the school rules, the consequences should be clearly displayed on the school's Positive Behaviour Plan Notice Board and in the School Behaviour Policy Document and will be implemented when necessary. These will take the form of:

- reminder;
- verbal warning;
- time out to reflect on behaviour;
- an introduction to the Social Skills Behaviour Programme;
- head teacher involvement.

Any incidents of serious misbehaviour will not necessarily follow the above criteria and the head teacher is likely to be involved immediately.

Challenging pupils

Pupils who consistently break school rules are placed on the school's Behaviour Programme.

Social Skills Behaviour Programme

Why will children be put on the Behaviour Programme?

- Continually failing to meet our school's expected standards of behaviour or repeatedly breaking our school rules.
- Pupils demonstrating serious misbehaviour will automatically be placed on the programme at the discretion of the behaviour management team.

What will happen on the Behaviour Programme?

- Pupils will be taught social skills to help them interact well with adults and other children during lunchtimes.
- Parents/carers will automatically be informed when their child is placed on the programme.

How do children come off the Behaviour Programme?

- Children will finish the programme when they have merited enough rewards to warrant integrating back with their peers.
- Parents/carers will be notified of completion of the programme.

The role of the head teacher

If the head teacher becomes involved, she liaises with the Inclusion Leader, SENCO and outside agencies to discuss the needs of individual pupils.

It is the responsibility of the head teacher, under the School Standards and Framework Act, 1998, to implement the school behaviour policy consistently throughout the school, and to report to governors, when requested, on the effectiveness of the policy. It is also the responsibility of the head teacher to ensure the health, safety and welfare of all children in the school.

The head teacher keeps records of all reported serious incidents of misbehaviour.

The head teacher has the responsibility for giving fixed-term exclusions to individual children for serious acts of misbehaviour. For repeated or very serious acts of anti-social behaviour, the head teacher may permanently exclude a child. The role of the governors is detailed in the exclusion policy.

Only the head teacher (or the acting head teacher) has the power to exclude a pupil from school. The head teacher may exclude a pupil for one or more fixed periods, for up to forty-five days in any one school year. The head teacher may also exclude a pupil permanently. It is also possible for the head teacher to convert a fixed-term exclusion into a permanent exclusion if the circumstances warrant. The chair of governors and the exclusion committee is to be informed of any fixed or temporary exclusions.

If the head teacher excludes a pupil, she informs the parents immediately, giving reasons for the exclusion. At the same time, the head teacher makes it clear to the parents that they can, if they wish, appeal against the decision to the governing body. The school informs the parents how to make any such appeal.

The head teacher informs the LEA and the governing body about any permanent exclusion and about any fixed-term exclusions beyond five days in any one term.

The head teacher monitors the effectiveness of this policy on a regular basis. She also reports to the governing body on the effectiveness of the policy and, if necessary, makes recommendations for further improvements.

If the school has to use correctives, it is expected that parents will support the actions of the school. If parents have any concern about the way that their child has been treated, they should initially contact the head teacher. If the concern remains, they should contact the chair of governors. If these discussions cannot resolve the problem, a formal grievance or appeal process can be implemented as set out in the school's complaints policy.

Agreed by staff: date
Reviewed annually: last review
Agreed by governors: date

D. PUPILS' BEHAVIOUR

There are various ways of categorising pupils' behaviour. For the purposes of this Handbook, we will consider the following labels:

- all children and young people in school;
- children who display low-level misbehaviour/disruption;
- children who display challenging behaviour;
- children and young people at risk of exclusion;
- children and young people educated outside school.

1. All children and young people in school

The vast majority of young children behave themselves very well both in and out of school. Nevertheless, there is a widely held public view that children's behaviour is deteriorating significantly. Whether pupils' behaviour is becoming worse or not is a difficult question to answer with certainty; it often depends upon your own perspective. Certainly, pupils' behaviour is constantly evolving and changing.

From a teacher's perspective, the advent of the National Curriculum (NC) brought coherence and continuity into the classroom in terms of what people are taught. At the same time, it may have reduced flexibility. But in this Handbook we are writing about the behaviour of primary school pupils. The overwhelming majority of primary schools are orderly and well managed and teacher–pupil relationships are excellent.

However, society and national cultures are changing and evolving, too. Society today is much more multi-cultural, pluralistic and diverse. The traditional nuclear family is breaking down increasingly and the values within some local communities have changed, such as the breakdown in extended family relationships. Within this context, within primary schools we are encouraging more children to participate more readily in discussion and decision-making, which may include, on occasions, challenging adults' opinions, requests and instructions.

If we were to compare teachers' experiences now with those of, say, forty years ago, it would prove an almost impossible task. More primary pupils now appear to have complex home lives, live in the 'computer age', become truants and absentees, have special or additional learning needs, mental health issues and, seemingly, literacy and numeracy difficulties. So how do we make direct comparisons?

At primary level, fortunately, the use of drugs, alcohol, knives and even serious cases of bullying are comparatively rare; although the latter, including cyber bullying and the misuse of social networking sites, are becoming more common. Therefore all we can do is reiterate that young children's behaviour is changing, often guided by their parents, carers, peers, the effects of the mass media, advertising and other societal pressures such as the fashion industry upon younger girls. But is primary-aged pupils' behaviour actually worse? Who knows?

2. Children and young people who display low-level misbehaviour/disruption

Elements of low-level misbehaviour can occur in any class at any time. The range of possible incidents caused by low-level misbehaviour includes:

- noisy entry into class;
- marginal lateness for lessons;
- lack of material or equipment;
- failure to do homework;
- calling out across the classroom;
- teasing or provoking other pupils;
- insisting upon a teacher's immediate response;
- moving around the classroom without permission;
- failing to listen to instructions;
- talking incessantly, unnecessarily;
- shouting or calling out.

In primary school classrooms, and in schools which are well managed and have a good school ethos, the impact of low-level misbehaviour is likely to be much reduced. The extent to which these low-level misbehaviours may occur more frequently and may develop seems to depend upon the culture of the school, an individual classroom teacher's skills and the composition of the class. Despite this, it is often continuous low-level disruption which can have a serious and cumulative effect upon both staff and other pupils. Tired, over-extended staff can at times respond to situations in ways they would never choose if they were relaxed and confident in the classroom.

The cumulative effects of pupils displaying the following behaviours can put pressure upon school staff and make the daily task of teaching a challenging one:

- attention-seeking behaviour;
- poor classroom survival skills;
- limited social skills.

3. Children who display challenging behaviour

What is challenging behaviour? It is difficult to define. Is it swearing at a teacher in the classroom? Is it victimising another pupil? Is it fighting? Is it tripping a classmate up? Is it a boy picking on girls? In fact, it is all of these things and more.

Challenging behaviour is any form of behaviour that interferes with children's learning or normal development, is harmful for the child, other children or adults, or puts a child in a high-risk category for later social problems or school failure.

The Elton Report defined challenging behaviour in a school setting thus:

> Any form of behaviour that causes concern to teachers. It can range from talking in class and not settling to work, to verbal and physical abuse, destruction of property and bullying.
>
> (Elton Report, 1989)

It is for this reason that challenging behaviour is so potentially widespread, and managing it is difficult and requires considerable skills; and so all teachers and senior teachers, including head teachers, require extensive training in and periodic updating of their classroom or school behavioural management skills and abilities.

4. Children and young people at risk of exclusion

Some children find school to be an unrewarding environment. In some cases, this may stem from them having unmet and, worse still, unidentified additional learning needs. There is good evidence from Howe and Mercer (2007) that many young children who misbehave in school lack the necessary literacy skills to engage in the curriculum at the level at which the teaching is presented to them. This can result in disaffection and ultimately lead to disengagement. When this occurs within the context of an inflexible curriculum (i.e. one that does not match their interest, enthusiasms and aspirations), it is likely that they will feel that:

- they cannot be successful;
- no one cares;
- they do not fit in;
- they are to blame in some way.

If this compounded by a peer-pressured 'try not to succeed' attitude or one where it is perceived to 'be cool to be difficult', it is even more likely that the young pupil will start to become disengaged from education.

A pupil with behavioural difficulties may be defined as follows:

> Any child with social, emotional or learning needs, whose behaviour and/or attendance adversely affects their learning and/or the learning of others.
>
> (NBAR, 2008: 48)

Children at risk of exclusion are normally drawn from this group.

It is clear from the above definition that pupils' needs are complex. Therefore managing individual pupils and groups of pupils is never easy; ask any parent! Some children with emotional difficulties may turn inwards and withdraw from others. Sometimes their problems may only become apparent in their reduced socialisation skills and/or disengagement from other members of their peer group. In fact, some pupils probably lack the social skills necessary to cope effectively within a classroom setting, such as those with Asperger's Syndrome.

It is evident and clear that better screening and detection techniques are required to accurately diagnose and establish better intervention strategies with some difficult pupils. Screening techniques need to be better able to detect subtle changes in pupils' behaviour and demeanour, depression and withdrawal. Whilst one child may be better able to cope with a sudden parental separation or divorce or a family bereavement, another may not and view the whole situation and life as a catastrophe. For all these reasons the availability of help, support and advice from appropriate professionals is a prerequisite both in and out of schools.

Some other pupils exhibit social and emotional difficulties that they 'act out' in their classrooms or schools. These are the ones who often cause us most concern. Also, there are children whose additional learning needs cause them serious problems. Often these pupils will react or 'lash out' in frustration, which causes behavioural difficulties within schools. Sometimes it is these kinds of pupils who will develop complex concerns or 'phobias' and who will graduate to become fully fledged troubled and exceedingly difficult children and young people during their secondary school careers. Reid (2012), in a study of young offenders in Swansea jail, found that the vast majority had serious histories of underachievement and behavioural difficulties whilst at school and many of them had committed the offence which led to their sentence whilst truanting from school.

5. Children and young people educated outside school

Pupils being educated outside schools include those pupils who are home educated, formally excluded from school, unofficially or illegally excluded from schools (although this should never happen), awaiting managed moves or moving into an off-site centre, pupil referral unit or alternative curriculum venue, amongst others. The costs of educating these pupils may be considerably higher than for mainstream primary schools.

E. THE ROLE OF THE BEHAVIOUR SUPPORT TEAM

The primary behaviour support team (PBST) is one part of an LA's overall behavioural support services. Figure 3.1 presents a fairly standard flow diagram of the organisation of a behavioural support team within an LA. It shows how action is taken within an LA from the point when initial concerns are raised to the time the case is referred to the Primary Behaviour Panel, as well as the targets and referral points engaged in this exercise. A typical example of the kind of posts and responsibilities of the people who comprise a PBST is presented in Figure 3.2. The PBST team is responsible for decision-making on pupils' behavioural support needs within an LA. It is an interesting phenomenon that many PBSTs throughout the UK are comprised of a high majority of women and some are exclusively female.

The PBST team consists of a range of specialist classroom teachers and support staff who, along with experienced LA personnel, make up the panel (see Figure 3.2). The PBST works in partnership with schools to:

- develop policy and skills for the effective management of challenging and more serious behaviour;
- bring about a sustainable, long-term impact upon teaching, learning and behaviour;
- develop the individual school's capacity to manage challenging and more serious behaviour and to reduce exclusions.

An important part of the work of the PBST is to help to provide professional development for teachers, school-based staff and governors, amongst others. PBST members are normally available to work with outside agencies, head teachers, senior staff, classroom teachers, non-teaching support staff, parents and carers, through either whole-school, whole-class, small-group or individual work with pupils.

In addition, the PBST is engaged in important work and interaction with the pupil support grant, the Outreach Team, the Most Challenging Pupils' Service, the Complex Case Team, SEN and ALN support, educational psychology, education social work, health, social services, and educated out of school and education otherwise teams, amongst a range of other possibilities. The PSBT also provides advice to schools on local needs, guidance and national legislation and regulatory requirements. The SEN Team and the SEN Code of Practice, for example, ensure that provision is matched to need and take responsibility locally for differentiation, School Action, School Action Plus, statutory assessment and Statement of Special Educational Need. Similarly, oversight of non-statutory guidance might involve developing the behaviour policy and communicating it to schools, overseeing the power of schools to discipline pupils and what it means, regulating pupils' conduct and disciplining them for misbehaviour outside school premises, promoting and rewarding good behaviour, punishing poor behaviour, the use of disciplinary sanctions, detention, the confiscation of inappropriate items, the use of force, restraint, violence reduction, safer school partnerships, bullying, attendance, exclusions, alternative provision, weapons searches, as well as provision for pupils with individual needs such as mental health or medical problems.

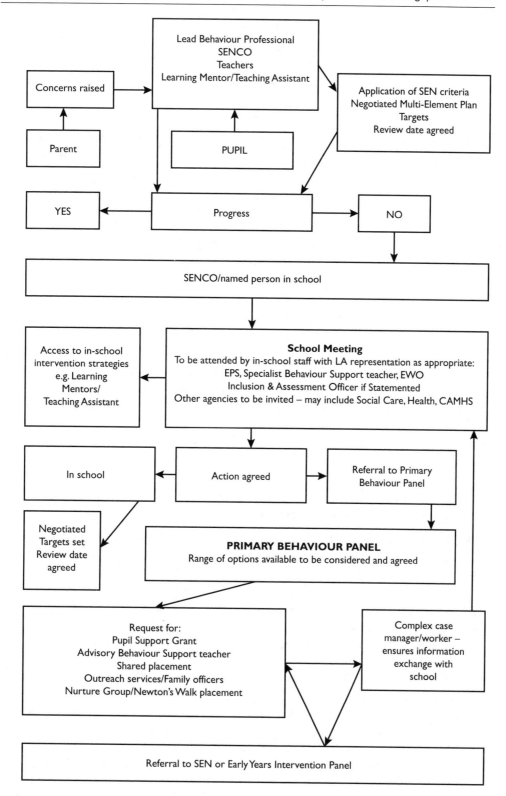

Figure 3.1 The typical organisation of a primary school behaviour management team: flow diagram for primary behaviour management

Chair of Primary Behaviour Panel		
Primary co-ordinator of behaviour provision and services		
Complex case manager	Teacher in charge, Specialist Team	Teacher in charge, Outreach Team
Complex case worker	Class teacher	Class teacher
Family officer	Class teacher	Behaviour support teacher
Consultant	Behaviour support teacher	Behaviour support teacher
	Specialist teaching assistant	Specialist teaching assistant
	Specialist teaching assistant	Specialist teaching assistant
	Specialist teaching assistant	Specialist teaching assistant
	Specialist teaching assistant	
	Specialist teaching assistant	
	Specialist teaching assistant	

Figure 3.2 Primary behaviour management support services team

Figure 3.3 provides an example of how a PBST might begin to undertake an audit of an individual pupil's behavioural needs. This is only one of a whole number of possible assessment strategies and forms which are used in the process, which may or may not be undertaken by the Most Challenging Pupils' Service, depending upon circumstances. Finally, Figure 3.4 presents a request form from a school for additional help and support from the LA's primary behaviour management support services team.

Most Challenging Pupils' Service: case example for a medium-sized LA in England

The Most Challenging Pupils' Service began as an LA project to reduce exclusions in primary schools and built upon the success and experience of earlier work led by the Educational Psychology Service. Initially, the project aimed to provide a rapid and effective response for key stage 2 pupils at risk of permanent exclusion. The intervention was time limited and based around a Multi-Element Plan, with support staff offering a consultation style of service to LA schools. Following a successful project year funded by the DfES Innovation Unit, the Most Challenging Pupils' Service became a core-funded service.

The Most Challenging Pupils' Service is focused on supporting primary-aged pupils by offering high-quality consultation to their teachers. It is used to help maintain the placement of pupils with challenging behaviour in primary schools. The service aims to help school staff to develop a detailed and effective behaviour plan for pupils by improving their understanding of the child's behaviour. This is achieved by collaborative working between the school's educational psychologist, Most Challenging Pupils' staff and school colleagues to assess the child's needs through a functional assessment and then to develop a Multi-Element Plan. Given the high demand for behaviour support across LA primary schools the support of the service is time limited and the four phases are normally completed over a twelve-week period.

Audit of Pupil Behaviour

Name	
Date	Year group

	Very good	Good (acceptable)	Satisfactory (improvement needed)	Unacceptable (action needed)
Arrival at school				
Entering the classroom				
Registration				
During the lesson				
Plenary				
First break				
Entering the classroom				
During the lesson				
Lunchtime				
Entering the classroom				
During the lesson				
At the end of the day				

Areas of priority:

Action steps:

Figure 3.3 Audit of pupil behaviour

Referral Form for Additional Services for Primary Behaviour Management

Date of referral	

Name of school	
Address	
Telephone number	

Name of head teacher	
Lead behaviour professional	
SENCO	

Identified needs

Include your school's behaviour needs as in your School Improvement Plan.

Whole-school input

Include any LA input over the last academic year regarding behaviour management, i.e. Educational Psychologist Services.

Intervention requested

For example training for midday supervisors.

Anticipated outcomes for the school

Include plans to ensure sustainability.

Completed by	
Position of responsibility	
Date	

Figure 3.4 Referral form for additional services for primary behaviour management

Access to the Most Challenging Pupils' Service is through the school's educational psychologist. The target population for this service would have the following characteristics:

- All children will be from the Foundation Stage, key stage 1 or 2 and the school should have completed two major intervention forms at School Action level.
- There will be documented evidence that the child is likely to engage in physically aggressive behaviour on a regular basis towards the staff who manage him or her and that this is a persistent problem.
- There will be documented evidence that the child is likely to engage in behaviour that prejudices his or her safety or the safety of others on a regular basis and that this is a persistent problem.
- The child's school will have indicated that it will co-operate fully in developing and putting into place measures designed to support the child by agreeing to co-operate in the assessment and carry out the recommendations made once the assessment is complete.
- The relationship between school staff and the child should not be at breaking point. Continued full-time schooling for the next ten to twelve weeks must be possible. This allows us to do a thorough assessment and deliver an intervention which should show signs of working.

Summary

In this chapter we have considered a respect and relationships and well-being policy, categories of pupils' behaviour and the role of the primary behaviour support team. In Chapter 4 we will conclude our tour of the essential background issues to understanding primary school behaviour management. In particular, we will consider such issues as the role of classroom assistants, learning school mentors, playground assistants, parents and carers and restorative justice.

Chapter 4

New approaches 4
Roles supporting classroom management

In this chapter we will bring together some of the key remaining pieces in the jigsaw that is all about managing primary pupils' behaviour. These sections will include important information and practical details about the following:

- school-based case conferences and the use of case data and case histories;
- making home visits;
- monitoring and follow-up;
- links with secondary schools;
- sharing good practice: top tips for managing behaviour;
- the use of websites;
- awards;
- training in primary school behaviour management;
- the role of school inspectors;
- the role of classroom assistants and learning or school mentors;
- the role of home–school liaison officers;
- the role of playground assistants;
- time management, decision-making and record keeping;
- restorative justice and restorative practice;
- the role of parents and carers.

For example, in the section on good practice (pp. 68–69) we present some of the top tips for managing pupils' behaviour in the classroom.

1. SCHOOL-BASED CASE CONFERENCES AND THE USE OF CASE DATA AND CASE HISTORIES

The use of case conferences in primary education amongst a range of caring and support professionals has mushroomed since the Children Act, 2004, legislation. Case conferences have been a standard plank of social care for a considerable period of time. They are now becoming much more widely used and are regarded as a useful tool both in supporting LA behaviour management services and during interdisciplinary and multidisciplinary work.

A case conference is a non-statutory meeting, often organised by social services or the 'lead professional', to consult with other agencies and professionals to collate information about the child and family. There are two types of case conference, the initial and the review case conference. The first case conference is undertaken very quickly when applied by social services following a referral. They consider the child and the family individually and as a unit. The people around the table are representatives of all the various agencies involved. These often include social services, police, education, health, and probation and/or the National Society for the Prevention of Cruelty to Children (NSPCC).

This is to establish the initial plan about what needs to be done about a case/child. This may result in a child being put on the 'at risk' register or, as a last resort, them being removed to a place of safety. The latter action might involve moving children out of the family home through the use of court orders and even seeking powers to ban certain adults from the home as well. Thereafter, all future case conferences, following the Every Child Matters agenda (2003), will be spaced at six-monthly intervals. Parents or carers invited to attend may bring their solicitor if they wish. The solicitor is normally allowed to advise her client but not speak on her behalf at the meeting. Parents and carers are entitled to read any pre-reports written about them before going into the conference.

Case conferences papers often include parents' and children's profiles as part of their case or case history data. For pupils' cases to be considered or for parents to be referred to a case conference because of their child's behaviour at or outside school, the conduct must, by definition, be serious, challenging and potentially place other pupils or teachers 'at risk'. Examples of such cases might be for anti-social behaviour, bullying, victimisation, threatening behaviour, the use of drugs, substance abuse, alcohol, sex-related activity, repeated misconduct in school. Fortunately, such referrals at the primary school level are comparatively rare, albeit increasing. Sometimes behaviour-related case conferences can invoke child abuse proceedings, as in the Bulger case.

Child protection case conferences

The child protection case conference has a specific role regarding the protection of children. The purpose is to allow the participants to pool their knowledge of the child's health, development and functioning, and the parents'/carers' capacity to ensure the safety and well-being of the child, as well as to minimise risk. It is a fact that classroom teachers and school support staff are often the first person/people to notice potential or actual abuse and schools therefore make a high percentage of initial child abuse referrals from a variety of angles. The key definitions of child abuse which may be detected by staff in primary schools revolve around significant harm or risk, physical injury, sexual abuse, emotional abuse, physical neglect or physical failure to thrive. The concepts and definitions to be followed by the members of the various agencies present are presented below.

Significant risk or harm

The concept of significant risk or harm is a complex matter. Much depends upon a professional's judgement based on an assessment of the child's and the family's circumstances. Significant harm may mean as a result of a specific incident or a series of incidents, or as a result of multiple concerns, which could even have occurred over a significant period of time. Case conferences should always ensure that the needs of the child are paramount. It is always essential, when considering whether there is significant harm, that the child's needs and circumstances come first rather than the view of the alleged abusive behaviour.

Physical injury

This covers actual or attempted physical injury to a child, including the administration of toxic substances, where there is knowledge or reasonable suspicion that the injury was knowingly inflicted or intentionally not prevented.

Sexual abuse

Any child may be deemed to have been sexually abused when any person(s), by design or neglect, exploits the child, directly or indirectly, in any activity to lead to sexual arousal or other forms of gratification of that person or any other person(s), including organised networks. This definition holds whether or not the child is said to have initiated or consented to the behaviour.

Emotional abuse

Emotional abuse is the failure to provide for the child's basic emotional needs so as to have a severe effect on the behaviour and development of the child.

Physical neglect

Physical neglect occurs when a child's essential needs are not met and this is likely to cause impairment to physical health and development. Such needs include those for food, clothing, cleanliness, shelter and warmth. A lack of appropriate care, including deprivation of access to health care, may result in persistent or severe exposure, through negligence, to circumstances which endanger the child.

Children's failure to thrive

Children's failure to thrive may be defined as their significantly failing to reach normal growth and developmental milestones, where physical and genetic reasons have been medically eliminated and a diagnosis of non-organic failure to thrive has been established.

2. MAKING HOME VISITS

A variety of professionals may make home visits to assess or contact pupil(s) and/or their parent(s) or carer(s) for a wide variety of reasons. These include health visitors, education welfare officers, education social workers, head teachers, a range of other school or LA staff such as members of the primary school behaviour support team (see Chapter 3), social workers, educational psychologists, various staff from voluntary agencies, home–school liaison officers, attendance officers, the police, GPs, amongst a range of others. One of the aims of the Children Act, 2004, was to prevent duplication and overlap between different agencies, but all the evidence (NBAR, 2008) continues to show that this and poor communication and different advice being given to families by different agencies continue to be amongst the reasons preventing the post-Every Child Matters (2003) agenda from becoming truly effective.

How professionals speak to children and parents and carers is equally important, alongside good listening and observation and recording skills.

3. MONITORING AND FOLLOW-UP

It is always important to establish who the 'lead professional' is when making links with a child and his or her family, following home visits or when compiling papers for case conferences, including the use of case histories. Recording the data accurately on the main file is important bearing in mind children's and parents' rights, the Data Protection Act, Freedom of Information Act, Disabilities Act, Race Relations Act, Human Rights Act, amongst many more, including the Children Act itself and its professional requirements. Care should be taken when transferring data and storing it in electronic files, and on data bases and hard drives. Child and adult confidentiality between and within services needs to be guaranteed and protected. Breaches of confidentiality are one of the main reasons for breakdowns or communication failures between parents and professionals. These unintentional lapses can cause serious divisions and destroy parents' and carers' respect for support professionals as well as their willingness to co-operate. In order to show continuity in support in both single- and multi-agency work with families, it is important that the same support professionals remain on a case whenever possible. Another frequent complaint from parents or carers is the constantly changing professional interface, which often leads to parents or carers supplying the same information to different staff on several separate occasions. It helps to plan follow-up meetings well ahead and to plan the papers for these meetings as early as possible. Too many sets of papers continue to be prepared at the last minute, for example on the day or night before a meeting.

4. LINKS WITH SECONDARY SCHOOLS

Links between primary schools have improved immeasurably in recent years. Nevertheless, the primary–secondary transfer scene has in some ways become even more complicated. No longer do all the pupils from local primary schools transfer automatically to their nearest neighbourhood secondary/comprehensive school and, in fact, the whole issue of admissions to particular secondary schools has become something of a political hot potato – at least in England.

How to choose a secondary school

Parents and carers will find out a great deal of information about their children's potential secondary school(s) from both their primary and potential secondary school(s) at specially convened meetings, in booklets and through a range of informal processes, such as talking to other parents. It is important to ask questions and gather certain information:

- Ascertain the views of the children themselves. For example, which school are their friends going to at the start of key stage 3?
- Ask about the strengths of the particular secondary school. Does it have a specialist curriculum area or interest/reputation? Would your child's temperament/personality suit the school?
- Are there challenges at the school? What is the behaviour, attendance, bullying like? Are staff–student relationships sound?
- What are academic standards like? What extracurricular activities do they offer?

Pupils' common worries before the transfer

Moving from the top class in year 6 of a primary school to the bottom year of a very much larger secondary school and into year 7 is probably one of the biggest educational challenges which both pupils and parents face. The first few days and weeks of secondary schooling are often a challenging period for both parties, and sometimes can be a taxing period for behaviour both at home and at school as various adjustments have to be made. Parents should never underestimate this transition period even if most or all their friends are having the same or similar experiences. Many children become particularly anxious and parents need to become good listeners and to hold intelligent conversations with their children, including asking the right questions.

Some of the most common worries which pupils have ahead of or just after the transfer include the following:

- Will I be bullied by older pupils?
- Will I get too much homework? Will I be able to keep up with it?
- Will I be forced to do some subjects I dislike, e.g. PE or swimming?
- Will I get to school on time?
- Will I be in the same class as my friends or my best friend(s)?
- Will I feel lost in school?
- Will I have my own locker?

These are some of the issues which primary and secondary schools, parents and children need to consider in advance of the transfer to ensure the transition period goes as smoothly as possible.

5. SHARING GOOD PRACTICE: TOP TIPS FOR BEHAVIOUR MANAGEMENT

An abundance of websites are available on good practice in managing pupils' behaviour in school, in the classroom and in different kinds of schools. Some of these sites have originated from national government departments or agencies. Others emanate from local authorities or individual schools or are established by consultants or specialists in behaviour management, such as our own Behaviour Stop Ltd. All these sites contain a vast array of useful information on good practice or sharing good practice. One of the most useful is the site prepared by Dave Stott (2009), who is the author of *50 Top Tips for Managing Behaviour*, from which the list presented below has been adapted.

Stott makes the point that all teachers have their own individual ways and styles of keeping order in the classroom. However, some techniques and processes are universally adaptable. As we feel that his advice is so practically useful, we would like to endorse it and, although some have been slightly adapted and reworded, and a couple even excluded, you may like to try the ideas for yourselves as the need arises.

TIP: Stott's top practical behaviour strategies in the classroom

- *Voice matching*: always ensure your voice is at the volume and has the intonation which you expect from the pupil. A loud and aggressive voice will usually result in a loud and aggressive response.
- *Self-calm*: practice all your self-calming skills. Remember that the first person who needs to calm down is you.
- *Move in*: if you are speaking to an individual pupil, do not shout across the room or remain rooted behind your desk; move in slowly towards the pupil in a non-threatening way.
- *Move out*: once you have spoken to the pupil, the temptation is to remain close by the pupil, awaiting compliance. You are much more likely to be successful if you move away, expecting compliance. This enables the pupil to make the right choice without 'feeling' the stress of your presence.
- *Personal space*: for most people, personal space is about the length of an outstretched arm. This is a good guide to use in the classroom.
- *Hurdle help*: use positive posters in the school and classroom as rule reminders (both written and illustrated) to help pupils overcome the hurdles that prevent them from complying with your rules and expectations.
- *Positive ethos*: always establish and maintain a positive ethos in your classroom. To help to achieve this, set a high standard. Always be on time, be well prepared, mark on time, use praise regularly with pupils, and concentrate initially on the pupils who are on task and complying with the classroom guidelines.
- *Proximity praise*: rather than giving random praise, spot the off-task pupil and make sure you praise the pupil nearby who is on task and complying; this is much better initially than highlighting the wrong behaviour.
- *Non-verbal language*: be aware that approximately 60 per cent of all communication is non-verbal. Keep asking yourself: what is my body language saying?
- *Antiseptic bounce*: this is a classic strategy. Send the target pupil to a colleague with

---

a note or message. The note says: 'Tell (pupil's name) "Well done" and send him or her back!' The pupil has been removed from the problem area, received praise and will usually return in a better state of mind.

- *Meet and greet*: some pupils are often simply not in the right state of mind at the start of a school day or the lesson. Establish a system whereby you, the CA or LSM meet and greet the pupil upon entry and create the right atmosphere.
- *Track pupils' behaviours*: it is essential that you have an accurate and objective system for tracking, monitoring and evaluating behaviour.
- *Refocusing*: don't be verbally misled by pupils' stories or arguments. Refocus them on the issue by using an empathetic statement which regains the initiative.
- *Broken record*: always avoid engaging in an argument. Be prepared to repeat your instruction(s) up to three times using the exact same wording before raising the level of your response.
- *Time out/change of seat*: a change of environment will often help to refocus a pupil. The emphasis should be on the word 'time'. Always ensure you have a plan of how to reintegrate the pupil into your teaching group.
- *Self-review*: give the pupil a self-review sheet and ask them to review their own behaviour/actions during class/the work they have completed.
- *Hierarchy of response*: have at least five levels of response and remember that your role is to use the responses to keep the pupil at the lowest level possible; try never to escalate the issues/problems.
- *Communicate*: always make sure you have systems in place to enable the sharing of information with parents, other staff and the named pupil. The competent classroom teacher should always be able to detect potential hotspots, problem issues or potentially difficult lessons or situations in advance.

The use of websites

There are a multitude of websites providing teaching and non-teaching staff with an array of ideas, resources, strategies and training to help effectively manage behaviour in the classroom. Two very good websites are www.behaviourstop.co.uk and www.tes.co.uk/teaching-resources.

Awards

There are a range of awards for primary schools in the United Kingdom or other countries for which it is possible to apply. Two of these are the Leading Aspect Award and the Times Educational Supplement (TES) National Schools Awards.

The Leading Aspect Award

The Leading Aspect Award is open to any aspect of education and allows the organisation to identify its leading practice.

TES National Schools Awards

The TES Awards, for which primary schools can apply and be judged in a national competition on an annual basis, include the Outstanding Primary School of the Year Award, the Outstanding Literacy or Numeracy Initiative, the Best School Website Award, the Outstanding Contribution to Education of the Year Award, amongst several others.

6. TRAINING IN PRIMARY SCHOOL BEHAVIOUR MANAGEMENT

Research indicates that many educational professionals receive too little training on behaviour and attendance (NBAR, 2007, 2008; Reid, 2004, 2005a, 2006a, 2010a, 2010b). We agree. Explicitly, the NBAR Report team found that 'some of the strongest evidence they received revolved around the need for more and better training, especially on behavioural management, at almost every level' (NBAR, 2008: 99). The report expressed concern at the lack of a clear qualifications framework and a linked professional development programme for a wide range of educational staff who work with attendance and behaviour issues in school. These personnel included school governors, midday and play supervisors, teaching assistants, learning school mentors, home–school liaison officers, education welfare officers, police officers who work in schools, practitioners from health care, social care, the voluntary sector and LA support agencies, as well as trainee teachers, probationary teachers, teachers in the early years, more experienced teachers, senior staff, deputies and head teachers. The NBAR Group were particularly concerned that most governors had received little or no training on the nature or understanding of challenging behaviour or school absenteeism. The group took the view that to provide effective services for securing good attendance and behaviour, it was essential that all those involved received adequate training on how to deliver their role and how to work effectively with each other. Whilst in some parts of the UK and elsewhere, primary staff receive better behavioural management training and support, it is clear that others receive very little. The NBAR team wondered how much better it might be if all education professionals had a right to receive the appropriate training, development and qualifications for their respective roles in behavioural management. Amongst primary staff many new and young teachers, classroom assistants and learning mentors were especially critical of the little training (or lack of it) which they had received in behavioural management.

Some of the issues or programmes which were found to be needed were:

- improving the behavioural climate within a school;
- how to engage pupils and raise their self-esteem;
- improving teachers' classroom management skills;
- assisting staff who are experiencing difficulties managing classroom behaviour;
- how to engage effectively with parents and carers;
- working with troubled individuals;
- securing change in a pupil's behaviour;
- engaging the support of parents in working for change;
- supporting colleagues and guiding them in ways of dealing effectively with individual pupils;
- involving external agencies and using them effectively to support children and young people in difficulty;
- the use of restraint;
- reducing the costs of school exclusions through better intervention and management techniques;
- how to implement the children and young people's rights agenda;
- how to make school councils more effective.

In England, the Department for Education and Schools manages a national behaviour and attendance strategy which operates at three levels: national, regional and local. This commenced in 2003. Its core aim is to 'improve pupil behaviour and attendance, supporting practitioners through developing a consistent approach building on the best current practice' (see www.dfes.gov.uk/behaviourandattendance). The main thrust of the programme is:

- to reduce behavioural problems, both serious and low level;
- to reduce exclusions;

- to provide high-quality alternative provision for those who are excluded, at risk of exclusion or at risk of dropping out of the system;
- to reduce truancy, tackle the root causes and improve school attendance levels;
- to ensure effective mechanisms are in place for identifying and re-engaging pupils who go missing from school;
- to improve perceptions of behaviour and attendance among school staff, parents and the community at large;
- to close the gap between behaviour problems shown by different groups of pupils.

A related DES website, Behaviour in Schools, provides official policy news and carries a range of case study examples. This can be found at www.des.gov.uk/ibis/index.cfm.

The DES in England also managed the Behaviour Improvement Programme (BIP) between 2002 and 2006. During this period around 450 secondary schools and more than 1,700 primary schools benefited from the BIP funding and related resources. Recognising the importance of developing social, emotional and behavioural skills (SEBS), this has been a core part of the National Strategy for School Improvement since September 2004. Specialist materials to develop the social and emotional aspects of learning (SEAL) have been available to primary schools since May 2005. Successful leadership by the SMT in primary schools is key to the effectiveness and wise use of the SEAL and SEBS programmes. The National Programme of Specialist Leaders of Behaviour and Attendance (NPSLBA), which started in 2004, is now a fully integrated part of the national strategies programme. It is designed to prepare specialist leaders for schools and LAs on behaviour and attendance.

7. SPECIALIST LEADERS AND SPECIFIC ROLES

Most lead behaviour professionals (LBPs) have other responsibilities in the schools they work in and some schools use alternative titles to describe the role. As a member of the SMT, the LBP oversees the school's behaviour and attendance and anti-bullying policy. The LBP supports all staff to ensure high standards of behaviour and attendance in school at all times, to ensure the best possible standards of teaching and learning.

The LBP's main functions are to ensure high standards of behaviour and attendance by:

- creating shared values, expressed as expectations and standards of behaviour and modelled through the consistent manner in which all staff manage behaviour and attendance;
- implementing a coherent whole-school policy, improvement plan and monitoring arrangements for behaviour and attendance;
- supporting all staff to improve learning and teaching through improved confidence and skills in behaviour and attendance management;
- organising a programme of CPD for all members of the school community;
- managing collaborative partnerships with other local schools, the local community, parents, agencies and other providers of support for improving pupil behaviour and attendance;
- facilitating the learning and teaching of SEAL, through a whole-school SEBS programme, with additional provision for pupils who need it;
- establishing and maintaining a school climate that is inclusive, safe and secure and one where positive behaviour and regular attendance are learnt and taught by all.

In turn, these LBP-led schemes are further enhanced by such schemes as Education Improvement Partnerships (EIPs), courses facilitated through the National College School Leadership programmes and by sponsored research. Scotland, Northern Ireland, Wales and other countries have their own national, regional, state and local programmes (Reid, 2010a).

The role of school inspectors

There is nothing which school staff and governors enjoy more than receiving a glowing report from school inspectors. How schools manage behaviour and attendance is a key part of a school's inspection processes. However, inspection criteria vary considerably from country to country. Also, some LAs conduct their own inspection regimes, often as a part of school improvement, enhancement or school effectiveness frameworks. Reid (2006b) showed how significant the impact of primary school inspections could be upon school attendance and the wide range of issues highlighted by inspection reports. He also reinforced how a poor performance on behaviour and attendance could lead some schools to be placed in special measures (Reid, 2005c, 2007a, 2007b).

It is interesting to observe how schools are inspected for behaviour and attendance. For many years it was often the lay inspector who fulfilled these roles. However, such has been the increased importance given to the area that there appears to be a swing back to the lead inspector or one of the registered specialist assessors fulfilling the role. A high percentage of schools placed in special measures have either an attendance- or a behaviour-related reason, or both, for being placed in this category, and these are frequently among the top three reasons given by inspectors for their decision.

The role of classroom assistants and learning or school mentors

Both classroom assistants (CAs) and learning school mentors (LSMs) or support mentors have a complex role and are used in a variety of different ways by schools and LAs and in specialist provision or in special educational needs (SEN) schools. Much depends upon their job description and terms of reference. Sometimes CAs and LSMs are appointed for their specialist work with pupils who have behavioural issues. The role and support of the CA or LSM can be of immense value in supporting pupils or groups with social, emotional and behavioural difficulties. However, there should always be close teamwork between the preparation and planning of the classroom teacher and her support staff for it to be truly successful and for them to establish the complete partnership.

In terms of behaviour the CA and/or LSM can offer or provide support in a variety of ways. These include:

- sharing responsibility with the teacher for monitoring, changing and redirecting behaviour, possibly by using an individual behaviour target programme;
- increasing the adult/pupil ratio and thus the amount of positive attention and support each pupil can receive;
- providing additional support for learning activities which individuals find particularly difficult and stressful;
- helping to de-escalate and diffuse potential problems;
- helping to resolve difficulties over equipment, space or activities;
- giving regular praise, support and encouragement to particular pupils;
- providing reward sessions when pupil(s) have achieved their behaviour targets;
- ensuring such schemes as 'time out' or other alternative behaviour or 'quiet room' activities are carried out properly;
- taking an individual away from the rest of a class, thereby allowing them to calm down without disrupting the rest of the class;
- being vigilant in watching out for any changes of behaviour or mood of pupils thought to be at risk of neglect, abuse or bullying;
- ensuring time is given to listen to the pupil and understand his or her views;
- befriending a pupil and helping to build trust (without causing the pupil to become over-reliant);

- helping an individual pupil to solve a situation and learn from their mistakes;
- supporting pupils at unstructured times (e.g. at lunchtime);
- modelling appropriate behaviour – incidentally, a sound professional working relationship between a teacher, CA/LSM or both can also model good communication and respect between adults, including parents, colleagues and other support professionals;
- participating in school in-service training, school review and pupils' assessments or case conferences;
- conducting activities with an individual or small group of pupils which will help develop social skills, raise self-esteem, improve emotional intelligence and/or develop co-operative play skills;
- accurately observing the behaviour of pupil(s) for an agreed period of time to provide a baseline of behaviour and to assess the effectiveness of practical interventions;
- recording incidents or utilising the antecedent, behaviour, consequence (ABC) format, or utilising other analyses of behaviour approaches or formats or by administering tests or questionnaires with pupils (e.g. Coopersmith, Brookover, etc.).

Therefore, CAs and LSMs can perform invaluable tasks in support of their classroom teacher, who acts as their professional leader.

The role of home–school liaison officers

The duties of the home–school liaison officer (HSLO) can vary between schools and LAs. In some areas they act solely as specialists in managing school attendance. They manage attendance and make home visits when pupils are not attending school. In this capacity, they act like attendance officers or education welfare officers (EWOs). Often senior staff or the head teacher will request a home visit when a pupil fails to attend school or because there is concern about the welfare of a pupil. HSLOs often write reports and progress reports on these pupils. Sometimes they make home visits because of pupils' behavioural or bullying difficulties or for other related issues.

Some schools also employ specialist support staff for pupils with specific or serious behavioural or other difficulties. Under the supervision and direction of a teacher, a school's specialist behavioural support worker assists in classroom activities, school routines, and the care and management of pupils with behavioural disorders and/or related disabilities or other specific needs.

The role of playground assistants

Play assistants generally support pupils with their play-related activities during breaks and at lunchtimes. Some play assistants have dedicated roles, such as helping to support pupils with special educational needs, disabilities or behavioural difficulties, including a wide range of social, emotional and psychological problems. Some nursery assistants undertake similar assignments in the classroom or during breaks or both.

8. TIME MANAGEMENT, DECISION-MAKING AND RECORD KEEPING

As mentioned in Chapter 1, maintaining appropriate records, evidence of meetings, decision-making, resolutions and subsequent actions and accurately mapping pupils' progress are an important part of today's managerial skills, as outlined in the Children Act, 2004, processes. It is also important how records are kept. It is equally important that they never contain personal comments, opinions or derogatory information. Education professionals need to remember that their schools, the SMT and their LAs have to comply with the legal requirements of the Data Protection Act, Freedom of Information Act, Human Rights Act, Race Relations Act, Disability Act, to name but a few. Doing so is sometimes not easy, especially when you are dealing with issues like pupils' misbehaviour, attendance, bullying, exclusions, mental health, disabilities, social, family and home background, psychological and medical histories. It is for this reason that all governors, head teachers, members of the SMT and staff involved in the management, care, record keeping and decision-making for these kind of issues should be properly trained for their tasks.

9. RESTORATIVE JUSTICE AND RESTORATIVE PRACTICE

In increasing numbers, schools and LAs in the UK, Europe, the United States, Canada and Australasia are looking towards the introduction of restorative justice (RJ) or restorative practice (RP) or similar approaches for dealing with the management of difficult pupils and their reintegration (Hopkins, 2004; Kane *et al.*, 2007). Partly, restorative justice schemes have been started as a result of the drive towards making schools more child-friendly places. The main reason, however, for the development of restorative justice approaches has been because of the need to re-establish relationships following a breakdown, possibly as a result of indiscipline.

Some schools, looking for solutions to concerns about indiscipline and disaffection, aggression and violence, now appreciate that there is a need to restore not only good relationships but also a positive school ethos, which reduces the possibilities of further conflicts arising again. The restorative justice approach seems compatible with the recognition that schooling in today's complex, modern, fast-changing and pluralistic society is increasingly difficult, demanding and stressful.

Many RP schemes are being introduced into schools using the basic principles but different formats, with different target groups and at differing levels. The manner in which RP schemes are introduced and developed in schools is exceedingly important. The training of staff using a whole-school approach to manage RP schemes well is essential.

Scotland has taken a lead on the introduction of RP schemes into schools (McCluskey *et al.*, 2008a). For example, the Scottish Project into RP (McCluskey *et al.*, 2008b) found that:

- RP seemed to be most effective when 'behaviour' was seen as an issue to be addressed through restorative strategies that involved active learning for all children and for staff across the school;
- this was most likely to happen when there was visible commitment, enthusiasm and modelling by the school management team and where the school had invested in significant staff development;
- in many schools there was a clear positive impact on relationships, seen in the views and actions of staff and pupils and in a reduction of playground incidents, discipline referrals, exclusions and the need for external support.

It is anticipated that many more RP schemes will be introduced into schools around the world in the foreseeable future. This is a fast-developing and emergent field in which much research activity is currently taking place (Morrison, 2007).

10. THE ROLE OF PARENTS AND CARERS

Background

Teachers and pupils are the two key components of learning and school-based relationships. But there is a third party in the equation: parent(s) and carer(s).

Some schools follow 'open' practice procedures with parents. This means that they are welcome to enter the school at any time. Other schools utilise 'closed' procedures. This means that parents are only welcome inside schools after making appointments or for set events, e.g. parents' evenings/afternoons, open day, etc. Some schools use a variation on both practices. That is, in the infant section parents are welcome at any time. But in the juniors they have to make appointments.

Variations on these practices occur almost from school to school. The reality is, however, that the better the communication is between school and home, the better the support the parents are likely to give the school. This applies not just in terms of parent–teacher associations but also when it comes to such features as discipline, attendance, exclusion and, where necessary, home visits.

Teachers and parents

Just as teachers need to feel confident in front of their class they also need to feel in control of managing pupils' behaviour. For this to work well, a good constructive relationship between teachers and parents can be invaluable. Building good relationships with parents can also have a considerable and beneficial effect on teacher–child relationships. For example, the children will often absorb their parents' comments and attitudes towards the teacher. When parents support teachers in the home with positive remarks, children are more likely to have respect for their teachers.

TIP: Five Golden Rules for managing pupils' behaviour in the classroom

1 Establish a close working relationship with parents. Explain to parents what is expected from each child, what the consequences are for inappropriate behaviour, learning and poor attendance, and what the reward structure is for good behaviour.
2 Communicate with parents on a regular basis informing them of their child's successes. For example, 'Megan was awarded the weekly certificate for improved behaviour in the playground', 'Charlie was awarded the termly certificate for best attendance in the final assembly of the term for coming to school every day, even during the snow'. Using the Home–School Link Book may be helpful for this activity.
3 In the event of a disagreement, it is counterproductive to argue with a parent(s). It is also helpful not to interrupt the parent when they are talking; allow them to inform you of their problem. Then you can put your viewpoint and inform the parent(s) of your common goal: wishing their child to succeed in school and later life.
4 Invite the parents to see their child's work. This helps build strong working relationships. The parents can imagine their son's or daughter's participation in the classroom. This helps to build up confidence and strong working relationships between teacher, parent and child. It provides 'conversation points' about school and learning in the home. If parents do not wish to meet in school (perhaps because they feel uncomfortable, probably due to their own negative experiences at school), then you could photocopy samples of their child's work and send it home.
5 Always comment positively on a child, regardless of the child's behaviour. Focus on the individual child's strengths (e.g. at football, at drawing or as a popular member of the class).

Communication with parents

Communication with parents occurs in five ways to a lesser or greater extent between home and school:

1   *Formal introductory all-school activities*: these include sessions learning about the school and the curriculum when the pupil first joins the school.
2   *Open days and parents' evenings*: schools vary on how these events are organised, e.g. through appointments, open procedures, after-school, evenings or termly events.
3   *School reports/assessments*: these are sent home at regular intervals.
4   *Individual appointments for parents or carers*: these are made as and when necessary. For example, 'John has missed a lot of school and needs to catch up'. Or 'we need to speak to you because Sally has been ill with glandular fever'. Or 'we need to see you because Wayne's behaviour has deteriorated'.
5   *Whole-class discussions with parents*: in these, teachers take the opportunity to show parents and carers the whole-class work, possibly through displays, and follow these displays up with discussions about the curriculum and teaching and learning processes. These sessions can provide opportunities for parents to gauge and to understand their children's work in its proper educational context. Although not all schools currently follow this approach, it is important, as Desforges and Abouchaar (2003) found that parental involvement in children's learning is a significant factor in pupil's educational achievement.

Parents and behaviour

Parental support is a substantial factor in enabling pupils to cope with and adapt to the demands of behaving appropriately in school. When a pupil exhibits behavioural difficulties in school, parents are a key resource in helping teachers to secure change in a pupil's behaviour. If it does not actively involve a pupil's parents in significant discussions about a pupil's misbehaviour, a school may reduce its own chances of securing improved conduct.

Schools need to understand that parents have much more time and more opportunities to influence and shape their own children's behaviour. A school's influence is for thirty-eight weeks out of fifty-two each year and, in most weeks, for up to five days. Parents, on the other hand, are actively involved every day for fifty-two weeks of each year.

When teachers think parents are contributing to the pupil's problematic behaviour, it becomes critically important that they try to engage with them. In the final analysis, a home appointment or visit may even be necessary.

Who holds parental responsibility?

In an area where family structures are evolving, and there are fewer and fewer traditional families, schools and teachers need to be clear as to who the parents are in a given family, especially to meet the requirements of the Children's Act, 2004. For example, the Welsh Assembly's Inclusion Strategy promotes working with all of those adults who carry 'parental responsibility'. In complex, non-nuclear families, it is important that teachers understand and recognise who holds specific daily parental responsibility.

The following may be helpful to schools in clarifying the position:

- In the event of separation or divorce, both parents retain responsibility for the child (unless a court determines otherwise).
- Where parents are unmarried, only the mother has parental responsibility (unless a court has ordered otherwise).
- Where a child is subject to a Residence Order and is, for example, living with grandparents, the grandparents hold responsibility for the duration of the order.
- Where a child is accommodated by the local authority, the parents and the local authority are likely to be working in partnership to meet the child's needs.
- Where the child is 'looked after' by the local authority and subject to a Care Order, the local authority holds parental responsibility for the child.

In these latter cases, the school and/or local authority can engage with:

- divorced parents – either separately or at the same time, depending on the extent to which they co-operate following the divorce;
- the mother – she determines whether to involve anyone else (especially for younger children);
- the grandparents;
- the parents and the social worker;
- the social worker and a carer, foster parent or prospective adopter.

Whoever holds responsibility, the principles of a school's approach to securing support for the child, especially one manifesting behavioural difficulties, remains the same. In effect, the school has an *in loco parentis* responsibility for the children in their care during the school day in term-time.

Information sharing with parents

It is always a good idea to build a history of positive contact with parents. When schools establish such a history, it is much more likely that the parents or carers will listen to their concerns and accept them should any problems with behaviour arise.

Early notification to parents or carers is normally best for two reasons. First, it helps to prevent behaviour from worsening. Second, schools and parents will start to work together at the earliest possible opportunity. Schools should try to avoid parents asking, 'Why weren't we told about this before now?'

What parents need to know

Schools should advise parents of the following:

1 *When there are difficulties*: all parents and carers need to know when their child is experiencing difficulties in school.
2 *The scope and extent of the problems or difficulties*: parents need to know the extent of any difficulties in school so that they can compare this with their child's behaviour at home. They can then make a judgement on the nature of their child's needs.
3 *The school's approach to responding to a pupil's behavioural difficulties*: parents need to be advised of how the school intends to react to the problem(s).
4 *Advice on working together*: how parents or carers can help and support the school and their child in dealing with and hopefully resolving the behavioural difficulties.

Types of parents

Not all parents will necessary react in the same way when schools advise them of their children's difficulties. Some parents may lack the skills, knowledge and insight to appreciate their significance for the learning and behaviour of their child. They may also lack the knowledge of how to equip their child to cope in particular settings (e.g. being bullied). Through sound interaction with parents and carers, schools can often be alerted early to actual or impending problems for their child.

Generally speaking, there are different types of parents. The vast majority of parents and carers are competent and capable and always ready to support their child through change. However, some parents may be unaware of their own significance in supporting their child in his or her learning and behaviour at school. Some may be struggling with poverty, low incomes, poor housing, illness, disabilities, unemployment, divorce, amongst other possible issues. The cumulative effect of all or any of these may be to reduce their capacity to work in active partnership with schools.

Some parents or carers may be wary of engagement with authority figures such as head teachers. This may stem from their own histories as pupils themselves or from other outside influences, or they may suffer from low self-esteem.

A very small minority may appear 'not to care' about their child's behaviour in school. This may stem from their own struggle to manage their child's behaviour at home.

Utilise a 'no blame' approach

Schools must be careful not to overtly blame parents or carers for the poor behaviour of their child. Otherwise, confidence will be reduced and tensions raised, and then co-operation is less likely to occur and remedial strategies to be effective either in the short or long term.

Summary

In this chapter we have considered a wide range of issues, from utilising school-based case conferences and case data to links with secondary schools, 'top tips' for implementing good practice in behaviour management in the classroom, training in primary school management, the role of CAs, LSMs and other key support staff, through to the emerging use of restorative justice and restorative practice schemes and the role of parents and carers. This concludes Part I of this Handbook on essential background issues to provide an understanding of behaviour management in the primary classroom. In Part II, we will consider more fundamentally the role of classroom management strategies and how to implement and utilise classroom management skills from a variety of perspectives.

Part II

Effective classroom management

Chapter 5

Tips for classroom professionals
Practical advice

The training of staff in positive behaviour management is essential not only for the effectiveness of the school but also for their health and well-being. In one recent survey, the Association of Teachers and Lecturers found that half of those it surveyed had considered leaving the profession because of bad behaviour (Association of Teachers and Lecturers' Survey, 2010). For this reason alone it is clear that effective and positive behaviour management in schools is an essential training requirement for all those engaged in teaching and working in the school and classroom situation.

The art of teaching and managing difficult behaviour can be stressful even for the most accomplished practitioner. If you prepare well, think positively and believe you are a winner, then you are more likely to win at changing the children's behaviour. Henry Ford once said, 'Whether you think you can, or think you can't – you're right.' Positive attitudes are contagious and will affect the children's outlook within the class. By and large, pupils take their lead from their teachers, especially in primary school classrooms.

In this chapter, we will consider the following five issues:

- tips for successful teachers;
- how to model appropriate behaviour;
- the use of body language;
- how to remain in control in class;
- the relationship between teachers and parents.

TIPS: Tips for successful teachers

Successful teachers:

- create positive learning cultures;
- take leadership of their class;
- organise and plan lessons effectively;
- believe all children have the ability to achieve;
- engage inattentive children;
- involve pupils in overall classroom management, giving them ownership and responsibility;
- have a sense of humour which can be used to disarm challenging situations;
- have positive body language;
- model the desired behaviour;
- welcome children into class;
- deal with behaviour fairly and consistently.

Modelling behaviour

The teacher's behaviour is the most significant influence in the classroom. By being a positive role model to children, you will help to encourage them to develop better social skills which enable them to make more positive choices. Pupils have both the right and need to feel safe, valued and respected. Therefore, teachers need to manifest the kind of confident approach which conveys these values.

TIP: Modelling the desired behaviour

Desired behaviour	Teacher modelling the behaviour
Respecting others	Do not ridicule a child in front of their peers. Instead, deal with the behaviour fairly and appropriately.
Resolving conflict	Deal with the situation in a calm yet authoritative way by applying the appropriate sanctions in a fair and consistent manner.
Listening to others	Provide support for a child by listening and showing interest in whatever she or he is talking about.

Do's	Don'ts
Remain in control	Lose control of the situation
'Catch' poor behaviour before it starts	Use sarcasm
Respect and acknowledge race, gender and culture	Personalise a pupil's behaviour
Be fair and consistent when issuing sanctions	Get irritated or angry
	Raise your voice
Inform parents of positive achievements	Be uncaring and distant
Listen attentively and show interest	Make threats or promises you can't keep
Look for the win–win solution	Condemn the individual's character
Evaluate what worked well	Reprimand individuals in front of their peers
Disapprove of the behaviour, not the child	Make personal comments in front of the whole class; instead, do this in one-to-one situations
Ignore minor misdemeanours	
Reward good behaviour	
Teach the child to self-manage their behaviour	

Body language

How teachers' personalities, appearance and temperaments are transmitted to their pupils is key to creating and maintaining a positive learning culture within a school and inside a classroom. An individual's body language (posture, eye contact, facial expression, head and body movements, gestures, touch, etc.) make up approximately 55 per cent of what we are communicating. Therefore, to be an effective communicator to pupils, it is important to understand and implement positive and effective body language.

Non-verbal communication is a useful tool in the classroom as it is possible to express, for example, approval or disapproval of a pupil's behaviour in an effective way without speaking. Below is a list of suggestions to improve body language.

TIP: Body language

Eye contact

- Eye contact is generally associated with trust, rapport and positivity.
- Too much eye contact can be intimidating and threatening.
- Looking away shows a lack of interest or deviousness.
- Looking down conveys submission.
- Develop a steady gaze, as an individual who makes frequent eye contact is seen as confident.

Facial expressions

- Facial expression can easily communicate, for example, mood, attitude, understanding, confusion.
- A smile can make others feel more at ease.
- A frown can convey aggression or suggest that the person is unsure of something.
- To convey that you are in control, display a calm, relaxed facial expression with a smile to confirm acceptable behaviour.

Posture

- Posture can convey a whole range of attitudes, for example lack of interest.
- A good positive posture takes up more space, so make yourself look bigger.
- A proud, upright stance makes you look more important.
- A sagging posture can mean lack of confidence.
- Standing and walking tall, with your shoulders back, shows confidence as a leader.
- A relaxed stance can be effective when dealing with a challenging situation.

Gestures

- Non-verbal gestures can be used to direct an activity.
- The flat of the hand can be used to signal to the class to calm down.
- To invite a child to sit down we can point with our hand.
- Putting a finger to your lips can signal quiet.
- A thumbs-up signals good work/behaviour.
- Avoid folding your arms as this can indicate a closed, defensive attitude and makes you appear unapproachable.
- Having your hands in your pockets, tapping on surfaces, fidgeting, scratching, etc. can give the impression of discomfort or embarrassment.

Proximity

- Where possible, allow pupils their personal space.
- Standing in a pupil's personal space can be deemed as threatening and could incite a situation.
- The more room you appear to occupy, the more confident and important you appear.

Tone of voice

- Your voice should be clear, positive and non-threatening.

- Warm and expressive voices, used in an imaginative way, draw pupils in and make them want to pay attention and listen.
- A lively voice will be motivating and encourage the pupils to readily engage in the activity.
- Speak at an acceptable speed so that pupils can understand the information given.
- Do not shout; instead, project your voice in an assertive manner.
- Do not use a patronizing voice as this can bring about negative pupil behaviour.

Mannerisms

- Move around the classroom in a comfortable fashion, smiling and making gentle eye contact with everyone.
- Be a visible presence by standing as long as possible through each lesson.
- Think about your breathing to help you calm down; take slow breaths until you start to feel relaxed.
- Clothes have an impact and convey an individual's personality. Smart, comfortable clothes in plain, darkish colours have been shown to work best.

How to remain in control

When dealing with a challenging situation it is important to remain detached and not take it personally. Instead, take a deep breath and display a calm and confident exterior as this may help to reduce a child's anxiety and his or her frustration and enable the child to feel more secure. Remember to keep your tone of voice low and calm no matter how frustrated or upset you may be feeling. Remember also to reassure the class or individual pupils that you care about them and that their display of misbehaviour has not affected your overall concern for their welfare. When pupils feel the teacher is in control they are more likely to calm down and make the right choice and so improve their behaviour.

Case study: Don't take it personally

Mrs Harris, class teacher

Mrs Harris had a pupil in her class who on occasion would engage in unacceptable behaviour in order to embarrass and/or get a reaction from her. On one occasion the pupil said to her for no apparent reason, 'Miss, do you know you're really fat?' Normally, Mrs Harris would have reacted negatively to this type of comment but instead she remained in control and responded with, 'Do you know, I have asked myself that question. I really don't understand it as I regularly go to the gym and I have a healthy diet. But no matter what I do I don't seem to be able to lose the weight.' The pupil was not expecting this type of response and immediately apologised.

This type of response from Mrs Harris prevented the pupil's behaviour from escalating and through her response she created a win–win situation. Answering in this way also made her feel in control, which resulted in an unexpected turning point in her relationship with the pupil.

It is a good idea to apply the following technique. When a behavioural incident occurs in class, immediately grade it and give it a score out of ten. A score of ten represents something very serious, while a one is only a very minor incident. When a situation arises, for example a child displaying high-level disruption in the class, would you score it a nine or eight? Then ask yourself at the end of the day, of the term or in a few months' time whether you would still see it as that serious. Next time a child displays similar challenging behaviour ask yourself again whether it is a nine or a five. This technique helps to put difficult situations into perspective.

TIP: Responding

- Start the day/lesson with a positive remark to any child who may display challenging behaviour.
- Welcome them at the door.
- Try to deal with minor misbehaviour non-verbally so that the child knows his or her behaviour is unacceptable and has the choice to turn it around.
- Deal with situations calmly, quietly and in a non-threatening way.
- Have a database of comments and commands you can use in trying situations.
- If/when a situation arises take a deep breath and count to ten before intervening.

Case study: You're not a teacher!

Mrs Cook, midday supervisor

Like most support staff in schools, pupils frequently make statements to midday supervisors such as 'You're not a teacher' when asked to follow an instruction. On one occasion, Mrs Cook stopped a child from running into the hall to have his packed lunch and asked him to walk in sensibly. The pupil responded with 'You're not a teacher' and refused to follow the instruction. Mrs Cook answered, 'That's correct, Keenan. I'm not a teacher. I'm a midday supervisor and I'm responsible for your behaviour during lunchtime.' As Mrs Cook remained in control and did not respond negatively to the situation, the pupil followed her instruction and walked into the hall sensibly.

This is an effective strategy to help defuse potentially difficult situations and challenging remarks from pupils which can otherwise lead to 'lose–lose' outcomes.

Managing emotions

Understanding and managing your own emotions brings a positive balance to the classroom. By displaying positive emotions a teacher will instil a feeling of safety and trust amongst the pupils.

Make time for yourself

It is important to de-stress after a working day, thereby helping to recharge the batteries. Looking after yourself will help to make sure you're fit and healthy and will put you in a better state of mind to help your pupils. Teachers sometimes feel guilty when they put their own needs before those of their pupils, but doing so will help you to provide more quality time and better teaching for your pupils.

McGee (2001) defines GUILT as follows:

- **G**ive yourself
- **U**ninterrupted
- **I**ndulgent
- **L**eisure and pleasure
- **T**ime at least twice a week.

You're only human

Not everything is going to go the way you anticipated, whether it's a lesson or a challenging situation. So don't pretend. Pupils have more respect for teachers who are human and communicate what went wrong and how it can be dealt with more effectively in the future, for example: 'Lana, I'm sorry I didn't get a chance to speak to you today about your trip to London, so what I need you to do is to find me tomorrow breaktime in the playground so we can have a chat.' We can achieve this by following our own social rules and by saying what we mean. It is important to mean what we say by developing our own self-awareness and expressing ourselves correctly.

Tell someone

We all encounter situations which give us concern, whether it is dealing with a difficult class or individual. When this happens we need to tell someone and talk through the issues with a colleague or friend in order to help gain a proper perspective and come up with solutions. Don't bottle things up. Instead be proactive and talk about it.

TIP: Believe in yourself

- Be positive and believe that you can make a difference.
- However small your achievements are, always acknowledge them and celebrate.
- Remember we all make mistakes and that's how we learn.
- It is important to understand that children's behaviour may only improve slightly or sometimes not at all. It may even get worse before it gets better, which can make us feel helpless, even inadequate.
- Remember it's not 'one size fits all' so be flexible, adaptable and open to change.
- Plan ahead, but be flexible and accept change. Remember it takes time to accomplish all your goals. Also, keep your goals realistic.
- Don't take it personally when sometimes children do not show appreciation for your efforts.
- If you feel overwhelmed, chat it through with another member of staff.
- Take time out to enjoy a healthy lifestyle, including exercise, healthy eating and sleep.
- And, finally, adopt a sense of humour and have some fun!

Summary

In this first short introductory chapter to Part II, we have considered a range of practical information for teachers to apply in the classroom. In Chapter 6, we will develop these themes by considering a whole-school strategy for positive behaviour management.

A whole-school strategy for positive behaviour management

This chapter focuses upon how to establish and manage a whole-school strategy on behaviour management. Effective behaviour management relies heavily on a school's overall strategy through its school policy document on behaviour management to provide a well-structured and consistent approach to dealing with pupils' difficulties. This policy should specify the correctives and rewards available for staff to use to deter negative conduct and promote positive behaviour. The strategy must be reviewed and the policy document amended and updated on a regular basis to ensure its maximum effectiveness.

More specifically, this chapter will focus upon the following issues:

- how to inform staff, parents, carers and pupils about the use of whole-school correctives;
- how to take steps to deal with unwanted behaviour;
- the use of reflective learning in managing behavioural matters:
- understanding emotional literacy;
- monitoring and evaluating pupils' progress through the use of such aspects as self-monitoring charts, behaviour contracts, Individual Learning/Behaviour Plans, Pastoral Support Programmes;
- requesting assistance in an emergency or a difficult situation.

Informing staff, pupils, parent(s)/carer(s)

Before the implementation of any new strategy within a school, it is important that all concerned are fully informed and participate in the process and understand the aims, procedures and outcomes.

Informing staff

One of the aims of the whole-school approach is to achieve consistency in the use of disciplinary processes by all staff. This gives a clear message to both staff and pupils that procedures are fair. There are occasions when school routines are disrupted, such as when a supply teacher is being employed in the school to cover sickness or staff are on day release to attend in-service courses. Quite often, these staff are unfamiliar with school routines and procedures and this can cause disruption in the classroom. To ensure continuity is maintained, it is important to induct supply staff and other support professionals in the procedures set out in the school's positive behaviour policy. This can be achieved by creating an overview of the procedures which they receive as part of their welcome pack when arriving at school.

Informing pupils

Pupils can be informed about the whole-school approach during an assembly and it can be reinforced throughout the year during class circle time. The school council can be involved in the decision-making, and all staff and pupils should also have an opportunity to participate in the establishment of a school's rules, correctives and positive reinforcements. With everyone working together, the implementation of the rules and school behavioural policy document should occur more smoothly, with a great deal of common ground between all the interested parties. This will also generate support for the monitoring processes. In order for children to take ownership they need to be involved in the following:

- how the strategy works;
- school rules and correctives;
- school positive reinforcements;
- the various stages of the approach, i.e. reminder, warning;
- the agreed list of 'serious' misbehaviour;
- how the approach deals with 'serious' misbehaviour;
- how parent(s)/carer(s) will be involved.

Informing parent(s)/carer(s)

Gaining parental support is a crucial factor in enabling pupils to cope with and adapt to the demands of behaving appropriately in school (see Chapter 4). When a pupil exhibits behavioural difficulties in school, parents are a key resource in helping teachers to secure a change in behaviour. If it does not actively involve a pupil's parent(s) in significant discussions about a pupil's misbehaviour, a school may reduce its own chances of securing change substantially. Schools need to understand that parents have much more time and many more opportunities to influence and shape their own children's behaviour.

Whole-school correctives

Correctives are only really effective when used in the context of a positive classroom culture, where clear rules and routines apply, as well as the use of rewards to reinforce positive behaviour. These should be used sparingly to achieve the best results and should not overburden the person imposing the corrective. When issuing correctives to a child because of inappropriate behaviour, you should not implement them in isolation. They must be paired with more positive responses which inform the individual child about the appropriate behaviour and the actual set of skills for which you are looking. Correctives need to be timely, specific, logical, reasonable and fair, with a clear beginning and ending.

It is important that correctives are:

- understood by pupils, staff and parents/carers alike;
- fair;
- consistent;
- appropriate;
- aimed at teaching appropriate behaviour.

Schools have a legal right, when a pupil misbehaves, to impose correctives which are reasonable and proportionate to the circumstances of the case. Schools should monitor the use of correctives carefully by taking account of the pupil's age, ethnicity, gender, special educational needs (SEN), disability and any unique family, social or psychological circumstances.

When and how to issue correctives

Correctives should be issued with more positive instructions about the behaviour which you are seeking and an explanation of the skills required to achieve this level. They need to be timely, specific, logical, reasonable and fair, with a clear beginning and ending. Correctives should be implemented when a pupil is engaging in any of the following:

- breaking school/class rules;
- affecting the education and well-being of other pupils;
- preventing the teacher from teaching;
- failing to follow instructions;
- a serious incident, e.g. fighting.

The types of redress issued need to be reasonable and proportionate to the situation. If they are too severe, delayed or inconsistently applied, they will probably fail to work.

To ensure consistency and fairness when issuing a corrective, a behaviour management team should be assigned. A member of this team can be consulted prior to a pupil receiving a corrective to ensure it is appropriate and a logical response to the misbehaviour displayed. The team can consist of any of the following members of staff:

- head teacher;
- deputy head teacher;
- SENCO (special educational needs co-ordinator);
- pastoral support worker;
- SMT (senior management team) member.

Serious misbehaviour

When a pupil's misbehaviour is deemed serious, then, after discussions with a member of the behaviour management team, he or she should be 'fast-tracked' straight onto the latter stages of the school's policy, which we call the Fifth Response (see p. 91). To ensure consistency of approach, a list of what the school considers to be serious misbehaviour needs to be devised, agreed and recorded.

TIP: A sample list of serious misbehaviour
- hitting;
- kicking;
- spitting;
- swearing;
- damaging school property;
- refusing a member of staff after three requests;
- using ICT equipment inappropriately;
- bullying;
- stealing;
- leaving without permission:
  - the classroom;
  - a school building;
  - the school grounds;
  - a school trip.

Sustaining motivation

When issuing correctives the child's motivation to learn and develop needs to be taken into consideration. The whole process of implementing correctives should be designed to ensure that a child understands when his or her behaviour is unacceptable and will not be tolerated again by the school.

When a child is given a corrective, they may feel as if they have 'blown it', which may result in a worsening of the behaviour and an 'I don't care' attitude. In order to keep the child focused and motivated, try implementing the 'Golden 5 Minutes Rule'. Here, within five minutes of the reprimand/corrective, try to find something about which to praise the child, for example sitting correctly, reading quietly, completing their work. This can be very effective at keeping the child motivated to engage in more appropriate and better behaviour.

A graduated response

When deciding on whole-school correctives, it is important that it includes an opportunity for a graduated daily response to ensure that the child has the opportunity to redeem him- or herself by making positive choices. For example:

- First Response;
- Second Response;
- Third Response;
- Fourth Response;
- Fifth Response.

First Response

Below are some suggestions for First Reponses to unwanted behaviour:

- issue and record the First Response;
- redirect the child's behaviour;
- make eye contact with the child to make them aware you have noticed and disapprove of the behaviour;
- use physical proximity, for example walk over to the child and mark their work;
- give the child a verbal prompt, for example: 'John I'd like you to listen so you'll know what to do for the next task, thank you';
- give a reminder.

Second Response

Below are some suggestions for Second Reponses to unwanted behaviour:

- issue and record the Second Response;
- one-to-one reprimands;
- miss x minutes of playtime;
- give a warning.

Third Response

Below are some suggestions for Third Reponses to unwanted behaviour:

- issue and record the Third Response;
- removal from the group/class;
- withdrawal from a particular lesson or peer group,
- withdrawal of access to the school IT system (if the pupil misuses it by, for example, accessing an inappropriate website);

- removal of break or lunchtime privileges;
- miss *x* minutes of playtime;
- give a time out.

Fourth Response

Below are some suggestions for Fourth Reponses to unwanted behaviour:

- issue and record the Fourth Response;
- meeting with head teacher;
- setting additional work;
- loss of privileges in class or in school;
- preventing participation in non-curriculum activities, for example a school trip or sports event;
- holding discussions with parent(s) or carer(s);
- miss *x* minutes of playtime;
- give a time out.

Fifth Response

Below are some suggestions for Fifth Reponses to unwanted behaviour:

- issue and record the Fifth Response;
- a variety of forms of detention, i.e. an emotional literacy behaviour preventative;
- SMT and SENCO to discuss next step for behaviour, i.e. monitoring and evaluating behavioural progress, for example Individual Behaviour Plans (IBPs);
- managed moves;
- a fixed-term exclusion;
- permanent exclusion.

Below are detailed examples of more carefully thought out and graduated responses:

Time out

If a child is engaging in undesired conduct give them time out either inside or outside the classroom. For infants this can be through the use of a simple hoop or a coloured spot. Time out should not be used as a punishment but rather as a graduated response to help to provide the child with an opportunity to make the right behavioural choice. In order for this to be effective, a designated area should be identified either inside or outside the classroom, free from distractions, for this purpose. In this area, it is sensible to display a poster guiding the child through the Reflective Cycle process. This Reflective Cycle can be simplified for key stage 1 children. Depending on the age of the child and level of misconduct displayed, this will determine the length of time spent in the time out area.

It is important that the corrective is given to enable the child to spend time reflecting and that the class teacher decides when they feel the child is ready to join the rest of the class/ group. Time for reflection is crucial in order for the individual pupil to recognise the implications of his/her behaviour and/or for both the teacher and the pupil to re-establish their own levels of self-control. It is also important to establish what types of behaviour warrant a time out in advance and this list should be included in a school's behaviour policy. These should always be discussed with the children to reinforce the class's expectations at least at the start of each new school year cycle.

TIP: Time out procedure

Issue a time out in a calm and assertive way.

Use a script when issuing a time out, for example 'Gareth, I am asking you for the first time to go to the time out area and think about your behaviour.'

When the child is in time out, inform them of the following:

- how long they will be in time out;
- that they need to think about the unacceptable behaviour displayed;
- what they need to do to put things right.

Return to the child after the designated time and ask:

- Why were you put into time out?
- What do you need to do to rejoin the class/group?

If the child is calm and apologises allow him/her to rejoin the class/group. If he/she is not ready, then extend the time out or move to the next graduated response.

When the child returns to the class/group repair the relationship and implement the Golden 5 Minutes Rule (see pp. 90–91).

Reflective learning

It is important for a child who has engaged in inappropriate behaviour to reflect and understand his or her actions. The reflective learning process helps pupils to do this by helping them to understand whether it was a good or bad experience, what came out of it and whether they could have handled events in a different way, as well as to understand better how it subsequently has made them feel. This can be readily achieved by using the model of the Reflective Cycle shown in Figure 6.1, especially when coupled with emotional literacy training tasks as a preventative against future inappropriate behaviour.

Loss of privileges

Planning to include daily, weekly, monthly and termly positive reinforcements in your teaching not only helps to keep the children motivated but also enables the school to enforce a 'loss of privileges' corrective, depending upon the form of the inappropriate behaviour.

The loss of privileges can include excluding a pupil from:

- a non-curriculum activity, i.e. attending a school/class fun day;
- after-school activities, i.e. orienteering;
- playtime with their peers;
- representing the school, i.e. at a concert or football match.

It is important never to remove a reward that a child has already gained. A child's conduct often improves over time when he or she starts to realise that a particular action may 'cost' him or her a loss of privileges which he or she enjoys or looks forward to taking part in. It is also important to note that taking away a longer-term reward (e.g. a trip to the pantomime) can sometimes worsen pupils' behaviour as the child will no longer have the motivation to try hard or to behave and may even feel victimised. In situations like this, the use of a 'strike' chart may be more appropriate because it is less instantaneous and gives pupils a period of

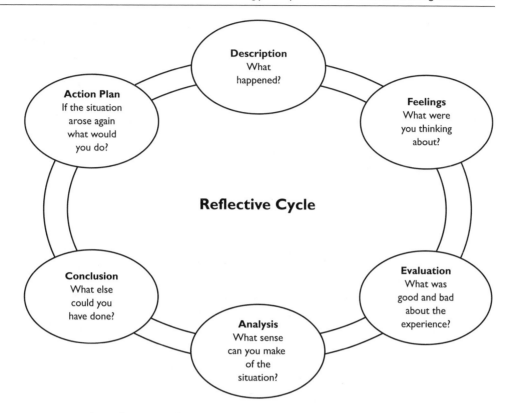

Figure 6.1 The Reflective Cycle

time to reflect upon their actions. For example, if the child receives three strikes on the chart, then the main reward is taken away. A strike can be issued if a child reaches a Fourth and/ or Fifth Response (see graduated responses on pp. 90–91). The use of strike charts usually gives a child up to three chances before he or she is penalised further. It is ultimately the pupil's choice whether to engage in positive or negative behaviour. There may be occasions, however, when major rewards may need to be removed when or if a child's misbehaviour is severe or they could benefit from having a significant corrective implemented.

Detention

Detention can be an effective corrective provided it is coupled with emotional literacy training (see the 5-Step Behaviour Programme in Chapter 7). When detention is part of the school's positive behaviour policy, potentially any pupil can be placed into it. Ideally, pupils in the early years should not be given detentions as they tend to be more suitable for junior-aged pupils. If the detention is outside normal school hours, then twenty-four-hour notice should ideally be given to parent(s)/carer(s) for safety reasons. When children are given detention in class, they must still receive time to undertake a form of play so that they can exercise. This can be achieved by supervising the child outside in a designated area for a specific period of time.

Emotional literacy

In order for children to make positive choices they need to understand what is acceptable and unacceptable as well as developing the skills to help manage their own behaviour. It is important to help children understand why they have behaved in a certain way. More often than not children are completely oblivious as to why their behaviour is sometimes unacceptable. Engaging children in emotional literacy exercises can help them to recognise the relationship between their thoughts, feelings and actions when responding to others.

> Your behaviour is based upon your feelings, which are based on your thoughts. So the thing to work on is not to change your behaviour, but those things inside of your consciousness that we call thoughts. Once your thoughts reflect what you genuinely want to be, the appropriate emotions and the consequent behaviour will flow automatically. Believe it, and you will see it!
>
> (Dyer, 2001)

What is emotional literacy?

Emotional literacy is the ability to express feelings using words. The ability to show emotions, to show others how they are feeling, is a basic emotional need of all adults and children. If these emotional needs are not being met children will express their emotions and feelings by displaying challenging and unwanted behaviour. Some children find it hard to talk about their emotions and how they are feeling. If they first of all identify how they are feeling they can be taught how to manage and control behaviours. A good starting point is to ask children to use 'I' statements such as:

- I feel sad;
- I feel unimportant;
- I feel hurt;
- I am unhappy;
- I am bored.

By identifying how they are feeling using these 'I' statements they are becoming more aware of their own feelings. The Emotional Literacy Programme addresses these feelings and helps to balance them first by identifying the following:

- the behaviour being displayed;
- the emotion – the way that the child feels before, during and after the behaviour has occurred;
- the skill and strategy needed to show the child how to regulate and motivate themselves through planned activities.

> Emotional Intelligence is a way of recognizing, understanding, and choosing how we think, feel and act. It shapes our interactions with others and our understanding of ourselves. It defines how and what we learn; it allows us to set priorities; it determines the majority of our daily actions. Research suggests it is responsible for as much as 80% of the 'success' in our lives.
>
> (Freedman et al., 2001)

Developing emotional literacy is an essential part of a child's education. Emotional literacy not only helps children to recognise their emotions and feelings but also helps them to understand how these can affect them individually as well as the people around them. This provides them with the ability to form and manage relationships, which is a key part of growing up.

Children's behaviour, academic performance and social relationships, both in and out of school, are influenced by their knowledge and understanding of their own emotions. It is clear that it is not only a family's responsibility to teach children about important interpersonal and conflict resolution skills, as this responsibility also rests with the school. Working together and promoting these skills both at home and at school will benefit the child and also help to create a strong home–school link.

Emotional literacy comprises one of four key areas of development, self-awareness, self-regulation, self-motivation, empathy and social skills. These are presented in Figure 6.2. In Figure 6.3, we provide a list of social competencies.

Providing children with a full range of these skills gives them the ability to make positive choices, which has great benefits for the school. Here are some of the benefits of developing children's emotional literacy:

- understanding of appropriate and inappropriate behaviour;
- being able to tolerate frustration better;
- helping to overcome stressful situations;
- getting involved in less unwanted behaviour;
- being able to express emotions, i.e. anger, in an appropriate and safe way;
- developing an understanding of how their actions can affect other people;
- becoming more able to communicate their needs and to express their feelings;
- taking personal responsibility for promoting a safe and positive school environment;
- being able to walk away from a situation and being able to request an adult's help;
- increasing willpower and self-control;
- increasing understanding of appropriate and acceptable behaviour;
- developing the ability to respect the needs and rights of others.

Self-awareness	Children are able to: • describe how they are feeling and why; • identify their emotions, i.e. happy, sad, angry; • understand how their feelings can influence outcomes; • make positive choices.
Self-regulation	Children are able to: • manage their feelings, emotions, thoughts and actions; • show respect towards others; • understand and accept when they are in the wrong; • accept changes in circumstances and changing routines.
Self-motivation	Children are able to: • set personal goals and work towards achieving them; • focus on long-term goals rather than short-term gains; • show flexibility in trying new approaches; • motivate others to achieve their goals; • overcome setbacks and failure to achieve their goals; • see setbacks as the result of circumstances and not personal flaws.

Figure 6.2 Personal competence

Empathy	Children are able to: • show an awareness of others' emotions and feelings.
Social skills	Children are able to: • build relationships with peers and adults; • respect the opinions of others; • share successes with others; • put over their point of view in a positive manner.

Figure 6.3 Social competence

Pupils with limited emotional literacy skills can:

- have relationship difficulties with parents, teachers and peers;
- engage in inappropriate behaviour on a regular basis;
- when older, and in adulthood, have a higher incidence of involvement in the criminal justice system;
- be depressed, aggressive and anxious;
- as an indirect consequence, have poor academic success.

Class activities to promote emotional literacy

This week's social skill

Choose a social skill from the list above and focus on it for the week, e.g. sharing. Introduce 'sharing' to the class and ask them to think about the answers to the following questions:

- What does it mean to them?
- How does it make them feel when someone shares something with them?
- What can they do to practise the social skill 'sharing'?

At the end of the designated week, ask the children to discuss with the class all their sharing experiences and activities. Get them to make lists in pairs or in groups.

I spotted you!

In the classroom keep a box with a slot in it and some 'I spotted you!' nomination forms. Encourage the children to look for anyone (including teachers) in the class/ school displaying good social skills. Get them to write their name and the social skill on a nomination form and post it in the box. A list of social skills can be written on the slips so that the child can tick off the appropriate one. At the end of the week, the teacher reads the slips and reinforces the correct behaviour through praise and/or by giving rewards such as a 'star'.

Secret friend

Put all the pupils' names in a box and each child in turn chooses a name and becomes that child's secret friend for the day. The secret friend then practises any of the agreed social skills on that child. For example, they can show good manners by opening the door for them or asking them to play a game in the playground, etc. At the end of the day each pupil tries to guess the name of their secret friend.

'Can we sort it?'

Keep a log, as a school, of incidents that have taken place in the playground, then during circle time present one of the incidents and ask the class, 'Can we sort it?' Ask the children to discuss or role-play how to come up with positive solutions and practical advice to help prevent the incident from happening again.

Meeting with parent(s)/carer(s)

Schools must be careful not to overtly blame parents or carers for the poor behaviour of their child. Otherwise, confidence will be reduced, tensions raised and both short- and long-term co-operation less likely to occur. Similarly, for remedial strategies to be effective, either in the short or long term, parents or carers must be fully 'on-side' and supportive.

The way parents and carers are invited by schools to help solve their child's behaviour or attendance problem is important. It is best not to do so by sending a message or letter through the child. If a letter is sent through the post, be careful about the contents of the letter. Make sure it is not perceived to be threatening. Always attempt to be constructive in your comments and in the search for solutions.

Normally, it is best to make contact with the parent or carer through a home phone call or by arranging a meeting with the parents or carers in school. This may need to take place in after-school hours if both parents are working.

If a meeting is arranged with a parent or carer to discuss their child's behaviour, it is best to follow this format:

- Note how the parents or carers seem as they enter the room.
- Provide a warm greeting to them. Keep the meeting between the head teacher (and occasionally) the class teacher with the parents. Do not invite third parties without the prior consent of the parents. Do not have too many 'unnecessary' adults in the room.
- Offer a polite recognition that you understand their concern as well as expecting them to appreciate the school's difficulties.
- Ask them for their insights into the situation. Seek their views of any issues or difficulties on which they need your advice.
- Explore what, if anything, they have done to deal with the problems to date.
- Present the school's view of their child's difficulties.
- Listen to their response with care.
- Discuss and agree what the school and the parents can do by working together to resolve any difficulties.
- When parents or carers seem overwhelmed by the range of difficulties being caused by their child or appear unable to cope, it can be productive to indicate how, where and when they can secure further help and advice. This help or advice may be provided by the local authority, social services, health or voluntary agencies. By offering such practical advice (and providing parents or carers with a relevant list of key names, addresses and telephone numbers), schools may help to lift some of the burden from themselves. Parents or carers may then be more ready to work more closely with the school. Sometimes the advice given by the relevant outside agencies can be practical or financial and may result in specialist support from, for example, an educational psychologist or social worker.

Action planning

Following the meeting, it is normally best to agree an action plan for improvement with the parents or carers. This can take several forms. Usually, it is likely to involve:

- agreeing on the behaviour which needs to change;
- specifying the behaviour that we want the child to exhibit;
- establishing a monitoring and/or reward system in a way that ensures the pupil can experience some initial success;
- agreeing on a reasonable form of corrective for any non-compliance;
- reviewing progress, possibly by arranging further meetings;
- setting out how progress will be judged, possibly by arranging further meeting(s).

Some challenges

Sometimes schools engage with parents or carers who:

- feel they are failing;
- have been battling with the child's behavioural difficulties at home long before their child exhibited them in school;
- have been trying a range of strategies at home already to improve their child's behaviour.

In such circumstances, head teachers can:

- emphasise any successes which the parent and/or the school may have already experienced;
- suggest ways in which either the school or parents might refine their approach;
- suggest to the parents or carers how much more effective the situation would be if both parties combined their endeavours.

If both parties share problems empathetically, practised solutions are most likely to emerge, confidence and self-esteem can be maintained, and neither party will feel alone in their plight.

Many schools now involve parents in a range of activities at school. These may include breakfast clubs, out-of-school clubs, weekend activities, societies, sports clubs, drama, amongst others. One of the very best ways of involving parents whose children have behavioural difficulties is through utilising the Family Values Scheme, which is described in detail in Chapter 12.

Monitoring and evaluating behavioural progress

Some unwanted behaviour is difficult to change. In these cases, behaviour plans may need to be implemented to help to monitor and evaluate the conduct. Before compiling these individual or group plans an antecedent–behaviour–consequence analysis needs to take place to help identify and understand the pupil's behaviour (see Chapter 9, pages 149ff.). There are many ways to monitor and evaluate a pupil's behaviour.

To ensure a behaviour plan is successful you need to:

- have a good understanding of an individual's conduct, e.g. the trigger points and reinforcers, noting that the frequency and intensity are imperative;
- use the ABC analysis – antecedent–behaviour–consequence;
- ensure that the pupil understands his/her behavioural difficulties;
- focus on the priority behaviour that needs to change;
- identify the desired behaviour you want the pupil to adopt;
- agree short-term SMART targets, which will reflect progress in achieving the desired behaviour (see pp. 98–99);
- involve the parents/carers in establishing ways to monitor, reinforce and reward the desired behaviour between the home and school;
- discuss appropriate correctives for dealing with inappropriate behaviour at home and at school;
- agree when the behaviour plan is reviewed;
- ensure the behaviour plan is signed and dated by key individuals.

SMART targets

When you set targets they need to be:

- *specific*: be specific and clearly define the behaviour required;
- *measurable*: decide on the criteria for measuring the pupil's progress toward achieving the goal;
- *achievable*: goals need to be set so that the pupil has a realistic chance of achieving them;

- *relevant*: focus on no more than three types of behaviour, which are relevant to the classroom;
- *time bound*: ensure there is a time limit, so the pupil has something to achieve within a fixed period.

The following can be used to help monitor and evaluate a pupil's behaviour:

- Home–School Link Books;
- self-monitoring profile;
- behaviour contracts;
- Individual Learning Plan (ILP);
- Individual Behaviour Plan (IBP);
- Pastoral Support Programme (PSP).

Home–School Link Books

Home–School Link Books are an effective way for parents, children and teaching staff to communicate with each other. The book can be used for a number of purposes, for example an update on behaviour and personal achievements. It may also be used by parents to give teaching staff information about significant events/incidents that may have happened at home that might affect the child.

Self-monitoring profile

Self-monitoring can be an effective tool to help the pupil to improve their self-awareness and to understand their behaviour by working with them as an individual to help them to resolve their difficulties. The benefits of a self-monitoring profile are:

- involving the pupil in deciding on the behaviour to be monitored;
- helping the pupil become more aware of his or her behaviour;
- providing the pupil with an awareness of the frequency of behaviour;
- actively involving the pupil in the process of behaviour modification.

Figures 6.4 and 6.5 present diagrammatical formats of how to use a self-monitoring chart and profile and illustrate the diagrams with exemplary data.
   To use the self-monitoring chart:

- focus upon no more than three forms of behaviour otherwise the exercise can become too complicated;
- encourage the pupil to complete the grid after each session;
- if the pupil displays the monitored behaviour the relevant code number is recorded in the appropriate time slot – for example, Jack Load leaves the classroom without permission at 2.30 p.m. on Monday, so the number 3 is recorded in the Monday 2.00–3.15 p.m. box on the chart.
- use the chart for just one week;
- assess the information on the chart and formulate appropriate strategies;
- celebrate, where possible, the pupil's ability to improve his or her behaviour;
- explore the strategies the pupil has used to improve his or her behaviour.

Behaviour contract

Figure 6.6 presents an example of an individual behavioural contract for a pupil. A behaviour contract is a written agreement between the pupil and teacher and can include the pupil's parent/carer. It provides the pupil with a structure to bring about behavioural change or

A Self-Monitoring Profile

Pupil's name:_____   Date:_____

Behaviour to be monitored:

1.

2.

3.

Behaviours monitored by:_____

Time	Mon	Tues	Wed	Thurs	Fri	Totals		
						1	2	3

Pupil's comments:

Completed by:_____

Totals: 1 = _____   2 = _____   3 = _____

Figure 6.4 A diagrammatical illustration of how to use a self-monitoring chart

A Self-Monitoring Profile
EXAMPLE

Pupil's name: Jack Load   Date: 15 February 2010

Behaviour to be monitored:

1. Calling out in class

2. Swearing

3. Leaving the classroom without permission

Behaviours monitored by: Mrs E Knight

Time	Mon	Tues	Wed	Thurs	Fri	Totals		
						1	2	3
8.45–9am				3	1, 2	1	1	1
9–10am	1, 3		1, 2			2	1	1
10–10.30am				3				1
10.30–11am	Break	Break 2	Break	Break	Break 2		2	
11–12pm								
12–1pm	Lunch	Lunch	Lunch	Lunch	Lunch 2		1	
1–2pm	3, 1			1	3	2		2
2–3.15pm	3, 1, 1	3				2		2

Pupil's comments: This week has been a bit better than last week. I didn't have a very good day on Monday because a year 6 girl started winding me up during lunchtime. I'm going to try to do better next week.

Totals: 1 = 7   2 = 5   3 = 7

Figure 6.5 An example of the use of a self-monitoring profile

My Contract

Pupil's name:_____   Date:_____

These are my goals:

1. _____

2. _____

3. _____

These are the consequences if I don't meet my goals:

_____

_____

_____

These are the rewards if I meet my goals:

_____

_____

_____

My contract will be reviewed on:_____

Signatures: _____

              _____

              _____

Figure 6.6 Behaviour contract

modification. Ideally, you should involve the pupil in the writing of the contract, including the consequences and rewards.

The contract should incorporate the following ideas:

- use of no more than three goals at a time, for example not calling out in class;
- the agreed consequences for not achieving the goals;
- the agreed rewards for achieving the goals;
- the agreed timescale, for example a day or a week;
- a definition of how and by whom the behaviours will be monitored;
- setting a date for reviewing the contract.

Individual Learning Plans with behavioural targets

An Individual Learning Plan is used when a pupil displays behaviour that causes some concern although the severity or the frequency of the conduct is not too great. The pupil's learning and behaviour targets can be incorporated into an ILP.

Consider the following issues when implementing ILPs:

- how to share the information and goals with parents/carers;
- how to involve the pupil in drawing up the plan, ensuring it is pupil friendly;
- how to include baseline information about the pupil's curriculum levels and needs;
- how to agree short-term SMART targets, which will reflect progress in achieving the desired behaviours;
- how to include three or four specific objectives which are related to the targets;
- the teaching strategies to be used;
- including the support and resources needed to help meet those targets;
- reviewing the ILP at least twice a year, but ideally termly.

Individual Behaviour Plans

Pupils whose behaviour is difficult to manage in school for a sustained period of time, despite the implementation of the ILP, or where a pupil's misbehaviour becomes more frequent, challenging and/or severe, will usually need to progress onto an IBP. The IBP is designed to record the strategies used to help the pupil to progress and it will set out the targets that the individual should be working towards. It provides more detailed planning and a greater level of differentiation than the ILP.

Consider the following when implementing IBPs:

- writing the plan in partnership with parents/carers;
- involving the pupil in drawing up the plan, ensuring it is pupil friendly;
- agreeing short-term SMART targets, which will reflect progress in achieving the desired behaviours;
- including three or four specific objectives which are related to the targets;
- the behaviour management strategies to be used;
- including the support and resources needed to help meet those targets, including any special arrangements or changes;
- providing ways for members of staff to recognise and praise the pupil's positive behaviour;
- listing proactive and reactive strategies to respond to unwanted behaviour;
- reviewing at least twice a year, but ideally termly.

Pastoral Support Programmes

The Pastoral Support Programme is intended for use with pupils whose behaviour is worsening rapidly either through a series of fixed-period exclusions (which may lead to permanent exclusion) or because they are at risk of failure at school through disaffection. A PSP must be drawn up and implemented if a pupil is at risk of being permanently excluded. It is designed to help pupils improve their social, emotional and behavioural skills so that they are able to manage their behaviour more effectively.

Consider the following when implementing PSPs:

- identifying a member of staff to co-ordinate and oversee the PSP planning and process;
- involving the local authority when planning how best to support the pupil through the involvement of Education Psychology, Primary Behaviour Support Service, specialist teacher advisers, exclusions and reintegration officers, education welfare officers or other agencies;
- co-ordinating agencies and family working with the child to ensure ongoing support;
- agreeing short-term SMART targets for the pupil to work towards;
- ensuring it acts as a preventative measure for pupils at risk of exclusion;
- making the PSP needs to be practical and manageable;
- developing and implementing the PSP in conjunction with other existing plans.

It is important that the PSP is not used to replace the SEN processes within either the school or the LA. The ILPs, IBPs and PSPs all conform with the Children Act, 2004, agenda and the requirement to monitor regularly each pupil who is considered to be 'at risk'.

Requesting assistance

There may be occasions in the classroom when a child displays behaviour which is very challenging, i.e. aggressive and violent conduct. If this happens, a procedure needs to have been previously established with the whole staff either to deal with emergency situations or for a teacher or member of the classroom support staff to request assistance. For example, at a school in Swansea, the father of a five-year-old child stormed into a class and started to physically attack a young teacher because she had told off his daughter for inappropriate behaviour the previous day. Various schools tend to use different approaches, for instance a set of coloured assistance cards can be used by every member of staff to show a member of the behaviour management team that they may require assistance. This is a very effective and efficient way of communicating the type and level of response needed, although in extreme circumstances it may not always be possible. Therefore some schools now use personal alarm systems or other electronic warning devices.

When cards are used, the member of staff must write his or her name and class on the back of each card so that it is known where assistance is needed. The card is given to another pupil or member of the support staff to take to one of the senior management team, normally the head teacher. Below are examples of what each card can request.

Green assistance

This card requests assistance when a member of the behaviour management team is available. This card is sent in the following circumstances:

- if you require a second opinion regarding a decision;
- if you have a query;
- if you would like a pupil's behaviour to be positively reinforced;
- if you have a concern regarding a pupil.

Orange assistance

This card requests assistance from a member of the behaviour management team as soon as possible. This card is sent in the following circumstances:

- if a pupil requires a time out outside the classroom;
- if a pupil is persistently displaying low-level misbehaviour;
- if a pupil is displaying defiance towards a member of staff;
- if an incident has taken place and has not yet been resolved.

Red assistance

This card requests immediate assistance from a member of the behaviour management team. This card is sent in the following circumstances:

- if a pupil has left the classroom without permission;
- if a pupil is displaying challenging behaviour;
- if a pupil is putting themselves or others in danger.

Summary

In this chapter, we have considered a wide range of different strategies for managing pupils' behaviour within the school and classrooms. These have ranged from the use of reflective learning and the use and understanding of emotional literacy to such practical issues as the use of self-monitoring contracts, behaviour contracts, individual support plans and requesting assistance in a difficult situation. In Chapter 7, we will present the 5-Step Behaviour Programme and discuss how to implement and use it.

The 5-Step Behaviour Programme

An example of a whole-school strategy for positive behaviour management

In this chapter, we will consider the 5-Step Behaviour Programme (which for younger children incorporates the Good Choice Teddy Approach). This is a useful programme for primary schools to use and apply, especially those schools which have a number of children with persistent low-level or challenging behavioural problems. The 5-Step Behaviour Programme was originally created to facilitate work with challenging pupils in difficult schools and is now in use throughout a number of schools and LAs in England and Wales (Morgan and Ellis, 2009).

About the programme

The 5-Step Behaviour Programme (5SBP) is a comprehensive scheme to support schools to achieve effective behaviour management through a simple step-by-step approach. The programme achieves this by encouraging schools to adopt an approach to behaviour management which is simple, effective and yet sustainable. It focuses on schools setting up effective systems for school rules, correctives and rewards linked to a whole-school positive behaviour policy. Using tried and tested strategies throughout the programme, it endeavours to show schools how to plan, implement and monitor these systems. All the strategies that are used in the programme are based on the philosophy that consistency in positive reinforcement and the development of a child's emotional literacy can change and improve pupils' behaviour. The programme promotes inclusion and identifies ways that this can be done giving particular attention throughout the programme to incorporate the requirements of children with special educational needs and to ensure that the programme meets the requirements in the Code of Practice.

The 5SBP includes an Emotional Literacy Programme (Step 5) to help individual pupils recognise and manage their behaviour. This part of the programme can be used independently to enhance existing good practice or as part of a whole-school approach to managing pupils' behaviour. Either way, it focuses upon children reflecting on their behaviour and identifying the correct way forward. It also looks at the school environment and shows schools how a positive learning culture can influence the way children behave in school (see Chapters 5 and 6).

The five steps

The five steps of the programme are:

- Step 1: Reminder.
- Step 2: Warning.
- Step 3: Time Out 1 (thinking time).
- Step 4: Time Out 2 (thinking time).
- Step 5: Emotional Literacy Programme.

The aim of the programme

The programme aims to achieve the following:

- to enable staff to manage pupil behaviour more effectively;
- to implement a fair and consistent approach in dealing with incidents;
- to adopt rules, correctives and positive reinforcements which are effective;
- to teach strategies to help children manage their behaviour;
- to help to develop children's emotional literacy;
- to raise self-esteem.

A behaviour management team

In order for any programme to be implemented successfully there needs to be someone in school who is responsible for leading and monitoring the system. In smaller schools this does prove more difficult but it is not impossible. This responsibility in this case normally would rest with the head teacher and one other member of staff, either a teacher or a member of the support staff. In larger schools this task proves easier and can be delegated to a senior person within the school to lead and manage. Whatever your type of school, location and pupil intake, there needs to be a group of staff responsible for managing the programme. For the purposes of this Handbook, we will call it a behaviour management team. It could just as easily be a project behaviour team. Whatever name you use, these persons are responsible for communicating information to the relevant parties. It is recommended that this team meet on a regular basis in order to carry out ongoing evaluations of the programme and to monitor the pupil outcomes.

Involving pupils

In order for the programme to be sustainable it is important that all the pupils are fully involved in the process. There are lots of different ways that this can be done, through the school council, school/classroom monitors, class assemblies or circle time sessions. The more that pupils are involved during the initial stages of implementation, the more effective the programme will be. Once pupils are engaged in the process they will want to be involved in the monitoring to make sure that everyone is carrying out their ideas. Pupils need to be involved in the following activities as set out in the programme:

- how the 5-Step Behaviour Programme works;
- using the class tracking sheet;
- preparing the card system;
- agreeing and implementing the school rules and correctives;
- discussing the types of fast-track behaviour;
- establishing the Emotional Literacy Programme;
- agreeing the school's positive reinforcements;
- agreeing how parent(s)/carer(s) will be involved.

Informing parent(s)/carer(s)

Gaining parental support is a necessity if pupils are going to conform to the expectations of behaving appropriately in school. When a pupil displays inappropriate behaviour in school, parent(s)/carer(s) play a key role in helping teachers to secure change in a pupil's behaviour. Therefore, parent(s)/carer(s) need to be kept up to date with any significant change in behaviour in order for maximum progress to be made. Thus, keeping parent(s)/carer(s) fully informed is an essential part of the programme (see Chapters 4 and 5).

Involving supply staff and other professionals

One of the aims of the programme is to have a consistent approach by all staff towards pupils and their behaviour in the school. This gives a clear message to both staff and pupils that procedures are fair. There are occasions when school routines are disrupted, such as when a supply teacher is being employed in the school to cover sickness or another member of staff attends an external course. Very often these staff can be unfamiliar with school routines and procedures and sometimes this can cause disruption in the classroom. To ensure continuity is maintained, it is important to keep the supply staff and other professionals informed of the procedures as written in the school's positive behaviour policy.

How the programme works: for key stages 1 and 2

When implementing a whole-school behaviour management system it is important to understand that children sometimes make mistakes and this is all part of their normal development. These mistakes can provide a valuable learning platform providing they are addressed in a positive way. For example, when a child engages in low-level misbehaviour the following strategies can be implemented to help the child to understand and learn from their own unwanted behaviour. Here are some strategies you may try to re-engage a pupil:

- redirect the child's behaviour;
- make eye contact with the child to make them aware you have noticed and disapprove of the behaviour;
- utilise the physical space in the classroom – for example, walk over to the child and mark their work;
- give the child a verbal prompt such as: 'John, I'd like you to listen so you'll know what to do for the next task, thank you.'

If these strategies prove unsuccessful and the low-level misbehaviour continues, the programme suggests reverting to the five steps of the programme, i.e. reminder, verbal warning, time out. An effective way of doing this is to use a coloured card system (see Figure 7.1).

Issuing the 5-Step cards

When issuing the 5-Step cards it is important to give the child space and time to make the right choices. For example, when issuing a 'Reminder' approach the child at eye level and say something like 'That's a reminder'. Then, walk away, record the Reminder next to the child's name on the tracking sheet and continue teaching the lesson. If, after a few minutes, the child is still engaging in unwanted behaviour, repeat the process by issuing a Warning card. The 5-Step cards are particularly useful for children with learning difficulties as they can easily recognise that a particular colour relates to each stage. It also gives teachers and support staff confidence by allowing them to use a learnt script.

Classroom tracking sheets

The tracking sheet is a useful tool for the classroom teacher in monitoring individual children's behaviour (see Figure 7.2). They are simple to use and can be applied daily. When a child breaks a school rule an appropriate corrective from one of the five steps is marked on the tracking sheet against the child's name. Maintained systematically, these tracking sheets can be useful in helping to highlight patterns of behaviour amongst different pupils over particular periods of time. For example, every Monday, John, a pupil in year 4, reaches a Time Out 1 (T1) and yet his behaviour is very positive for the rest of the week. There could

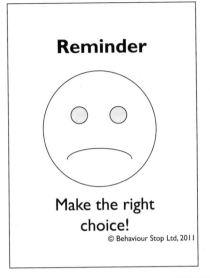

Figure 7.1 The 5-Step class cards

be a number of reasons which explain this pattern of behaviour. For instance, it could signal his unhappiness at a change which is taking place in his family life at the end of a weekend or maybe it is to do with starting school without breakfast. Such a pattern of behaviour would need to be investigated to see if it could be changed.

To effectively use and monitor the tracking sheets:

- The teacher/teaching assistant and not the pupil must record the behaviour on the tracking sheet.
- Two highlighting colours should be used, to show the difference between playground and classroom behaviour.
- All class teachers should hand in the tracking sheets to a member of the behaviour management team at the end of the week. This can be done through a class filing system or by using a central filing system. The sheets are also useful evidence to show external professionals and/or parent(s)/carer(s) when necessary at a later date.

Tracking Sheet
The 5-Step Behaviour Programme

Class_____   Week beginning_____

Name	Monday					Tuesday					Wednesday					Thursday					Friday				
	R	W	T1	T2	ELP	R	W	T1	T2	ELP	R	W	T1	T2	ELP	R	W	T1	T2	ELP	R	W	T1	T2	ELP

Figure 7.2 A class tracking sheet for key stages 1 and 2

At the end of the week, month or term the tracking sheet(s) can be used to positively reinforce pupils who have not received any correctives as well as the pupils who have achieved the goals set out in their Individual Learning Plans or Individual Behaviour Plans.

Recording class behaviour

It is good practice to record any behaviour that causes concern which is not usual for a particular pupil. This could mean that there are issues either at home or at school and this would need to be investigated and, if necessary, discussed with a member of the behaviour management team. A record can be kept in a class behaviour book or on the back of the tracking sheet. Child protection incidents must follow a school's child protection procedures.

Using the 5-Step card system

Step 1: Reminder

If a pupil displays unwanted behaviour show them the Reminder card and say, 'That's a reminder.' Then, next to his/her name on the tracking sheet circle the letter 'R'.

Step 2: Warning

If a pupil displays unwanted behaviour for the second time during the same day show them the Warning card and say, 'That's a warning.' Then, next to his/her name on the tracking sheet circle the letter 'W'.

Step 3: Time Out 1

If a pupil displays unwanted behaviour for the third time during the same day, show them the Time Out card and say, 'Go to the time out area and think about your behaviour, thank you.' Then, next to his/her name on the tracking sheet circle 'T1'. After between two and five minutes ask the pupil why they were given a Time Out card. If they are able to say why they were given the Time Out card and agree to make the right choices, then invite them to rejoin the class/group.

Step 4: Time Out 2

If a pupil displays unwanted behaviour for the fourth time during the same day, then show them the Time Out card and say, 'Please go to the time out area and think about your behaviour.' Afterwards, next to his/her name on the tracking sheet, circle 'T2'. After between two and five minutes ask the pupil why they were given a Time Out card. If they are able to say why they were given the Time Out card and subsequently agree to make the right choices, invite them to rejoin the class. Remind the pupil that if they continue to display unwanted behaviour they could be put on the Emotional Literacy Programme, which is Step 5 of the programme.

Step 5: Emotional Literacy Programme

If a pupil displays unwanted behaviour for the fifth time during the same day, then inform the child that their behaviour could result in them being placed on the Emotional Literacy Programme. A member of the behaviour management team will then need to discuss the pupil's behaviour with the member of staff and make a decision about whether they should be placed on the Emotional Literacy Programme. If it is agreed that the pupil is to go on the Emotional Literacy Programme, the letters 'ELP' are circled next to the pupil's name on the tracking sheet (see p. 110).

Using the 5-Step cards and the class tracking sheet together

When a child reaches a step on the programme by being given a coloured card the step must be recorded against the child's name on the class tracking sheet. This way behaviours are easily monitored and tracked throughout the day and the week. For example, a child reaching Step 3 of the programme, Time Out, will have a T1 circled against their name on the class tracking sheet.

These tracking sheets may give some added clues to an individual pupil's problems. For example, on every Monday morning, John's behaviour was poor. It soon emerged that he was unhappy to leave the family home as his parents were contemplating a divorce.

Either at the end of the week or at the start of a new week, month or term, the tracking sheets can be used to positively reinforce those pupils who have not received any correctives as well as those pupils who have achieved the goals set out in their Individual Learning Plans or their Individual Behaviour Plans.

How the programme works: playtime

Playtime procedures

In order to ensure a consistent approach to the management of pupils' behaviour from the classroom to the playground, the 5-Step cards are used in the form of coloured slips. Figure 7.3 presents the 5-Step cards for use in overseeing the pupils' behaviour in the playground. These coloured slips enable a member of staff to record the following information, which can then be handed to the class teacher at the end of play to record on the class tracking sheet:

- name of pupil;
- class;
- type of unwanted behaviour.

Designated time out area

To implement Steps 3 and 4, a time out area needs to be identified. This can be a round spot or a painted square located in a secure part of the playground. It is important that all children understand where the area is and what it is used for. The same procedure is then applied to time out in the classroom and time out in the playground.

How the programme works: for nursery/reception children

Not all children start school knowing what is acceptable and unacceptable behaviour. Creating a positive environment in school and in the classroom with clear expectations which are understood by pupils, parents and staff is fundamentally important to the primary aims of helping pupils to develop thinking skills, to learn how to learn and to enjoy the learning process.

Play provides opportunities for children to learn through imitation, imagination and fun and to learn about experiencing the consequences of their actions. There are a number of behaviour hotspots within the Foundation Years which need to be

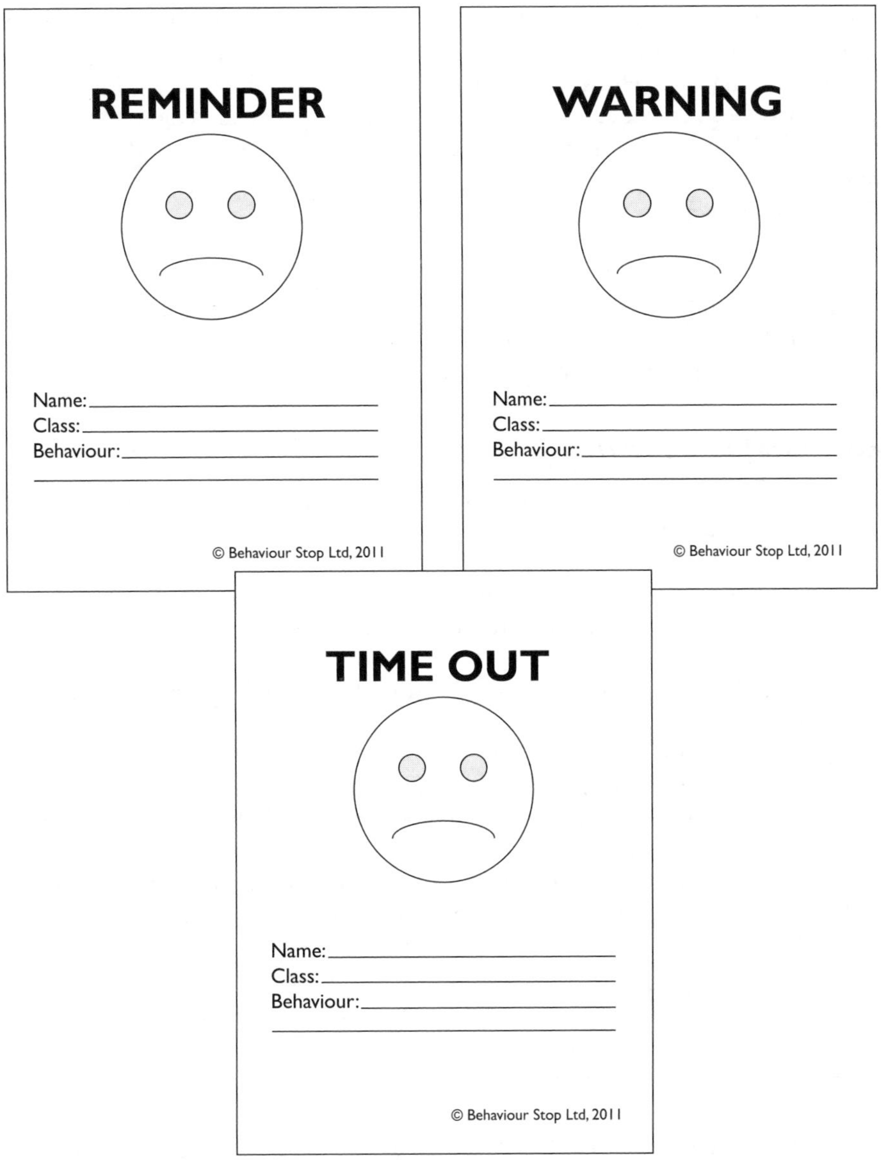

REMINDER

Name:_____
Class:_____
Behaviour:_____
_____

© Behaviour Stop Ltd, 2011

WARNING

Name:_____
Class:_____
Behaviour:_____
_____

© Behaviour Stop Ltd, 2011

TIME OUT

Name:_____
Class:_____
Behaviour:_____
_____

© Behaviour Stop Ltd, 2011

Figure 7.3 5-Step cards for the playground

taken into consideration to ensure a positive learning environment is created as well as preparing pupils to progress throughout the school. The hotspots are:

- following class rules and routines;
- entering and exiting the classroom successfully;
- sitting on the carpet sensibly;
- respecting one another;
- paying attention when the teacher signals for attention;
- asking questions/asking for help/asking for permission;
- turn taking, sharing and co-operation;
- getting ready for home time.

For much younger children the philosophy of the programme still applies, which is to encourage children to make the right choices and to praise and reward them when they are behaving well. However, for when a younger child breaks a school rule the five steps have been modified to four steps. Coloured cards or the Good Choice Teddy Approach (see Figure 7.4) are used to show a child which corrective they have been given.

The modified steps are:

- Step 1: Reminder.
- Step 2: Warning.
- Step 3: Time Out (thinking time).
- Step 4: meeting with parent(s)/carer(s).

Unacceptable behaviour

If a pupil displays unacceptable behaviour, before using the 4-Step cards and/or the Good Choice Teddy Approach:

- try to redirect the pupil's behaviour;
- make eye contact with the pupil to make them aware you have noticed and disapprove of the behaviour;
- use physical proximity for your own benefit – for example, walk over to the pupil and mark their work;
- give the pupil a verbal prompt such as: 'John, I'd like you to listen so you'll know what to do for the next task. Good boy';
- if a pupil continues to display unwanted behaviour give them a verbal reminder.

If the above fail to work, start using the stages in the 4-Step procedure and/or the Good Choice Teddy Approach. See the cards in Figure 7.4 and the tracking sheet in Figure 7.5.

Figure 7.4 The 4-Step class cards

Tracking Sheet
The 5-Step Behaviour Programme

Class _____   Week beginning _____

Name	Monday				Tuesday				Wednesday				Thursday				Friday			
	Reminder	W	T	P/C	Reminder	W	T	P/C	Reminder	W	T	P/C	Reminder	W	T	P/C	Reminder	W	T	P/C
	Reminder	W	T	P/C	Reminder	W	T	P/C	Reminder	W	T	P/C	Reminder	W	T	P/C	Reminder	W	T	P/C
	Reminder	W	T	P/C	Reminder	W	T	P/C	Reminder	W	T	P/C	Reminder	W	T	P/C	Reminder	W	T	P/C
	Reminder	W	T	P/C	Reminder	W	T	P/C	Reminder	W	T	P/C	Reminder	W	T	P/C	Reminder	W	T	P/C
	Reminder	W	T	P/C	Reminder	W	T	P/C	Reminder	W	T	P/C	Reminder	W	T	P/C	Reminder	W	T	P/C
	Reminder	W	T	P/C	Reminder	W	T	P/C	Reminder	W	T	P/C	Reminder	W	T	P/C	Reminder	W	T	P/C
	Reminder	W	T	P/C	Reminder	W	T	P/C	Reminder	W	T	P/C	Reminder	W	T	P/C	Reminder	W	T	P/C
	Reminder	W	T	P/C	Reminder	W	T	P/C	Reminder	W	T	P/C	Reminder	W	T	P/C	Reminder	W	T	P/C
	Reminder	W	T	P/C	Reminder	W	T	P/C	Reminder	W	T	P/C	Reminder	W	T	P/C	Reminder	W	T	P/C
	Reminder	W	T	P/C	Reminder	W	T	P/C	Reminder	W	T	P/C	Reminder	W	T	P/C	Reminder	W	T	P/C
	Reminder	W	T	P/C	Reminder	W	T	P/C	Reminder	W	T	P/C	Reminder	W	T	P/C	Reminder	W	T	P/C
	Reminder	W	T	P/C	Reminder	W	T	P/C	Reminder	W	T	P/C	Reminder	W	T	P/C	Reminder	W	T	P/C
	Reminder	W	T	P/C	Reminder	W	T	P/C	Reminder	W	T	P/C	Reminder	W	T	P/C	Reminder	W	T	P/C
	Reminder	W	T	P/C	Reminder	W	T	P/C	Reminder	W	T	P/C	Reminder	W	T	P/C	Reminder	W	T	P/C
	Reminder	W	T	P/C	Reminder	W	T	P/C	Reminder	W	T	P/C	Reminder	W	T	P/C	Reminder	W	T	P/C
	Reminder	W	T	P/C	Reminder	W	T	P/C	Reminder	W	T	P/C	Reminder	W	T	P/C	Reminder	W	T	P/C
	Reminder	W	T	P/C	Reminder	W	T	P/C	Reminder	W	T	P/C	Reminder	W	T	P/C	Reminder	W	T	P/C
	Reminder	W	T	P/C	Reminder	W	T	P/C	Reminder	W	T	P/C	Reminder	W	T	P/C	Reminder	W	T	P/C

Figure 7.5 A class tracking sheet for use with the 4-Step card procedure

TIP: 4-Step card procedure

Step 1: Reminder

If a pupil displays unwanted behaviour show them the Reminder card and say, 'That's a reminder.' Then, next to his/her name on the tracking sheet, record the word 'Reminder'.

Step 2: Warning

If a pupil displays unwanted behaviour for the second time during the same day, then show them the Warning card and say. 'That's a warning.' Then, next to his/her name on the tracking sheet, highlight the letter 'W'.

Step 3: Time Out

If a pupil displays unwanted behaviour for the third time during the same day, then show them the Time Out card and say, 'Go to the reflection area and think about your behaviour.' Then, next to his/her name on the tracking sheet, record the letter 'T'.

After between two and five minutes encourage the pupil to think about why they were given a time out and ask them if they are ready to make the right choices and return to the group/class. At the end of the day inform the parent/carer of their child's behaviour and ask them to reinforce making the right choices at home. A useful strategy is to use a home–school link reward chart which shows both school and parents whether a child has made the right choices. The Good Choice Teddy Approach can also be used to help reinforce positive behaviour. For more information go to www.goodchoiceteddy.co.uk. It also shows children that a consistent approach is being used by both home and school.

Step 4: Meeting with parents/carers

If the pupil has frequently received a number of time out sessions in school, then the parent(s)/carer(s) will be invited to attend a meeting with the class teacher and a member of the behaviour management team to discuss a way forward. Next to his/her name on the tracking sheet, highlight the letters 'P/C' to indicate that the parent/carer has been informed.

4-Step Good Choice Teddy Approach

The Good Choice Teddy Approach is based on a traffic light system (Reid, 2003). The teddy wears a green tee-shirt when the child is behaving well. This changes to orange if the child starts to display unwanted behaviour, and if after the child has been asked to make the right choice they do not listen, then the colour changes to red. When Teddy is wearing the red tee-shirt, the child is given a time out to reflect on their behaviour. If after time out they are ready to make the right choice, they put the green tee-shirt back on Teddy to signal they are ready to change their behaviour.

This strategy can work with an individual child, a small group or a whole class. The cards are shown in Figure 7.6 and an example of the strategy's use with an individual child is shown in the tracking sheet in Figure 7.7. For more strategies and resources on how to use Good Choice Teddy go to www.goodchoiceteddy.co.uk.

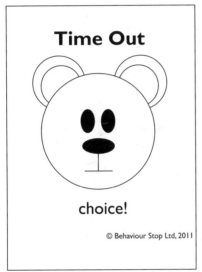

Figure 7.6 Good Choice Teddy class cards

4-Step Good Choice Teddy Approach

Step 1: Reminder

If the pupil displays unwanted behaviour, show them Good Choice Teddy and say, 'That's a reminder. You need to think about making the right choice otherwise teddy is going to feel sad.'

Step 2: Warning

If the pupil displays unwanted behaviour for the second time during the same day, then show them Good Choice Teddy and say, 'That's a warning. Teddy wants you to think

Tracking Sheet
The 5-Step Behaviour Programme: Good Choice Teddy®

Name of pupil _____   Week beginning _____

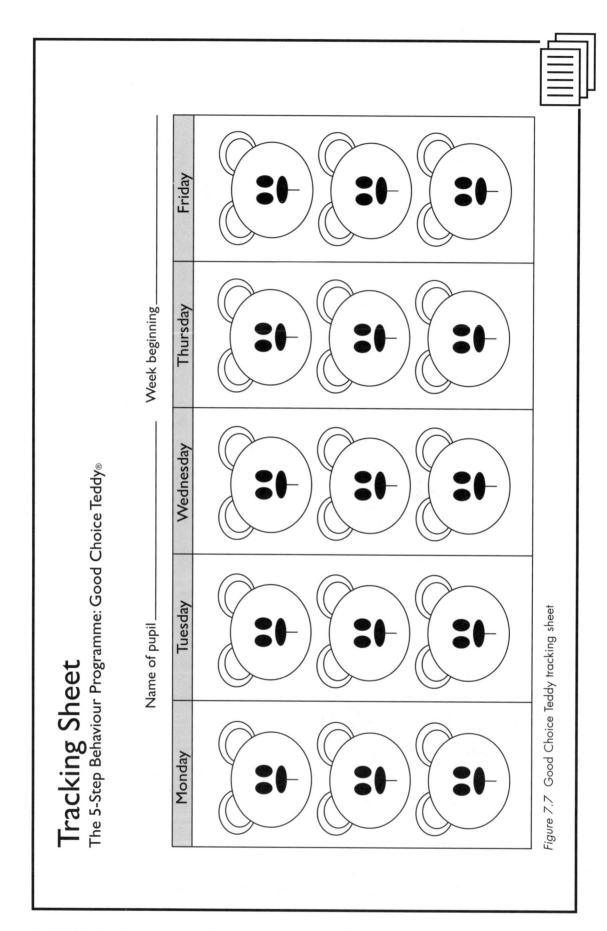

Figure 7.7 Good Choice Teddy tracking sheet

about making the right choice because he's feeling very sad.' Teddy's tee-shirt changes to orange. Then, on the tracking sheet, record a sad mouth on Teddy's face.

Step 3: Time Out

If the pupil displays unwanted behaviour for the third time during the same day, then show them Good Choice Teddy, change his tee-shirt to red and say. 'Teddy is feeling very sad. You now need to sit on the reflection spot and think about how you can make Teddy happy again.' Then, on the tracking sheet record a sad mouth on Teddy's face.

After between two and five minutes encourage the pupil to think how they can make Teddy happy again so he can wear his green tee-shirt. If the child makes the right choice – for example 'I won't throw sand at my friends' – he changes Teddy back to the green tee-shirt to signal he is ready to change his behaviour.

Step 4: Meeting with parents/carers

If the pupil has frequently received a number of time out sessions in school, then the parent(s)/carer(s) will be invited to attend a meeting with the class teacher and a member of the behaviour management team to discuss a way forward.

Positive reinforcement

The 4-Step Good Choice Teddy Approach tracking sheet can also be used to positively reinforce the child's behaviour. For example, if at the end of the day the child has not received a reminder, warning or time out they can take Good Choice Teddy home. There are a variety of resources to help reinforce positive behaviour at home. These can be found at www.goodchoiceteddy.co.uk.

How the Emotional Literacy Programme works

Before a pupil is placed on the Emotional Literacy Programme (Step 5), a member of the behaviour management team needs to be consulted to ensure consistency and fairness. Before the final decision is made the behaviour management team must check with all members of staff involved to ensure that they agree with the decision to be made. The following questions can be asked to help reach a decision:

- What is the age and stage of development of the child?
- Have any changes taken place at home?
- How is the child communicating his/her behaviour?
- Does the child have special or additional needs?

A pupil could be placed on the Emotional Literacy Programme if they have:

- engaged in a fast-track behaviour programme;
- reached the letters 'ELP' (Step 5) on the tracking sheet. Note this only applies to key stages 1 and 2, see Figure 7.2;
- recorded a frequent number (to be decided by behaviour management team) of time out sessions (Steps 3 and 4) in one week and subsequently still displayed unwanted behaviour.

Pupils with special educational needs

It is the special educational needs co-ordinator's (SENCO's) responsibility to adapt the Emotional Literacy Programme to address the needs of any pupils with special and/or additional needs. For pupils with special and/or additional needs who are likely to be put on the Emotional Literacy Programme, it is suggested that their parent(s)/carer(s) are invited to attend a meeting. During this meeting, the 5-Step Programme can be discussed and adapted where necessary and an intervention strategy and support package jointly agreed for the pupil.

The special educational needs co-ordinator (SENCO) must always be consulted before any pupil with special and/or additional needs is placed on the Emotional Literacy Programme. This is to ensure that the pupil's needs are being met and the level of corrective measures used to overcome the unwanted behaviour is justified.

Informing parent(s)/carer(s)

Once the decision has been made by the behaviour management team to place a child on the Emotional Literacy Programme, it is important that the parents are immediately informed. A letter should be sent to the home on the same day to inform them why their child has been put on the programme and, if necessary, a meeting arranged to share with them their child's misbehaviour and to explain how the programme will support the child. For infants this letter can be handed to the parent/carer; for juniors the letter is posted.

On successful completion of the programme, the pupil is awarded a certificate and a letter is sent home to his/her parent(s)/carer(s) to confirm satisfactory endeavour.

Programme requirements

The Emotional Literacy Programme is implemented during breaks and lunchtimes and the number of missed breaks and lunchtimes will need to be agreed by the school in line with their positive behaviour management policy.

Once the criteria of the programme have been agreed, they will be written into the school's positive behaviour policy and all parents in the school will be informed so that any misconceptions are addressed prior to any subsequent events taking place.

When a pupil is placed on the Emotional Literacy Programme, it must be agreed by all staff that he/she must:

- successfully complete x sessions in key stage 2/x sessions in key stage 1;
- not take part in any non-curriculum activities, e.g. Friday fun;
- not represent the school, e.g. school choir competition;
- not take part in after-school clubs, e.g. football.

These correctives are the foundation to the effectiveness of the programme and must not be diluted. Prior to a key non-curriculum event or activity, for example a trip to the pantomime, it is good practice to remind the pupils of the importance of making the right choices and not reaching Step 5 on the tracking sheet. It is also advisable to inform parent(s)/carer(s) that pupils on the Emotional Literacy Programme will not be able to take part in the activity/event. These points can be addressed via the weekly school newsletter.

Implementing the Emotional Literacy Programme

The Emotional Literacy Programme (ELP) is intended for those children who find it difficult to manage their emotions in and outside the classroom, which results in them displaying unwanted behaviour.

The programme is tailored to meet an individual child's emotional needs. The Emotional Literacy Programme co-ordinator teaches the pupils how to manage their behaviour independently. This is done in three ways:

- reflecting on their behaviour;
- practising the strategy;
- independently managing their behaviour.

This programme gives children the knowledge and confidence to make the right choices within a small group. During the ELP there is a need to work closely with parent(s)/carer(s) to ensure that the same form of misbehaviour does not recur time and again. This can be achieved by the parent(s)/carer(s) reinforcing the emotional literacy exercises at home.

The role of the Emotional Literacy Programme co-ordinator

The programme is led and managed by two members of staff, who share each session. The co-ordinators are responsible for the following:

- assessing children;
- keeping detailed records;
- involving and communicating with parents/carers;
- sharing information with all staff to keep everyone up to date;
- planning and delivering emotional literacy activities/exercises;
- ensuring all pupils have supervised play and toilet breaks;
- regularly communicating with the behaviour management team and SENCO;
- monitoring individual children.

Recording behaviour on the programme

It is advisable to record why a child has been put on the Emotional Literacy Programme to help monitor the behaviour and also to inform parent(s)/carer(s). This is the responsibility of the co-ordinators leading and managing the programme. When recording incidents it is important to include the following:

- a detailed description of the incident, including names of witnesses;
- what triggered the incident;
- whether the pupil was given time to calm down;
- who was consulted from the behaviour management team;
- the outcome.

Emotional literacy assessment

When a pupil has been put on the Emotional Literacy Programme they are required to complete an emotional literacy assessment. This is to establish the type of intervention needed to help support the individual in changing their behaviour. The NFER Emotional Literacy Assessment and Intervention Package (Ages 7 to 11) Service is an excellent resource to use on assessment.

Running the Emotional Literacy Programme

In order for the programme to be successful there are several issues that need to be considered to run a good session. These are:

- planning;
- rules;
- format;
- evaluation.

Planning

Planning is an essential part of the session. It is important to take the following into consideration:

- seating arrangements for pupils who have the potential to display unwanted behaviour;
- the organisation of the main activity;
- the resources needed.

Rules

Rules create clear expectations for the pupils and need to define what is acceptable behaviour. These must be reinforced on a regular basis and placed in a visible place. The same school rules apply to children on the Emotional Literacy Programme. The reason they are on the programme is that they have broken school rules and gone beyond the boundaries of what is acceptable behaviour within the school.

Format

The format of the session will inevitably vary according to the type of pupils. The sessions must be motivating to maintain the pupils' attention in order for them to benefit from the input. Here is an example of a session format:

- Welcome the pupils and recap on the aims and school rules.
- Introduce the session through discussion, worksheet, board game, etc.
- For the main activity, introduce a coping strategy to help them understand and maintain their behaviour.
- Hold a session plenary.
- Remind the pupils to make the right choices and try out their new coping strategy.

TIP: Ideas for emotional literacy activities

- Identify different types of feelings or emotions. Make a list of as many emotions as possible.
- The emotional literacy co-ordinator chooses an emotion and the group expresses that emotion non-verbally, for example write 'happy' on the board and have pupils act that emotion out, use a feelings chart.
- Do an emotional alphabet activity. Have pupils identify as many emotions as they can for each letter of the alphabet.
- Ask the pupils to identify different situations where people feel common emotions such as happiness, sadness, anger, fear and excitement. Ask the group how they behave in those situations.
- Differentiate between feeling anger and manifesting the behaviour of anger. Inform pupils that it is OK to be angry, but it is not OK to hit, call people names or yell at people. Spend time discussing and using examples that distinguish bad

behaviour from 'bad' emotions. Encourage the group to provide examples from their own experiences.

- Ask the pupils to keep a diary for the duration of the programme and record how they feel at different times during the day. They can use simple faces to express the feeling, for example happy, sad, angry, etc. Encourage them to tell someone what has caused them to feel this way. For instance, maybe they feel happy because their teacher gave them free time, maybe they feel sad because someone said something unkind to them. During the emotional literacy session ask the pupil to share their feelings.
- Some children find it difficult to know how someone is feeling. Give the child a mirror and ask him/her to make different facial expressions, for example happy, worried, sad and angry. Ask the child to look around the class and identify how other children might be feeling.

TIP: Ideas for a coping strategy to help with anger

- Walk away from the situation and sit quietly and comfortably.
- Close your eyes and think about your breathing.
- Count your breaths as you are breathing and this will help you calm down.
- Go and tell a teacher what has made you angry so they can deal with the situation.

(Morgan and Ellis, 2011b)

Assessment/evaluation

To assess the session ask the following questions:

- Did the pupils understand the new skill introduced?
- Did everyone take part?
- Did the pupils behave positively?
- What skills can the pupils benefit from learning in the next session?

Low-level and challenging behaviour on the programme

During the programme pupils may display low-level or challenging behaviour, thereby preventing the Emotional Literacy Programme co-ordinator from teaching and the pupils from learning effectively. This must be addressed immediately to ensure a positive learning environment is maintained.

If a pupil displays unwanted behaviour, the 5-Step approach is started. If a pupil receives a Warning card during the session, a member of the behaviour management team should be called to observe the behaviour. They will then decide with the Emotional Literacy Programme co-ordinator whether to:

- give an extra session;
- give one-to-one supervision away from their peers to complete the remainder of the sessions.

Extra sessions on the Emotional Literacy Programme

An extra session can be given to a pupil if they have received a Reminder and Warning from any member of staff while on the Emotional Literacy Programme. If the behaviour management team decides to give the pupil an extra session the reason must be recorded and made available to discuss with the child's parent(s)/carer(s) if necessary. If an extra session is given to a pupil, the class teacher must be informed straightaway. One possible consequence may be that the session will result in the pupil missing out on a key non-curriculum activity, in which case the parent(s)/carer(s) must be informed.

Third time on the programme

If a pupil is placed on the Emotional Literacy Programme for a third time or more in one academic year, it may be necessary to implement other strategies to help the pupil manage their behaviour. We now present a few examples:

- Parent(s)/carer(s) are requested to attend a meeting to discuss their child's behaviour and the ways in which by working together it can be improved.
- The pupil's behaviour is recorded in an ongoing chronology report.
- The pupil's behaviour is discussed with the school's SENCO and a decision made regarding whether he/she should be given an Individual Learning Plan or an Individual Behaviour Plan.

Chronology record

If a pupil is placed on the Emotional Literacy Programme for the third time a chronology record is set up for that pupil. This records, for example, all behavioural incidents which are a cause for concern. Such potential issues might include: possible exclusions, meetings with parent(s)/carer(s), observations of a pupil's behaviour by key professionals (e.g. educational psychologist). Figure 7.8 presents an observation chronology report form which is used for this purpose.

Monitoring school behaviour

Number of pupils on the Emotional Literacy Programme

It is suggested that an acceptable number of pupils on the Emotional Literacy Programme at any one time should not exceed 2 per cent of the total number of pupils in a school. If this number is exceeded the following questions should be asked:

- Are the 5-Step cards being used correctly?
- Are the behaviour management policy and practice in the school fair and consistent?
- Is the use of the school's positive reinforcements consistent and appropriate or are they used too frequently?
- Are the staff repairing their relationships with the children after disciplinary action is taken?
- Is pupils' positive behaviour being rewarded, or sufficiently rewarded?

Maintenance programme

When pupils complete the Emotional Literacy Programme it is important to help them manage their positive behaviour by reinforcing the learnt behaviour. This can be achieved through regular contact with the child either by the class teacher or by a member of the behaviour management team, and by keeping in regular contact with the parent(s)/carer(s).

Monitoring and evaluating behavioural progress

Some behaviour is difficult to change. In these cases, behaviour plans need to be implemented to help monitor and evaluate the pupils' conduct. Before compiling these plans an

Pupil Chronology Record
The 5-Step Behaviour Programme

Name: Jack Smith   **Class:** 3J

Date	Name of person reporting	Incident/event	Actions taken
15/05/10	RD	Involved in an incident with MC and KA. MC was calling JS names during playtime, JS tapped MC on the ankle, causing him to fall to the ground. JS and MC apologised.	JS and MC put on to Step 3 on the 5SBP.
18/05/10	TD	JS refused to follow the supply teacher's instructions when asked to return to his seat. This escalated to him answering the supply teacher back and causing disruption to the class. The supply teacher followed the 5-Step Behaviour Programme.	JS was given time out (Step 3). Following time out he chose to change his behaviour, apologised and returned to his group.
11/06/10	TD	During playtime JS became aggressive on the football pitch when his goal was disallowed. As a result he kicked KF (the goalkeeper) and used inappropriate language (f**k off), which was overheard by a group of children.	JS was put onto the Emotional Literacy Programme (Step 5). A letter has been sent to his parents requesting a meeting to discuss his behaviour.
12/06/10	RD	During the Emotional Literacy Programme (lunchtime) JS displayed inappropriate behaviour (shouting out, refusing to complete the task, being disrespectful to RD). SD (member of the behaviour management team) was requested to observe the behaviour.	SD and RD decided to give an extra session.

Figure 7.8 An observation chronology report form

antecedent–behaviour–consequence analysis needs to take place to help identify and understand the pupil's behaviour (see Chapter 9).

Summary

In this chapter, we have considered the 5-Step Behaviour Programme, which we have pioneered and used with extremely positive results in selected primary schools. The text describes the scheme and how to use it effectively within schools. For younger pupils, we advocate the Good Choice Teddy Approach, which is a similarly creative scheme. Further details of both approaches can be found on our website at www.behaviourstop.co.uk.

Chapter 8

Effective whole-school and classroom management skills

In order to create a positive learning culture within a school it will be necessary to make effective interventions from time to time. In this chapter, we will consider the following classroom intervention strategies:

- whole-school and classroom management skills;
- establishing positive relationships;
- making successful transitions.

Effective whole-school and classroom management

Effective whole-school and classroom management interventions are based on teachers' skills to successfully create well-managed and structured environments in which pupils can learn effectively. Creating a positive learning culture for a large number of children with different learning needs, abilities and attention spans is never easy and can often be challenging. However, children will learn better in classrooms which are orderly. Therefore pupils need to know and understand what is expected of them. This includes understanding the school and classroom rules and how they are expected to participate and behave during lessons.

Establishing well-managed schools

Well-managed schools have a small number of whole-school rules in place which are relatively simple to implement and administer effectively. These rules are overseen by the head teacher and senior management team but agreed and endorsed by the entire staff.

Ideally, well-managed schools and classrooms:

- begin the year with a set of rules and routines which are understood by all pupils;
- have a system of agreed rewards in place (e.g. showing a DVD as a reward for repeated good behaviour);
- use positive reinforcement to encourage pupils when they have participated well, through, for example, the use of praise;
- have an agreed and negotiated set of 'corrective consequences' or correctives for pupils' misbehaviour;
- have a selection of options at their disposal for dealing with potential and actual disciplinary problems;
- make sure interruptions do not interfere with or stop the flow of the lesson;
- make appropriate use of the classroom's physical space;
- have teachers who always prepare well-planned lessons;
- encourage a classroom environment of respect, which will help to develop positive relationships between teachers, CAs, LSMs and pupils, and help pupils to foster good pupil–pupil relationships between themselves.

Rules

School rules create expectations and provide boundaries for children. The best way for school rules to be successful and to be successfully established is to involve the children in creating them as well as the staff, perhaps by using the school council. This way the pupils will be involved in the decision-making processes, which should encourage them to take ownership of the rules. There is nothing more demoralising than creating a rule which has no relevance or impact. Involving the school council in organising, collating and helping finalise rules is often a very effective way forward. The discussion which takes place about the rules can provide helpful insights for pupils and children alike. Rules need to be clear, concise and constructed in language that all children understand. Following rules provides a learning opportunity for children of all ages to develop self-regulatory and social skills, which are two of the key components of children's emotional literacy development.

One practical suggestion is to keep overall school rules to a minimum. Therefore it may be best to create a maximum of five rules for the whole school to use, as not only is their application manageable but children will easily remember them. Of course, some rules may need to be differentiated between the infant and junior phases. Having a command of the phrasing used in creating school rules is often a skill in itself. The wording used needs to be positive. For example: 'Please listen to instructions first time' rather than 'Don't forget to listen!'

Here is an example of school rules for infants and juniors:

- Follow instructions first time.
- Keep hands, feet, objects and unkind words to ourselves.
- Respect one another and our surroundings.
- Be ready when an adult signals for attention.
- Use correct voice levels.

Once rules have been created and agreed by all the staff and pupils they need to be prominently displayed within the school. One good way of achieving this is to give behavioural rules a high priority in the school by having a dedicated display board in each classroom. School rules also will need to be displayed in the school entrances, school corridors and halls. For children with special needs and/or additional needs, a pictorial representation of the rules is recommended. These can even be designed by the children themselves and then laminated and displayed. The continuous and consistent reinforcement of school rules will help to maintain high standards of pupil behaviour and give a clear message that positive expectations of pupils' behaviour are a top priority in the school.

TIP: Making good rules

- When designing your classroom rules, they should be:
  - clear;
  - comprehensive;
  - enforceable.
- Write the rules in a positive way and avoid using 'don'ts'. For example: 'I will walk sensibly around the school' rather than 'Don't run around the school.'
- Give the pupils clear, simple instructions. The rules need to be specific and explainable, e.g. telling pupils to 'Be good' or 'Don't do that' is too vague.
- Display the class rules and go over them with the pupils on a regular basis.
- Check pupils' understanding of the rules.
- Explain the rationale behind the rules.
- Be consistent in enforcing the outcomes for breaches of the rules at the time.

Routines

Effective everyday school routines are activities carried out on a regular basis which are designed to help minimise difficult challenges from pupils in the school. They are critical for establishing well-managed and well-organised schools and classrooms. Establishing effective school and classroom routines is necessary for reasons of both common sense and health and safety. If pupils all ran into a class someone might fall, get squashed or otherwise injured! Therefore it is necessary, for example, to have agreed ways of entering school buildings at the beginning of the day and after breaks.

Establishing routines can also help children to build confidence in themselves and their peers. Studies undertaken by the Centre on the Social and Emotional Foundations for Early Learning have shown that implementing successful routines positively influences children's emotional, cognitive and social development. Pupils enjoy regular daily routines which are easy to understand and accomplish, yet are flexible enough to alter if circumstances ever change. The predictability and consistency of school routines gives children the confidence and security to help them learn what to expect, what is expected of them and how to manage their time effectively. For a practical way to help reinforce school routines, see the positive behaviour hotspot poster which is shown on p. 133 (Figure 8.1).

We will now provide some tips on how best to establish and manage school routines easily and flexibly.

TIP: Establishing and managing school routines

- Establish where potential trouble spots could occur within the school and why.
- Design routines to help minimise these potentially difficult situations, for example to prevent running down the corridor in order to avoid accidents.
- Check pupils' understanding of the routines.
- Explain the rationale behind each routine, e.g. if you run into the classroom someone else may get hurt.
- Model or illustrate the routine or procedure for the pupils.
- Be consistent. Take time to reinforce the routines, because if they are established at the beginning of the year they will help to ensure the rest of the year is more enjoyable and productive for both teacher and pupils alike.
- Display the school/class routines on the designated noticeboard and go over them with the pupils on a regular basis to reinforce the key points.

The use of positive reinforcement

The use of positive reinforcement enables us to strengthen a desired response. The use of positive reinforcements can therefore be a powerful tool in helping pupils to internalise the effects and consequences of their own behaviour. In order for positive reinforcement approaches to operate successfully staff need to be aware of what it is they are trying to achieve in the first place. Teachers, CAs and LSMs need to be consistent in their approach to achieve the best outcomes. Once the desired consequences have been achieved and become embedded a different form of pupil behaviour can be targeted.

In order to help to focus the pupils' attention, it is usually a good idea to display the week's/month's positive reinforcement strategies on a poster in the classroom and in other key areas throughout the school. This is a great tool to use when a pupil(s) starts to display unacceptable behaviour as you can show them all the previous strategies which they have successfully learnt earlier during the session.

In order for positive reinforcement strategies to have the desired effect they need to be applied in an immediate, consistent, achievable and fair manner. Often the best possible reward is a quick bout of praise or encouragement.

Immediate

When a child, for example, holds a door open for a member of staff they should be rewarded immediately so that the desired behaviour is reinforced and the child becomes more likely to repeat it time and time again. A delay in rewarding the desired behaviour lessens the impact and the likelihood of that behaviour being repeated. Keeping a supply of reward tokens on hand for later use is a great way of positively reinforcing immediately.

Consistent

A consistent approach is essential to ensure positive behavioural changes take place. It is very easy for teachers with heavy everyday workloads to forget to reward the targeted behaviour. Displaying posters in the classroom and in key areas throughout the school is a good way to remind both staff and pupils alike of the targeted improvement in behaviour, and it makes it more likely that a consistent approach will be implemented.

Achievable

We all enjoy being challenged. However, if a target or challenge is impossible for us to achieve we tend to become less motivated and even frustrated, which can result in unwanted behaviour. If a child can achieve a goal nine times out of ten, then this suggests it may be a good place to start. As the child grows in confidence and ability, the goal can be raised and become even more challenging. If a child becomes less motivated and/or frustrated, resulting in poorer behaviour, then it is likely the goal set is too challenging and it may need to be reassessed.

Fair

The concept of fairness is key to establishing trust and respect for both teacher and pupil. When a child perceives an approach to be fair, his or her response is more likely to be positive and accepting. Discussing what a fair approach is with the children during circle time in class is an effective way for everyone to agree and understand the rationale behind the idea.

Positive reinforcements can be divided into three categories, which we will now consider in turn. These are:

- social;
- tangible;
- activity.

Social

PRAISE

The selective use of praise is one of the best and most effective weapons in a teacher's armoury. Praise is an effective way to encourage children to engage in the desired behaviour as it focuses on a child's effort rather than on what is actually accomplished. When teachers give genuine praise that is specific, descriptive, spontaneous and well deserved, it encourages continuous learning to take place. It also decreases competition amongst children. So, for example, 'I liked the fact that you noticed that Ahmed was on his own during playtime and you included him in your game. That was very thoughtful.' This type of praise not only tells the pupil what they have done well but also about the school's values and expectations.

Too many teachers (like far too many parents) are regularly and often continuously negative with their pupils. Children like to know when they are doing well and appreciate being told so. Sometimes it is appropriate to praise a pupil in a one-to-one situation. Sometimes it is better in whole-class situations. It all depends upon what you are praising the pupil (and/or whole class) for. Is it for good work? It is for an out-of-school activity? It is for scoring three goals in a school football match or for playing the piano well in assembly? Think about the situation first before deciding what to say and when to say it.

Although praise can normally lead to positive outcomes, it is important to understand that some children do not respond well to praise in public, especially when they are quite shy. Therefore this type of positive reinforcement needs to be adapted to address that individual child's needs. Over-praising a pupil for doing something they are already good at and/or enjoy can, in some circumstances, also decrease their motivation (Henderlong and Lepper, 2002). Using positive praise well does encourage most pupils to take on new challenges without feeling afraid of making mistakes and/or failure.

PEER PRAISE

Encouraging children to praise each other not only creates a positive, fun environment but also motivates individuals to make positive choices. Children need to be taught how to praise their peers by clapping or cheering when they see a fellow pupil doing something positive. Below are two examples of using positive social reinforcers.

SPECIAL DAY

Special Day provides a cheerful start to each day and is an ideal way to reinforce all the positive behavioural changes each pupil has made over a period of time. Imagine having between ten and thirty pupils in the class saying something positive about one particular child. The beneficial effect can be amazing as it boosts self-esteem and, more importantly, acts as a powerful reinforcer for good behaviour. Every day a different pupil is chosen for attention on each Special Day and stands in front of the class. Then, in turn, the pupils, including the teacher and support staff, make a positive comment about the child. For instance: 'I like Elli because she shares her sweets with me in the playground.' The child whose special day it is receives a series of privileges for the day such as always being first in line or always being chosen to go on errands for the teacher. This idea has been adapted from *A Kit Bag for Promoting Positive Behaviour in the Classroom* (Morgan and Ellis, 2011b).

A TIME TO CELEBRATE!

Children need to be rewarded on a regular basis to show them that they are making the right choices in their behaviour. A weekly, monthly or termly celebration assembly where the whole school comes together to share pupils' achievements is certainly something very worthwhile. Family members can also be invited to join in the celebrations. The celebration assembly can also be linked to the positive behaviour hotspot (see p. 132) or to any other school-led initiative for which the children can be nominated by their peers and/or staff. Examples of celebration assembly rewards might include such achievements as making 100 per cent or improved school attendance and outstanding achievements in music, drama or sport, in academic work, in literacy or numeracy or in improved behaviour.

TIP: Using praise effectively

- Identify the behaviour you are praising.
- When a child displays the desired behaviour, immediately follow it with praise.
- Be creative and use different ways to praise.
- Relating praise to effort helps motivate children rather than comparing themselves to others.
- Encourage the child to become more independent in their achievements.
- Praise loses its effectiveness if it is given continuously and without reason.
- Never follow praise with a negative comment or criticism.
- Be sincere and specific when giving praise.
- Do not give praise continuously and without good reason.

Tangible

Tangible reinforcement, for example the use of tokens, lucky dips, raffle tickets, stickers, needs to be made desirable; something which the pupils aspire to and want. Children in key stage 1 will prefer different rewards from children at key stage 2. Below are some examples of tangible reinforcement which can be used by schools or in the classroom:

POSITIVE BEHAVIOUR HOTSPOT

Focusing on a form of misbehaviour which needs to improve is a very powerful way of reversing the undesired behaviour. Involving staff, pupils and the school council in a practical manner is a good way of transforming pupils' behaviour. Collectively, for example, the school council could discuss one or all of the following issues:

- Is it too noisy when classes walk in and out of assembly?
- Do all classes walk sensibly down the corridors and/or up the stairs?
- In the playground, when the whistle blows for the first time, are all pupils ready to return indoors?
- Are all cloakrooms tidy?
- Do all pupils return to class on time?
- Is rubbish picked up in the playground and in the canteen?
- What should happen if a pupil swears at a teacher or a dinner lady?
- What should happen if a pupil starts making mobile phone calls in class?

When a comprehensive list of behavioural hotspots has been compiled and the action agreed upon by staff, pupils and the school council, they can then be implemented one at a time or all at once over a week, a month or a term. Usually, one at a time is best. The agreed strategies should be disseminated throughout the school, perhaps by informing pupils of the collective decisions in a school assembly to begin the process. Having a common consensus throughout the school is very advantageous for everyone. The chosen hotspot (see Figure 8.1) can be further reinforced during class circle time as well as by displaying hotspot posters around the school to inform visitors and supply staff. Pupils are rewarded by staff with tokens/raffle tickets when they are seen to be following one of the chosen positive behaviour hotspots. At the end of the agreed timescale, the tokens can be put into a raffle and prizes given out to the lucky winners. Tokens can also be used to gain such things as house points. You can also discuss the chosen hotspot at the start of the school day following registration.

DYNAMIC DISCS

Visual reinforcements are another great way to motivate children. Dynamic Discs are designed so that each class has a set quantity of round wooden discs with a hole in the middle (rather

Figure 8.1 Positive behaviour hotspot poster

like Polo mints) which are placed on a metal stand to hold them in position. When the class or an individual child behaves well or achieves work of a very high standard, a disc is placed onto the metal stand. At the end of the week, perhaps during assembly, a child is nominated from each class to call out the total number of wooden discs achieved by their class. These scores can be recorded in a whole-school monitoring book to tally each class's progress over the term. When a class achieves the highest number of discs for the term they are rewarded with a whole-class prize such as a visit to the local cinema, with popcorn or ice cream as a treat.

Children who have not followed school rules during the week should not take part in the reward because otherwise this becomes counterproductive.

Activity: Friday Fun

Friday Fun (also referred to as Golden Time, Free Time or Enrichment Afternoon) is a fun way to help to engage and encourage young children. As members of staff we all look forward to Fridays as we consider the two-day break at the weekend to be our reward for the week. Pupils are no different and feel exactly the same. To ensure a consistent approach, all members of staff should be encouraged to choose an activity which they are interested in organising. Examples might include face painting, dodgeball, movie club, laptop games, biscuit decorating or class rounders. On a Monday morning pupils are asked to list their first, second and third choice of preferred activities on a piece of paper, which is then handed in to the Friday Fun co-ordinator. This way all year groups can be mixed up, which is a great way for the younger children to work with the older children. Every child is then fairly allocated their chosen activity, which is recorded and displayed in each class to help to reinforce the expectations of the school. On every Friday afternoon, at an agreed time, lessons conclude and the children take themselves off to their nominated member of staff for their chosen activity (see Figure 8.2).

Every week, month or term the activities are changed to ensure the children's motivation and interest continue. It is important that the children get a reasonable opportunity to rotate between activities.

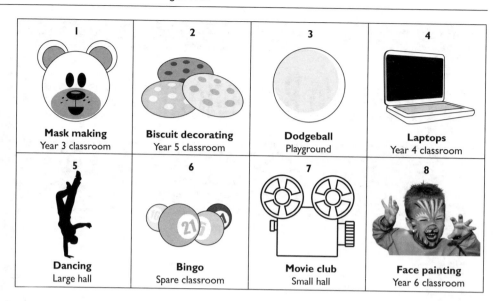

Figure 8.2 Friday Fun timetable

This type of activity can be very effective for a number of reasons:

- children can engage in an activity of their choice;
- children can take part in an activity with their chosen member of staff;
- children who have not followed school rules during the week do not take part;
- Friday Fun takes place at the same time each week and is a good way to round off every week on a positive note.

Establishing positive relationships

You as the teacher: self-management

Teaching children and managing sometimes difficult situations is never an easy job. Teaching can sometimes become stressful even for the most accomplished teacher. It is vitally important that teachers believe and think that they are in control all the time. Positive attitudes are contagious. By being positive, you will affect and change the children's outlook within the class in an empathetic and forward-looking manner. Never let the children know you have doubts in your own ability or are unable to cope in particular situations. Exude confidence at all times.

TIP: The golden rules of teaching

- Believe you can make a difference.
- Celebrate all your achievements, however small.
- Understand that you are human and you will inadvertently make some mistakes; we are all only human! Remember, mistakes are merely the portals to learning.
- It is important to understand that children's behaviour may only improve slightly or sometimes not at all. It may even get worse before it gets better, which can make us feel helpless, even inadequate.
- Keep a flexible approach and do what works best for you and the children.
- Plan ahead but be flexible and accept change. It will take time to accomplish all your goals. Remember to keep your goals realistic.

- Don't take it personally when children sometimes do not show appreciation for your efforts.
- If you feel overwhelmed, it is often best to talk the situation through with a colleague.
- Take time out to enjoy a healthy lifestyle, including exercise, healthy eating and sleep.
- Never overreact in particular situations; it usually makes things worse.
- Adopt a sense of humour and have some fun!

(Morgan and Ellis, 2011b)

Teacher–child relationships

The teacher's skills in managing her class depend upon the quality of her relationship with the children. It is essential to start with a new class in the right way by building positive and respectful relationships from the outset. Over time, a teacher must build up trust and empathy with the children as this establishes the basis for all tasks involving future behaviour management and change activities.

Fundamental to success is the building of strong interpersonal relationships with the children, thereby creating a caring, loyal and respectful bond. These empathetic bonds should form a strong foundation from which any necessary future behavioural changes can take place. In return, and by her displaying this empathy and care for all the children in the class, the pupils will gain respect from their teacher.

Morgan and Ellis (2011b) indicate that there are a number of ways to build a strong and respectful relationship with the class. These include:

- being a positive role model for the children – for them to be respectful to others they must be treated with respect;
- creating a caring, supportive and fair environment where every child feels accepted, that he or she belongs and can be relaxed;
- recognising every child's strengths and ensuring that every child feels he or she has the ability to learn (especially pupils with special educational needs and disabilities);
- acknowledging, reinforcing and sharing all successes with the class in as positive a manner as possible;
- involving the children in making decisions regarding the rules and the management of activities within the classroom – this helps them to 'own' their own rules;
- taking time to speak to every child individually to find out about their interests, talents, goals, likes and dislikes;
- discussing classroom rules and consequences so that all children are clear and understand what is expected of them;
- never embarrassing or ridiculing the children when reprimanding them;
- interacting with the children during playtime (e.g. joining in a game of football or 'hopscotch') or by just having a chat – children naturally enjoy this kind of interaction, which helps to give them confidence, and you are also showing that you have a legitimate concern for their needs.

Research (Reid, 2012) indicates that pupils like teachers:

- who are empathetic;
- who they can trust;
- who have a sense of humour;

- who encourage and promote interesting discussions and set worthwhile tasks and assignments;
- who teach well at all times;
- who give pupils praise when it is deserved;
- who show they like and understand children;
- who are warm, enthusiastic and show they enjoy their job;
- who are consistent and fair;
- who treat pupils with respect;
- who create a sense of 'freedom' in class;
- who listen to children's views and act accordingly;
- who vary their teaching styles and in interesting ways;
- who can laugh at themselves.

Knowing your children

If you are a new teacher or are given a new class, it is important to get to know the children reasonably well as soon as possible. Reid (2012) and Morgan and Ellis (2011b) suggest the following ideas:

TIP: Knowing your children

One way of achieving this is to give your children a clean sheet of paper. Then ask them to write down the following:

- your name;
- your birthday;
- your best friend(s) in class;
- your favourite television programmes;
- your favourite kind of music;
- your favourite singers or groups;
- your interests outside school (e.g. what you like doing at weekends or in school holidays);
- the names of your pets and what type of animal they are (e.g. dog, cat, hamster);
- the first names of your parent(s) or carer(s);
- where you like to go on holiday or where you would like to go;
- your favourite football or rugby team or your favourite sport or pastime;
- your favourite foods;
- your biggest dislikes;
- your favourite activity/subject in school;
- your idea for a school/classroom trip.

Take time to read all the children's answers. You can have a lot of fun by engaging the class with some of their answers, e.g. who said their favourite food was black pudding? Whose favourite sport is snooker? Who owns a pet snake? Whose favourite television programme is *Gardening Time*?

By remembering the children's responses (why not keep them in your desk drawers) you can have a conversation with them at the start of the day, in playtime, after the weekend or at the start of a new term. How is your pet snake, Holly? I see Manchester United lost again, Alex. JLS are number one in the charts, Sarah. Has your cat had her kittens yet, Alisha?

Children like to know that you as a teacher have an interest in them as a person and not just as a learner. They will naturally respect your interest in them and respond in kind.

TIP: Building relationships

- Welcome the children as they enter the classroom.
- Ensure all children understand what is expected of them.
- Create a positive environment where each child feels relaxed and accepted.
- Show an interest in each child's family, talents, goals, likes and dislikes.
- Engage with the children during lunchtime and playtime.
- Treat each child with respect; never embarrass or ridicule them.
- Share all successes with the class.
- Believe that every child has the ability to learn and achieve by recognising their strengths.
- Involve the children in making decisions regarding rules and activities within the classroom.

The systematic approach and displays

Getting to know pupils well means understanding them in a variety of ways. These include: as being part of their family, their immediate friends, within the class and school, and within the community.

Does the child in your class have older or younger brothers or sisters in the school? If so, engage in discussion with them about their brother(s) or sister(s). Just as you as a teacher have a life outside the school, so your pupils also have their lives as part of family and community groups. Their outside-school lives are exceedingly important to them and should always be respected.

Equally, the use of light, temperature, colours and display features can be important to both a child's mood and learning. The use of displays within the classroom is an important part of its organisation. The use of displays not only reflects the curriculum but also presents children's achievements. Good displays can be utilised as follows:

- as a curriculum resource;
- as a prompt or reminder for pupils;
- as a celebration of individual pupil achievement;
- as evidence to others of the work done by the class (e.g. other pupils, parents, the head teacher, local authority staff, school inspectors, visitors, etc.).

By visibly displaying their work, teachers' signal to their class that they value their pupils' efforts and are giving recognition to their achievements. Used in this way, display features in the classroom are as much a 'reward' as the use of certificates, prizes, merits, stars or other incentives.

Don'ts

Some teachers inadvertently destroy their relationships with individuals or whole classes of children through their own negative reactions or overreactions. These should be avoided at all times as once a relationship is 'broken' it is much harder to fix. Some teachers regularly spoil their own relationship with children by sending out mixed or confusing messages (e.g. by alternating between shouting at them and praising them). Reid (2012) and Morgan and Ellis (2011) suggest that teachers avoid the following:

TIP: Don'ts

The list now presented provides some ideas on the activities to be avoided and which most children tend to dislike:

- Do not shout or raise the voice unnecessarily. It is a good rule never to shout at all except in an emergency (e.g. a school fire). Never shout or call out remarks or 'names' of an abusive nature.
- Do not ever victimise or hit a pupil for any reason. Keep calm even in the most difficult of situations.
- Do not attribute bad behaviour to unrealistic isomorphisms (e.g. 'You are just like your older brother Adam, and he could never behave either', 'I'm not surprised at your behaviour considering where you live and the state of your family', 'You're going to get into the same trouble as your sister, Sian').
- Do not rip up children's work in front of them or their classmates, however poor it may be. Suggest that they start again and give them time to do so.
- Do not have an argument with their parent(s) or carer(s) in the classroom within sight or earshot of the child or their classmates.
- Do not tell the head teacher your views on a pupil in front of their classmates.

Warning signs

Teachers should also always be on the lookout for warning signs of child abuse, bullying, eating disorders, illness, stress, self-mutilation, harassment, underachievement and anxiety. For example, a child falling behind with her school work or failing to complete homework may indicate a problem in the family home (e.g. divorce, separation, parental break-up, imminent house move, etc.).

By getting to know pupils well and being aware of their personalities, moods and feelings, teachers are in the best position to spot or detect potential warning signs for major problems, often before they occur. By talking to a pupil and finding out the cause of the problem, a teacher can inform the head teacher, who, in turn, may need to contact outside agencies. Schools, head teachers and LA staff should be very keen to promote early intervention approaches in the interests of the child or the child's own safety or future personal development, including his or her best learning opportunities.

Positive talk

It is important to focus on positive rather than negative statements when interacting with children. This will guide them towards making positive outcomes rather than highlighting their mistakes. Conversely, it is wrong to 'label' children inappropriately, especially in front of classmates. For example, calling a child a 'hooligan' is likely to have the following results:

- the pupil is more likely to behave like a 'hooligan' in the future;
- the term 'hooligan' invokes a form of ridicule within the class and it can even 'backfire' on the teacher who has used it;
- the status of the 'hooligan' is raised temporarily amongst his or her peers and becomes a term of affection in playground banter.

TIP: Positive talk

Positive talk	*Negative talk*
'Craig, I'd like you to look at the board. Thank you.'	'Craig, stop chatting and look at the board.'
'Jody, if you know what day of the week it is, raise your hand. Good girl.'	'Jody, I've told you before, *don't* shout or *call out.*'
'Peter, remember to walk down the corridor sensibly. Thank you.'	'Hey, Peter, stop running down the corridor.'

Pupils' manners and respect

Many children do not have good manners instilled in them at home. It is therefore important for teachers to manifest and reinforce good manners to help to develop pupils' appropriate social skills. Good manners not only make a positive impression on others but also make us feel good about ourselves.

TIP: Manners and respect

- When a child demonstrates good manners always positively reinforce them.
- Model the desired behaviour to encourage children to practise good manners.
- Discuss with children in circle time the importance of treating others in the same way as they'd like to be treated.
- For younger children, engage in role-play activities to demonstrate appropriate responses.
- Ask children to think of creative ways to show respect to others, e.g. by writing thank-you notes.

Making successful transitions

It is important to create a positive and well-structured environment within the school and classroom right from the start of the year and each lesson/session. Self-categorisation theory (see Witte and Davis, 1996) states that people strive to conform to their representation of the group norm. Hence, based on this theory, school and classroom behaviour can be established and improved by using examples based upon what the majority of the children are doing and how they are behaving.

TIP: Arrival at school

Establish clear routines and expectations when pupils arrive at school at the start of each day, for example the procedure for when it's raining

Create a staff rota for the beginning of the day to greet pupils as they come into school.

Allocate staff to potential behaviour hotspots.

Design a personalised plan for pupils with challenging behaviour, for example:

- ask their parent/carer to escort them to and from school;
- arrange different times for them to arrive, i.e. just before registration;
- allocate a job to complete first thing in the morning, i.e. hand out milk during breakfast club.

When transitions from one activity to another are not managed effectively they can result in confusion, frustration and even unwanted behaviour. Transitions become part of the school's or classroom's routine to ensure a flow between each activity, whether it's entering the classroom, walking into assembly, moving from group work to individual tasks or when leaving the classroom to take part in physical education.

When establishing effective transitions ask the following key questions:

- What are the expectations of the school/classroom?
- Has adequate transition time been allocated?
- Are the children aware of the transition routine?
- Have the needs of children with additional/special needs been met?
- Are the transitions designed to make the children more independent?
- Are there activities arranged for children who are waiting for their peers?

There are a number of strategies to help prepare children for the respective transition to ensure they are aware of what is expected of them as well as the timeframe in which the changeover needs to be completed. Below are a few examples:

- the five-minute reminder; for example: 'You have five minutes before it's time to pack away ready for break';
- a pictorial cue displayed on the board;
- the ringing of a bell or the playing of a set piece of music;
- teacher claps a rhythm and the children join in;
- in the playground during breaktime, three short blasts of the whistle are sounded a few minutes before the final whistle is blown.

Welcoming the children into class

The teacher needs to immediately establish respect in a calm, reasonable but assertive manner. Make it clear from the onset that the classroom has set rules and routines. This needs to be practised every time the pupils enter the classroom, such as at the beginning of school, after playtime.

Entry times into the classroom can sometimes be an occasion when pupils bring their concerns, anxieties or unresolved issues into the classroom with them. For example, if pupils leave home for school after witnessing an argument between their parents or after observing some form of domestic violence at home, a disagreement between peers or an act of bullying, they are likely to feel emotionally ill at ease, even seriously concerned. Such unresolved issues can greatly impact on a child's behaviour and subsequently create challenges within the school and/or classroom, which more often than not impacts upon the teaching and learning. By building in reflection time before the start of a new activity/lesson, a teacher can calm a potentially difficult situation. Observant teachers who know their pupils well may notice something is wrong with a pupil and will be able to arrange to have a discreet talk, perhaps by asking the CA or

LSM to take over the class for a while. Creating a positive atmosphere in a classroom in which the children are ready to engage and learn will be helpful to everyone's cause; not least the teacher's. Successful transition strategies can be managed in many ways and include the use of, for example, circle time, peer massage and listening to appropriate music; all methods which are designed to give the children a greater awareness of themselves and other people.

Morgan and Ellis (2011b) suggest some ideas.

Welcoming the children into class

When greeting the pupils from outside the classroom you should stand at the door and welcome them in. Ask each child to enter, one at a time, informing them of the set task.

It is highly likely that one or two (or maybe more!) children will decide to 'test' boundaries and will not enter the classroom in the desired way, e.g. they may start talking or shouting out, trying to jump the queue, etc. When this happens, you should very promptly and assertively inform the child, 'You're not ready to come into our classroom. Please wait there until you are ready to come in', then direct the child to wait outside the classroom in clear view of the teacher.

When all the children have entered the classroom and they are engaged in the set task, praise and reward the desired behaviour from the majority of the class. In this way, the children are more likely to be motivated to carry out the task.

Return to the child whom you have asked to wait outside the classroom and ask them if they are ready to come into the classroom. It is highly likely that the child will now be ready and will enter the classroom in a calm and focused manner. If the child is not ready, then give them a further period of time for reflection (always ensuring they are in eyesight of the teacher) and then return and repeat the process.

Strategic seating

Seating plans and layouts in classrooms can vary tremendously. Teachers should consider the following when seating children:

- Can I see pupils' faces? Can they see me?
- Can everyone see the board (if you're planning on using it)?
- Can the pupils see one another?
- Can I move around the room so that I can monitor effectively?

Strategic seating also needs to be taken into consideration during such times as school assemblies, sports day, school productions and in everyday classroom lessons, especially with pupils who are hyperactive or who have known behavioural or mental health issues. A teacher should ask:

- Is there enough space between each row?
- Are potentially disruptive children sitting next to each other?
- Are members of staff strategically placed to monitor positive and negative behaviour?

Position of the teacher

The position of the teacher is key to establishing a positive learning environment within the classroom.

TIP: Position of the teacher

- Try to stand or sit facing all the pupils.
- Move around the room to establish the whole area as your territory.
- Periodically scan the room with your eyes to reinforce positive behaviour and nip unwanted behaviour in the bud.
- When using a board, write at an angle so you have a full view of the classroom.

The lesson

In order to create a positive learning environment it is important to gain the pupils' attention. This can be achieved in a number of ways and below are a few suggestions.

TIP: Ready to start the lesson

- Only start the lesson when you have the full attention of all the pupils.
- Take time to explain the task and also ensure the pupils understand what to do.
- Inform the pupils of the appropriate voice level for the task being undertaken. To help reinforce this expectation catch a child using the appropriate voice level, stop the class and reward that child, for example with a token reward. This will motivate the whole class to engage in the desired behaviour.
- To ensure late arrivals do not impact on the lesson implement a procedure which is understood by all pupils.

Getting pupils' attention

Below are a few suggestions adapted from *A Kit Bag for Promoting Positive Behaviour in the Classroom* (Morgan and Ellis, 2011b) on how to help get pupils' attention.

Keep the Beat game

1 Let the class know that when you want their attention you'll clap a rhythm and they must copy that beat. When you stop clapping you want their eyes on you and no talking.
2 Reward the children who complete the task with the chosen token reward.
3 Make it challenging for the children by clapping more complicated beats.
4 When increasing difficulty levels remember to provide them with challenges that they are able to complete without feeling frustrated, otherwise this will have a detrimental effect on their behaviour.

Silence All Around game

1 Let the class know that when you want their attention you'll say, 'One, two, three, three, two, one. Silence all around has begun.' The children must then freeze with no talking.
2 The children who freeze the longest complete the task and are rewarded with the chosen token reward. If all children freeze for a set time they are all rewarded.
3 Time the children to see if they can break their best record. If they break the record they can be rewarded with extra token rewards.

Give Me Five

Let the class know that when you want their attention you'll hold up your hand and say, 'Give me five.' Everyone holds their hand up and begins to count down from five to one, getting progressively quieter until they whisper 'one'.

Statues

This is a great game to play at the end of a lesson to get the class's attention again in a fun and calm way. When the children hear 'One, two, three, statue!' they freeze in a statue-like position. The children who are the stillest and quietest are chosen to, for example, line up by the door first. This game can be repeated until all the children are lined up.

Heads Down, Thumbs Up

A maximum of four children are chosen to stand at the front of the class. The rest of the children place their heads on their desk with their eyes closed and thumbs in the up position. The four children secretly and gently squeeze one child's thumbs and return quickly to their place at the front of the class. The teacher asks if any of the students can correctly guess the person who squeezed their hand. If they are right, they can then swap places and become the new champion. Used correctly, this can help to settle a chatty class brilliantly!

Apple Pie

A child is chosen to stand with his or her back to the class, blindfolded. The teacher signals to one of the children to say the words 'Apple pie' in a voice different from their own. The blindfolded child must then guess which child said 'Apple pie'. If they guess correctly they score a point. If the blindfolded child guesses incorrectly, that child they named takes their place and the game continues.

TIP: The end of the lesson

- Bring the class back together at the end of the lesson with a discussion, game or task.
- Feed back to the class what went well with the lesson and what could be improved.
- Dismiss the pupils in small groups to prevent congestion in the corridor.
- Stand by the door and either say something positive to them or give them a smile and say or wave goodbye. This is a good opportunity to check they are walking sensibly through the corridor to their next lesson.

Summary

In this chapter we have considered many of the fundamental principles for schools and teachers to manage pupils effectively within the classroom. We will now continue with and develop this theme in Chapter 9 by looking in more detail at how to manage specific classroom difficulties.

Dealing with specific classroom difficulties

Practical solutions

Every teacher is aware that teaching children can be both difficult and demanding. Without the correct skills, attitude and resourcefulness, pupils will invariably start to take advantage of particular situations and start to disrupt classes. These disruptions can be very time consuming. They can also affect the learning and well-being of the whole class, including pupils who are able and those with special educational needs or additional learning needs alike.

In addition, responding to challenging behaviour can cause individual teachers (or all the teachers in a school) stress and make them feel anxious about coming to work. In extreme cases, it can cause illness or stress-related symptoms.

Many teachers feel ill prepared for managing pupils' behaviour when they start to teach. Trainee teachers tend to have received very few sessions on managing pupils' behaviour. Normally, they develop their skills either on teaching practice or in the early years of teaching. The induction period in schools is particularly crucial in developing teachers' classroom management skills. Research indicates that some teachers who fail to manage their classrooms successfully either fail their teaching practice(s) or probationary period or leave the profession early, often frustrated or exhausted. This is a waste both of time and of crucial resources.

When dealing with disruptive conduct, a school's behaviour policy document must include an effective whole-school approach to ensure consistency and continuity of rules, correctives and rewards. Behavioural change doesn't happen overnight, so patience and a consistently positive approach are often two of the essential prerequisites to achieving the desired goals.

Low-level misbehaviour

Low-level misbehaviour can occur in any class at any time. In classrooms with a strong ethos and culture of managing attendance and behaviour, the impact of low-level misbehaviour is likely to be markedly reduced.

The range of low-level misbehaviour/disruption includes:

- noisy entry into class;
- marginal lateness for lessons;
- not having appropriate materials or equipment;
- failure to do homework;
- calling out across the classroom indiscriminately;
- teasing and provoking other pupils;
- moving around the classroom without permission;
- using mobile phones;
- failing to listen to instructions;
- talking unnecessarily or incessantly.

Hence difficult to manage low-level misbehaviour can range from mild disruption to attention seeking. Low-level misbehaviour is often fuelled by hyperactivity, being withdrawn, low self-esteem or ebullience. These factors can, in turn, be exacerbated by problems at home, in school or in the classroom or by pupils having learning difficulties, physical, psychological or mental health problems. Illness or medical treatments (e.g. taking certain kinds of tablets) are another factor.

Often, tired, over-extended staff can unwittingly make things worse for themselves. Sometimes, teachers respond in ways in which they would never do if they were feeling more relaxed, refreshed, less stressed or more confident in the classroom. It is often these internal psychological and stress-related features which make teaching such a challenging profession.

Challenging behaviour

Serious misbehaviour

Behaviour starts to become more challenging when the teacher's strategies (providing they are appropriate) fail to operate effectively in the classroom. It is often for this reason that a pupil who is classified as challenging by one teacher can be regarded as a 'lovely child' by another. Many pupils react to situation-specific trigger points.

Qureshi and Alborz (1992) and Hastings and Remington (1994) defined five types of challenging behaviour. These are:

- aggressive behaviour;
- destructive behaviour;
- self-injurious behaviour;
- stereotype behaviour;
- socially or sexually unacceptable behaviours.

Emerson was one of the first to define challenging behaviour. His definition was:

> Behaviour of such intensity, frequency and duration that the physical safety of the person or others is likely to be placed in serious jeopardy or behaviour which is likely to seriously limit or delay access to, and use of ordinary facilities.
>
> (Emerson, 1995: 234)

All behaviour is relative and situation specific. It is affected by social, environmental, cultural or historic factors. It is the contextual situation which determines whether behaviour is appropriate or inappropriate. For example, what is deemed acceptable in the playground may be unacceptable in the classroom.

Unwanted behaviour starts to become a concern if the following increase:

- frequency;
- intensity;
- duration.

Frequency

The frequency is the rate of reoccurrence at which the unwanted behaviour takes place. If a pupil, for example, repeatedly disrupts the class he or she may be seen as exhibiting unacceptable behaviour.

Intensity

The intensity is the level or the seriousness of the unwanted behaviour. Helen, for example, can engage in positive behaviour for weeks. But if she starts to get angry her behaviour may involve biting, shouting, spitting or hitting another pupil. Her outbursts can cause physical harm. They also upset the other pupils and/or parents.

Duration

The duration is the length of the time the unwanted behaviour lasts. For example, Brandon has had a disagreement with a friend. He will not follow his teacher's instructions. He refuses to return to class. When he does so, he becomes sulky and argumentative. His poor behaviour often lasts for long periods and he will continually disrupt the class.

Understanding behaviour

Understanding the root cause of the child's behaviour is essential. Not doing so often means that teachers are unlikely to implement appropriate behaviour strategies which are sustainable. Evidence from the literature suggests that there are five basic models which are useful in understanding children's behaviour. These models are:

- biological;
- behavioural;
- cognitive;
- systemic;
- psychodynamic.

Biological

The child has a tendency to interact with the environmental influences around him or her and this interaction informs his or her behaviour. Research evidence has come from studies around twins separated at birth and in early infancy. This goes to show that both nature and nurture are involved in children's development.

Behavioural

Behaviour can be modified through 'conditioning'. This is achieved by another event following an action. There are two types of 'conditioning':

- *classical conditioning*, where a response is connected with a certain stimulus; for example a child feels happy and excited on a Friday afternoon as this is the time the whole class has Fun Friday;
- *operant conditioning*, where a desired response is induced and repeated by regularly rewarding the positive behaviour and issuing correctives for the negative behaviour; for example, if a dog sits and offers its paw when instructed it will be rewarded with food.

Cognitive

The cognitive approach helps children to learn to judge and reason effectively and to gain a picture of their surroundings, views and beliefs. This means that the way in which we behave is influenced by our thinking.

The cortex is the conscious, rational-thinking part of the brain and determines the child's response to certain situations. Research has shown that if an infant is constantly being subjected to negative situations, for example experiencing domestic violence and/or neglect, then the connections that form the cortex to help deal with situations in a rational way are limited. In situations such as these, children are left to rely on their limbic system, which is the body's alarm system. So when a child is faced with the person sitting next to them taking their pencil without asking, instead of the rational-thinking cortex being engaged the limbic system is triggered, displaying the flight/fight reaction.

Systemic

The systemic approach looks at targeting the individual's behaviour within the system. These systems can include:

- their family;
- their friends;
- their school;
- their classmates;
- their community;
- their outside-school clubs, for example Scouts.

The quality of these systems is a great influence on the child's behaviour. For example, a child living in a family where domestic violence takes place will naturally struggle within another system, i.e. school. The behaviour which that child experiences at home, for example shouting, violence and aggressiveness, will not work in a school or classroom context. This may cause some children from difficult or unhappy home backgrounds to experience adjustment difficulties at school, which, if not resolved in the early stages, can lead some pupils to start manifesting behavioural difficulties or disorders at an early stage in their school careers. In these situations, working with the family in order to help them to understand how their own behaviour and environment is affecting their child is paramount in finding solutions to help to resolve their child's behaviour. However, this is both a skilled and delicate task.

Psychodynamic

The psychodynamic approach is one used in a clinical setting as it focuses on understanding and intervening by unravelling past conscious and unconscious experiences in order to help the child deal with them.

TIP: Behaviour theory

- A child will repeat a behaviour if it is being rewarded.
- A child should be less likely to repeat a behaviour when appropriate correctives are issued.
- If there is no consistency with rewards and correctives it is likely the child will continue to display the unwanted behaviour.
- The more attention the teacher gives to a child's poor behaviour, the more likely it is that the unwanted behaviour will be repeated.

Children and young people at risk of exclusion

The vast majority of primary school pupils attend school and behave well. However, a minority of children find school to be an unrewarding environment. In some cases, this may stem from unmet and, worse still, unidentified learning needs. There is good evidence from

Howe and Mercer (2007) that children and young people who misbehave in school lack the necessary literacy skills to engage in the curriculum at the level at which it is being presented to them. This can result in disaffection and ultimately, in extreme cases, to disengagement and serious disruption to classes.

When this occurs within the context of an inflexible curriculum (i.e. one that does not match a child's interest, enthusiasms and aspirations), it is likely that they will feel:

- that they cannot be successful;
- that no one cares;
- that they do not fit in;
- that they are to blame in some way.

When this experience is compounded by a peer-pressured 'try not to succeed' attitude and/ or by a lack of parental involvement and lack of interest in the young person's learning, it is likely that he or she will become further disaffected and disengaged from education. Evidence from research suggests that many young people who have become disaffected often become disengaged from schooling because their additional learning needs have never been assessed, diagnosed or met (NBAR, 2008: 48).

It is becoming increasingly evident that better detection skills and screening techniques are required, in order to improve both pupils' behaviour and attendance, allied to early intervention policies in accord with the Children Act, 2004, agenda. Skilled screening can detect subtle changes and differences in pupils' behaviour, irrespective of cause (e.g. medical, social or familial).

Troubled children

Most schools keep a register of pupils considered to be 'at risk' or severely troubled, whether for emotional reasons or otherwise. Staff in classrooms who suspect that a pupil has a serious behavioural disorder or troubled background should speak to their head teacher in the first instance.

In turn, the head teacher may decide to involve the local authority, for example the educational psychology or behavioural support services or medical or social services staff or, in extreme cases, each of these agencies. Sometimes, calling an inter-agency or LA-organised case conference is necessary, normally requiring the attendance of parents and/or carers.

In the most extreme cases, there are a few examples of seriously disruptive pupils who are being educated otherwise than at school. These include pupils who are being educated in alternative curriculum centres, pupil referral units or, in certain circumstances, at home.

A problem-solving approach

When formulating strategies to help children understand and manage their behaviour, it is unlikely that prescriptive approaches will work. Instead the strategies need to be specific to the individual's needs.

To identify the behavioural needs of a child a problem-solving approach needs to be implemented. Formulating appropriate strategies requires an examination of the child's behaviour, which can be achieved by asking a series of specific questions. The answers should help to understand the nature and causes of the behaviour and what they might mean for that particular child.

By being aware of the antecedents to a child's unacceptable behaviour it is possible to reduce or even avoid the child developing future conduct problems. This can be established by utilising a problem-solving approach. Some of the questions which you might like to ask are:

- What seems to be the underlying cause of the child's behaviour?
- Where and when does the child display this behaviour?

- What are the triggers for the behaviour?
- In order for the child to get their needs met, what acceptable behaviour can they use?
- What strategies can be implemented to create behavioural change?
- How can the child's progress be monitored?

The antecedent–behaviour–consequence chart

It is important to try and identify the reason for misbehaviour occurring. Remember, all types of behaviour have meaning and are communicating something, perhaps a message. The antecedent–behaviour–consequence (ABC) chart (see Figure 9.1) is one approach which can be used to formulate a clearer understanding of the meaning of a particular form of behaviour.

The ABC chart is used to collect information through observing events that are occurring within a child's environment, as follows:

- A = antecedent: what happens before the behaviour occurs;
- B = behaviour: the observed behaviour;
- C = consequence: the positive or negative results of the behaviour.

ABC analysis: unwanted behaviour

The ABC chart is useful in helping teachers to identify why a child is likely to behave in a particular way or to repeat those unwanted behaviours. A classic example might help Liam who is seeking attention from his teacher. When he displays his normal good behaviour he receives no attention from the teacher. However, when he displays poor, unwanted behaviour, the teacher immediately gives him attention by staying in with him during breaktime and by sitting next to him in class. In this case the unwanted behaviour is more likely to continue. Ideally, the opposite should apply.

ABC analysis: reducing unwanted behaviour

Analysing the ABC chart helps to identify why a child's unwanted behaviour is more likely to decrease over time. The teacher gives Liam positive attention for good behaviour but when he displays unwanted behaviour the teacher implements the whole-school correctives and

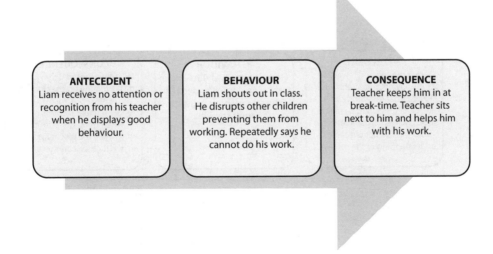

Figure 9.1 The antecedent–behaviour–consequence chart

he receives little or no attention. In this example the unwanted behaviour is more likely to decrease (see Figure 9.2).

Preventing disruptive behaviour

Proactive strategies

Proactive management strategies are designed to equip the teacher with an array of preventative measures to implement before a behaviour problem occurs. These strategies create a sound routine, clear expectations and coping strategies designed to reduce pupils' frustrations and outbursts. The key to successful proactive interventions is advanced strategic planning. Otherwise teachers are put in a situation where they have to react to the unforeseen behavioural disorder. All too often this unplanned reaction from an inexperienced teacher tends to be emotionally loaded. Therefore, it is always best to try and focus on increasing pupils' positive behaviour through the use of praise and encouragement instead of trying to focus (often solely) on reducing pupils' undesired conduct. Proactive behavioural techniques are key to the management of good conduct in the classroom. Sometimes, however, even for the most experienced teacher a quick dose of negative reinforcement is necessary. Generally speaking, the best and most experienced and successful teachers will use large doses of positive reinforcement in their daily teaching. Poor, often weak and failing teachers will do the reverse.

Redirection

It is important to understand that we cannot always control a child's behaviour, but we can redirect it. Children can display conduct that warns us that they are about to lose control. By recognising these 'early warning signs', we can stop the behaviour from getting worse, for example by rechannelling the emotion in a positive manner. Try not to put too much time and energy into managing unwanted behaviour. Instead, try to implement the appropriate correctives in as calm a manner as possible. As soon as the child displays more appropriate behaviour, celebrate his or her achievement through positive comments such as praise, and do so in a dynamic way. The pupil will soon appreciate the different and positive strategy and act accordingly in the future.

ANTECEDENT	BEHAVIOUR	CONSEQUENCE
Liam is praised and rewarded for displaying good behaviour. The teacher frequently gives him attention when he makes good choices i.e. completes set task. The teacher checks his understanding of the set task.	He occasionally shouts out in class. If he doesn't understand the set task he can disrupt other children.	When unwanted behaviour is displayed the teacher ignores, uses 'time out', follows the whole school sanctions policy. When good behaviour is displayed the teacher praises through celebration and rewards.

Figure 9.2 Reducing unwanted behaviour using the antecedent–behaviour–consequence chart

---

TIP: Redirection

1   If a child shouts out to answer a question, remind them how they were sitting with their hand raised ready to answer the question. Then give them another chance to answer the question by displaying the desired behaviour.
2   If a child becomes disruptive at the beginning of the lesson when the books are being handed out, it could be useful to redirect their attention by choosing them to hand out the books to the remainder of the class.
3   If a child finds it difficult to line up sensibly, ask them to stand at the front of the line and lead the other children into the classroom.

Choices

It is important to understand that we cannot completely control children's behaviour, but we can enable them to make their own more informed choices and then to understand the consequences of that conduct. Encouraging children to make decisions is an important skill that they develop as they grow up, helping to make them independent thinkers. It is very difficult for a child to argue when they are given a choice, as choices help children feel they are in control of their lives, and so they are more likely to respond in a positive way. Involving a child in the decision process gives them ownership and so they are more likely to stick to the choice made.

The ability to make choices and accept the outcomes is a measure of the child's confidence and self-esteem. Making choices can be practised in a variety of situations, for example during breaktime asking a child to choose a snack. Using the language 'John I can see you chose an apple today' makes the child familiar and confident with the process of choice making. To help children in the Foundation Years manage their behaviour, see the Good Choice Teddy Approach (Chapter 7).

Unwanted behaviour

When a child is displaying unwanted behaviour the delivery of choices needs to be structured so as to ensure a positive outcome, as follows:

1   Decide on the choices being offered.
2   Ensure the outcome of the choice is acceptable.
3   Limit the choice to avoid overwhelming the child.
4   Approach the child in an unthreatening manner.
5   Deliver the choice at their eye level.
6   Immediately walk away from the child in order to give them time to think about the choice.
7   Praise the child if they have made a positive choice.
8   Follow the school's correctives if they make a negative choice.

If necessary the choices can be repeated by working through points 4 to 6 again.

Before giving a child a choice, first decide on the desired outcome. It is important that the child knows that their choice will be allowed. Giving a choice rather that telling a child what to do will help ensure the outcome is positive rather than negative. Telling a child what to do can be seen by the child as quite confrontational and also gives them the option of defying the member of staff.

Choices need to be age appropriate since too may choices can be overwhelming for a child and as a consequence can have a negative outcome; for example: 'Tom, you can play with the cars or you can draw' rather than 'Tom what would you like to play with?' To help younger children, limit the choices to two; for older children more options can be given.

TIP: Positive choices

Positive choices (it is likely the pupil will comply)	*Negative choices (it is likely the pupil will become confrontational and/or refuse to comply)*
'Would you like to complete your work on your own table or next to me so that I can help you?'	'Either complete your work now or you can stay in at playtime to complete it.'
'Ben, put your toy car either in your bag or on my desk.'	'Ben, give me that toy car.'
'Lisa, you can either sit and listen to the story or choose a book and read/look at it on your own.'	'Lisa, stop poking Sam in the back or you'll lose five minutes off your playtime.'

Dialogue

Using key pre-prepared scripts when dealing with unwanted behaviour can prevent emotions from escalating, and it is one way of enabling staff to deal with situations in a calm, assertive and fair way. Scripts also create a familiar base which a child can understand.

If a child is engaging in unwanted behaviour, for example is sitting under a table instead of completing their work, you could say, '*The instruction is* to sit on your chair.' If the child fails to follow the instruction, then you might proceed to the script 'Not following direction'.

Not following direction

The script below has been adapted from *A Kit Bag for Promoting Positive Behaviour in the Classroom* (Morgan and Ellis, 2011b) and can be used if a pupil refuses to follow a direction, for example will not move to a designated area of the classroom as directed by the teacher. After each time of asking the adult must walk away from the pupil to allow them enough time and space to think about making the right choice.

TIP: Getting a child to follow direction

Asking a pupil to follow direction when they are calm

1 *'I'm asking you for the first time to{…}'*
   Walk away from the pupil and return within one or two minutes.
2 *'I'm asking you for the second time to{…}Remember, if you do not follow my direction when I ask you the third time I could{…}(follow the school's correctives).'*
   Walk away from the pupil and return within one or two minutes.
3 *'I'm asking you for the third time to{…}'*
   If the pupil follows the direction, praise them for doing so. If the pupil does not follow the direction, issue the appropriate sanction.

Asking a child to follow direction when they are not calm

1   *'I'm going to give you five minutes to calm down and think about making the right choice, then I'm going to ask you to follow my direction. Remember, if you don't follow my direction when I ask you for the third time I could{...}(follow the school's correctives).'*
    Walk away from the pupil and return within five minutes.

2   *'I'm asking you for the first time to{...}'*
    Walk away from the pupil and return within one or two minutes.

3   *'I'm asking you for the second time to{...}Remember, if you do not follow my direction when I ask you the third time I could{...}(follow the school's correctives).'*
    Walk away from the pupil and return within one or two minutes.

4   *'I'm asking you for the third time to{...}'*
    If the pupil follows the direction, praise them for doing so. If the pupil does not follow the direction, issue the appropriate corrective.

(Morgan and Ellis, 2011b)

TIP: Reducing the likelihood of situations arising which might spiral out of control

Although preventative measures will not always work, there are a number of steps which schools can take to help reduce the likelihood of situations arising where the power to use force may need to be exercised:

- creating a calm, orderly and supportive school climate that minimises the risk and threat of violence of any kind;
- developing effective relationships between pupils and staff that are central to good order;
- adopting a whole-school approach to developing social and emotional skills such as the Social and Emotional Aspects of Learning (SEAL) programme;
- taking a structured approach to staff development that helps staff to develop the skills of positive behaviour management, to manage conflict and also to support each other during and after an incident;
- effectively managing individual incidents: it is important to communicate calmly with the pupil, using non-threatening verbal and body language and ensuring the pupil can see a way out of a situation; strategies might include, for example, going with the staff member to a quiet room, away from bystanders or other pupils, so that the staff member can listen to concerns, or being joined by a particular member of staff well known to the pupil.

Responding to challenging behaviour

Reactive strategies

Responding correctly to an incident of unwanted behaviour is vitally important. Reactive strategies are designed to manage the behaviour at the time it occurs. These strategies are effective providing they are planned for and used correctly. Reactive strategies should ensure that staff:

- are non-confrontational;
- follow the national guidance/local education authority/school policy document on behaviour management and how to handle incidents effectively;

- follow the school's own guidelines on dealing with challenging behaviour;
- ensure the individual child is safe;
- ensure the safety of the staff and other children.

Dealing with challenging behaviour

When dealing with a situation it is important to wait for a child to calm down fully, to get back to 'baseline', before discussing the incident. This prevents the situation from escalating out of control. The time–intensity model (Smith 1993) illustrates the course of an anger-fuelled behavioural incident (see Figure 9.3).

The 'recovery phase' following an incident is a risky time to discuss the incident and to start requesting apologies. This is because it is a time when further incidents are highly likely and emotions are fully charged.

Using force

The judgement on whether to use force and what force to use should always depend on the circumstances of each case and, crucially in the case of pupils with SEN and/or disabilities, information about the individual concerned.

TIP: Reducing the likelihood of situations occurring that require the use of force

Although preventative measures will not always work, there are a number of steps which schools can take to help reduce the likelihood of situations arising where the power to use force may need to be exercised. These are the same as for situations that might spiral out of control, with one additional point:

- wherever practicable, warning a pupil that force may have to be used before using it.

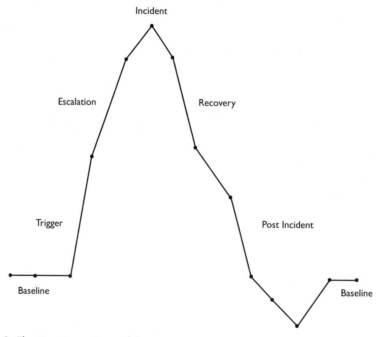

Figure 9.3 The time–intensity model

Situations where staff should not normally intervene without help

An authorised member of staff should not intervene in an incident without help, unless it is an emergency. Schools should have communication systems that enable a member of staff to summon rapid assistance when necessary. Help may be needed in dealing with a situation involving an older pupil, a large pupil or more than one pupil or if the authorised member of staff believes he or she may be at risk of injury. In these circumstances he or she should take steps to remove other pupils who might be at risk and summon assistance from other authorised staff, or, where necessary, phone the police.

TIP: Examples of situations where it is admissible to restrain a pupil

Examples of situations that particularly call for judgements of this kind include the following:

- when a pupil attacks a member of staff or another pupil;
- when pupils are fighting, causing risk of injury to themselves or others;
- when a pupil is committing, or is on the verge of committing, deliberate damage to property;
- when a pupil is causing, or at risk of causing, injury or damage by accident, by rough play or by misuse of dangerous materials or objects;
- when a pupil absconds from a class or tries to leave school other than at an authorised time;
- when a pupil persistently refuses to follow an instruction to leave a classroom;
- when a pupil is behaving in a way that seriously disrupts a lesson;
- when a pupil is behaving in a way that seriously disrupts a school sporting event or school visit.

Refusal by a pupil to remain in a particular place is not enough on its own to justify use of force. It would be justifiable where allowing a pupil to leave would:

- entail serious risk to the pupil's safety (taking into account age and understanding), to the safety of other pupils or staff, or of damage to property;
- lead to behaviour that prejudices good order and discipline, such as disrupting other classes.

In these examples use of force would be reasonable (and therefore lawful) if it was clear that the behaviour was sufficiently dangerous or disruptive to warrant physical intervention of the degree applied and could not realistically be dealt with by any other means.

Wherever possible, these judgements should take account of the particular characteristics of the pupil, including his or her age, understanding and any SEN or disability that he or she may have. This would include the outcomes of any risk assessment and, as appropriate, any specific strategies and techniques set out in the pupil's positive handling plan.

Before using force staff should, wherever practicable, tell the pupil to stop misbehaving and communicate in a calm and measured manner throughout the incident. Staff should not act out of anger or frustration, or in order to punish a pupil, and should make it clear that physical contact or restraint will stop as soon as it ceases to be necessary.

TIP: Types of force that might be used

The types of force used could include:

- passive physical contact resulting from standing between pupils or blocking a pupil's path;
- active physical contact such as:
  - leading a pupil by the hand or arm;
  - ushering a pupil away by placing a hand in the centre of the back;
  - in more extreme circumstances, using appropriate restrictive holds, which may require specific expertise or training.

Where there is a high and immediate risk of death or serious injury, any member of staff would be justified in taking any necessary action (consistent with the principle of seeking to use the minimum force required to achieve the desired result). Such situations could include preventing a pupil running off the pavement onto a busy road or preventing a pupil from hitting someone with a dangerous object such as a glass bottle or hammer.

Staff should make every effort to avoid acting in a way that might reasonably be expected to cause injury. However, in the most extreme circumstances it may not always be possible to avoid injuring a pupil.

Staff should always avoid touching or restraining a pupil in a way that could be interpreted as sexually inappropriate.

Recording and reporting incidents

Schools are strongly advised to keep systematic records of every significant incident in which force has been used, in accordance with the school's policy and procedures on the use of force and its child protection requirements. The purpose of recording is to ensure policy guidelines are followed, to inform parents, to inform future planning as part of school improvement processes, to prevent misunderstanding or misinterpretation of the incident and to provide a record for any future enquiry.

Behaviour management strategies

This section includes practical tried and tested strategies designed to manage pupils' behaviour and to quickly re-establish appropriate conduct. When implementing appropriate strategies it is always important to understand that the behaviour can sometimes get worse before it gets better. Therefore consistency and patience are imperative for success in changing negative behaviour into positive conduct. The information below is for guidance only and can be found in more detail in the book by Morgan and Ellis (2011b).

Attention seeking

Providing attention can be a powerful tool in encouraging positive behaviour and reducing unwanted conduct. Children enjoy receiving positive attention for a variety of reasons. If certain children do not receive enough positive attention they will often resort to behaviour that results in negative forms of attention, for example making noises or calling out. Some pupils would appear to prefer to receive this negative form of attention rather than not to receive any attention at all. Teachers should realise that giving positive attention and deliberately ignoring minor inappropriate behaviour at the right moment can be equally effective, depending upon the situation. The pupil soon learns to distinguish between positive behaviour that results in favourable attention and negative behaviour that results in either unfavourable or no attention. Most young children prefer to receive and enjoy receiving positive reinforcement, which normally makes them feel good about themselves.

Here are some possible reasons for attention seeking:

- lack of rules and boundaries;
- no sense of belonging;
- low self-esteem;
- a degree of immaturity.

(adapted from Morgan and Ellis, 2011b)

TIP: Attention seeking

- First carry out an ABC analysis to collect information about the child's behaviour.
- Put aside a few minutes a day one-to-one time with the child. If the child then looks for attention, remind them of their specific time. For this strategy to work consistency is imperative.
- Ignoring the behaviour can be a powerful strategy although it may have its drawbacks:
  - the child's behaviour can escalate – this is because they are trying to receive the attention they are used to and are testing the new rules that have changed;
  - other children may repeatedly bring the behaviour to the teacher's attention;
  - the behaviour may become a risk to the health and safety of others.
- If a child has displayed unwanted behaviour, withhold attention for about thirty seconds. For example, after unwanted behaviour the child should exhibit at least thirty seconds of good behaviour before you provide them with positive attention.
- 'Catch them being good' before things go wrong. For example, say, 'Sam, well done, you've worked very hard.' Pay lots of attention when the child is behaving well and reward often.
- Let the child know about the behaviour you wish to encourage; for example: 'Well done for putting up your hand to answer the question.' Make eye contact with the pupil, give a simple smile or nod of the head.
- Put more energy and attention into rewarding good behaviour than reinforcing bad behaviour. Give attention and make positive comments immediately following the behaviour that you liked and wish to encourage further.
- Try to provide positive attention to the class at least once every five minutes.
- If necessary, implement the whole-school correctives policy.
- Devise a behaviour plan with the child to help them take control of their own behaviour.
- Make sure the child knows you care about them. Remember the child took a long time to develop this unwanted behaviour, so be consistent and patient as the behaviour sometimes takes time to change.
- If the behaviour continues, a meeting with the parent(s) or carer(s) may be advisable to establish the cause.

Leaving class/school without permission

For a child to leave the class without permission is not only unacceptable but also a health and safety concern. Here are some possible reasons for leaving the classroom without permission:

- lack of rules and boundaries;
- trying to gain the teacher's attention;
- being upset by something going on in class;
- wanting to go somewhere more appealing.

(adapted from Morgan and Ellis, 2011b)

TIP: Leaving class without permission

- First carry out an ABC analysis to collect information about the child's behaviour.
- As soon as a child leaves the classroom their whereabouts must be established. This can be achieved by informing the head teacher immediately.
- Give the child a pass card which they can use if they feel they want to leave the classroom. This pass card will allow them to have a few minutes quiet time in their classroom. This is a good opportunity for the teacher to ascertain why they wanted to leave.
- If the child leaves the classroom because they are trying to gain the teacher's attention, when they are returned to class have minimal interaction with the child and involve them in the class task. The reason for this is to avoid letting them believe that they will get attention by leaving the room.
- If necessary implement the whole-school correctives policy.
- Devise a behaviour plan with the child to help them take control of their own behaviour.
- Make sure the child knows you care about them. Remember, the child took a long time to develop this unwanted behaviour, so be consistent and patient as the behaviour sometimes takes time to change.
- If the behaviour continues, a meeting with the parent(s) or carer(s) may be advisable to establish the cause.

Swearing

One of the most common behavioural problems plaguing teachers today is swearing, probably because it often becomes part of children's everyday language. The language and behaviour that children use can be influenced by their environment. Here are some possible reasons for children swearing:

- lack of rules and boundaries;
- to gain attention;
- to make friends or to impress their friends;
- to express anger, frustration or fear;
- as part of role-play, mimicking behaviour in the media;
- because they're upset;
- to explore cause and effect;
- because they wrongly think it makes them sound more adult;
- copying a family member's everyday use of language in their home.

TIP: Swearing

- First carry out an ABC analysis to collect information about the child's behaviour.
- Let the child know it's OK to feel angry, frustrated or frightened but swearing is not acceptable (Morgan and Ellis, 2011b).
- Check the child's understanding of the word and why he or she uses it. The child may think the word is OK because he or she heard his or her parent(s) or carer(s) or friends use it. Help him or her understand that these words can hurt other people's feelings (Morgan and Ellis, 2011b).
- If a child swears because they feel angry, frustrated or frightened provide them with other ways to express their feelings, for example ripping a sheet of paper (Morgan and Ellis, 2011b).
- If a child swears as part of their everyday language, talk about how inappropriate words make people feel and what words can be used instead. A meeting with the parent(s) or carer(s) would also be advisable.
- If a child swears for attention, inform them in a calm, brief manner that their language is unacceptable and that there are more appropriate ways to gain your attention (Morgan and Ellis, 2011b).
- If necessary implement the whole-school correctives policy.
- Devise a behaviour plan with the child to help them take control of their own behaviour.
- Make sure the child knows you care about them. Remember, the child took a long time to develop this unwanted behaviour, so be consistent and patient as the behaviour sometimes takes time to change.
- If the behaviour continues, a meeting with the parent(s) or carer(s) may be advisable to establish the cause.

Lack of motivation

Children lack motivation to do their schoolwork for a number of reasons. It is therefore important to ascertain the reason and also to understand what motivates the child to achieve. Children need to feel that they have the ability to achieve as well as internalise the satisfactions of successfully completing and/or participating in tasks. Here are some possible reasons for a lack of motivation:

- low self-esteem;
- learning difficulties;
- lack of enthusiasm;
- unhappy home background.

TIP: Lack of motivation

- Understand exactly where the child is academically and if necessary consider referring them for a learning disability evaluation, as their motivational problem may be linked to a learning difficulty. This can be done through the school's SENCO (Morgan and Ellis, 2011b).
- Recognise all efforts and attempts at improving and completing work by praising and positively reinforcing (Morgan and Ellis, 2011b).
- Help focus the child by using a five- or ten-minute sand timer and a tracker sheet. Place the timer in front of the child and inform them of the work they need to complete within the set time. If they complete their work a sticker/stamp is placed

on their tracker sheet. When they receive, for example, four stickers/stamps they are rewarded with five minutes free time (Morgan and Ellis, 2011b).

- Where appropriate, use a buddy system for completing a set task (Morgan and Ellis, 2011b).
- Pay attention to the child's positive abilities and not to their shortcomings.
- Provide opportunities for the child to take risks in new learning situations (Morgan and Ellis, 2011b).
- Provide opportunities throughout the day for the child to experience success and send home positive progress notes or set up a Home–School Link Book.
- Devise a behaviour plan with the child to help them take control of their own conduct.
- Make sure the child knows you care about them. Remember the child took a long time to develop this unwanted behaviour, so be consistent and patient as the conduct sometimes takes time to change.
- If the poor behaviour continues for a while, a meeting with the parent(s) or carer(s) may be advisable to establish the cause.

Activities to help motivate pupils

Children who are well motivated and who feel good about themselves can find handling conflicts and resisting negative pressures easier to manage. They tend to be happier, smile more and enjoy life. Ways to encourage this are by rewarding the desired behaviour and, by doing so, motivating the child to make positive choices and enjoy positive outcomes. Some ideas to help motivate pupils in a positive way, adapted from Morgan and Ellis (2011b), are now presented.

Money, money, money!

Collecting plastic money for good behaviour is an exciting way to keep children on task. At the end of the day/week the money can be counted and spent in the class shop. This is an effective reward as children, like adults, are often very motivated by money. In a class of older children, a tally can be kept to record how much money each child has accumulated and spent. If the class shop contains a lot of desired 'goodies', this can help pupils to become motivated to behave well.

Raffle tickets

Rewarding good behaviour with raffle tickets is a great motivator for children of all ages. The children experience the 'feel-good factor', knowing that the more raffle tickets they receive the greater the chance they have of winning a prize. Arrange a raffle draw at the end of the day, week or term, with great prizes. Involve the school council to decide what prizes to give and how to arrange them, for example by using donations from home, through school fundraising, or by writing to local or national companies (e.g. MB Games) to ask for sponsorship.

Music Marbles

Marbles are placed in a jar as a potential reward for the future positive behaviour of an individual or class. When the jar is full the class's reward is to choose their favourite music, which is played at different times during the day. Children can be encouraged to bring in their own music. As most children love to listen to the latest chart hits, this is a great motivator.

Calling out

Calling out in class is a common problem facing teachers today as it can disrupt the flow of the lesson and prevent other children from participating. It is important to deal with this behaviour immediately as other pupils may be encouraged to call out as well. Here are some possible reasons for calling out:

- lack of rules and boundaries;
- to seek the attention of the teacher for particular a reason – the recurrence of this can create difficulties for the teacher;
- to gain recognition from their classmates;
- they are not aware of the class rules (hands up if you have something to say);
- to feel they have accomplished something good, especially if they knew the right answer;
- in the case of children with attention-deficit disorder, they may have poor impulse control and just say what comes into their head without thinking first; these children will need help to develop their skills in self-control.

(Morgan and Ellis, 2011b)

TIP: Calling out

- First carry out an ABC analysis to collect information about the child's behaviour.
- Review your classroom rules regarding calling out at the beginning of every week, if appropriate. Then explain the rewards for putting hands up and the consequences for calling out. Explain why it is important to raise your hand. Tell the children that they need to learn how to raise their hand so you can choose them to answer a question. Inform them that it is not fair to others in the class when children call out. Explain that you will not call on someone who does not have their hand raised.
- Phrase your questions thus: 'If you know what day of the week it is, raise your hand.' If you say, 'Raise your hand' last, they remember what to do and very rarely call out.
- Actively look for good behaviour and praise it, especially among children who sometimes find it difficult, for example, to put their hands up instead of calling out.
- If a child says they call out because they are afraid they'll forget what they want to say, encourage them to write what they want to say on paper, then put their hand up. Remember to reward when they display the correct behaviour (Morgan and Ellis, 2011b).
- Try ignoring those who shout out and call on the one child who remembers to raise their hand, or say, 'I'm waiting for someone to raise their hand before I take the answer.'
- Be creative and instead of asking the children to raise their hand change it to, for example, fold your arms, touch your ear, stand up.
- If necessary implement the whole-school correctives policy.
- Devise a behaviour plan with the child to help them take control of their own conduct.
- Make sure the child knows you care about them. Remember, the child took a long time to develop this unwanted behaviour, so be consistent and patient as the behaviour sometimes takes time to change.
- If the bad behaviour continues, a meeting with the parent(s) or carer(s) may be advisable to establish the cause of the conduct.

Activities to help use up excess energy

Don't Let It Drop

Each child stands in a space with a beanbag on their head. The teacher then gives instructions, for example: 'Sit down', 'Stand up', 'Arms out', etc. The children must follow the instruction without dropping their beanbags. The instructions become more and more challenging as the game progresses, requiring the children to listen and concentrate. If a child drops her beanbag, then she must leave the game.

Making unwanted noises

Low-level disruption can be caused by pupils making a range of noises in class, for example clicking their tongue, cracking their knuckles. If these noises persist, the child could be ridiculed by their peers, which is damaging to self-esteem; get told off by the teacher; or it could lead to even worse disruption and even become the catalyst for a more serious incident.

Here are some possible reasons for making unwanted noises:

- lack of rules and boundaries;
- attention seeking;
- the pupil is stressed or bored and looking for subconscious ways to distract themselves from the lesson or trying to learn.

TIP: Making unwanted noises

- First carry out an ABC analysis to collect information about the child's behaviour.
- Check the child knows he or she is making a noise. Some children make noises without realising they are doing it (Morgan and Ellis 2011b).
- Talk to the child about the noises they are making and sensitively discuss that they are not appropriate in class and are disturbing learning and concentration. It would be important to emphasise that together both teacher and child will work on raising the child's awareness of the behaviour and eradicating it through the use of a reward scheme (Morgan and Ellis, 2011b).
- The reward scheme to support this approach could be devised together with the child, but a simple toy safe or similar could be placed on his table, which would ideally be near to the teacher to ensure easy access to praise, reward and remind him without doing so publicly across the classroom. Start the process using five-minute intervals, so if he has not make a noise for five minutes place a token in his safe. Continue this for the duration of the lesson/day. At the end of the day he counts his tokens and if he has received the pre-agreed number he gets the overall reward of, for example, free time. Again, this reward could be decided with the child to give him ownership (Morgan and Ellis, 2011b).
- If, however, the child makes a noise within the five minutes the time must be decreased to three minutes in order to find an achievable target so he has confidence in his ability to reach it. The timeframe would then be increased as he is succeeding, ideally in increments of five minutes until he completes a whole lesson/day without making a noise (Morgan and Ellis, 2011b).
- If necessary, implement the whole-school correctives policy.
- Devise a behaviour plan with the child to help them take control of their own conduct.

- Make sure the child knows you care about them. Remember the child took a long time to develop this unwanted behaviour, so be consistent and patient as the conduct sometimes takes time to change.
- If the behaviour continues, a meeting with the parent(s) or carer(s) may be advisable to establish the cause.

Activities to help reduce restlessness

Can You Keep Up?

Ask the children to find a space in the room facing you. Explain you are going to take them through a series of exercises to see if they can keep up with you. Start by jumping, running on the spot, doing star jumps, etc., all at a moderate pace. Then speed up. When the children are beginning to tire, introduce slower movements to create a sense of calm, for example stretching. This process helps to reduce restlessness and should help to create a sense of calm amongst the children.

Aggressive behaviour

Aggressive behaviour can be displayed physically and/or verbally, which makes this type of behaviour very challenging within a school environment. Some children lack the inner self-control to deal with their anger as well as the inability to express their feelings verbally and constructively (see the section on emotional literacy, p. 94). Here are some possible reasons for aggressive behaviour:

- a build-up of frustration;
- being bullied;
- not being understood;
- feeling a lack of justice and fairness;
- lacking in confidence;
- having had a disagreement at home.

(Morgan and Ellis, 2011b)

TIP: Aggressive behaviour

- First carry out an ABC analysis to collect information about the child's behaviour.
- Encourage the child to talk to their friend when they feel angry. Help the child count to ten and take slow deep breaths between each number. This helps to counteract the fight or flight stress reaction that underlies anger. Deliberately taking a slow, deep breath not only brings a soothing sense of relaxation, but will also help to focus attention in the present moment.
- Talk to the child about anger using an analogy with which they can easily identify, for example anger can be like a 'firework' or a 'volcano'.
- Teach the child empathy. They will be more likely to understand other people's feelings and become less aggressive towards them.
- Give the child a small ball to keep on their desk and squeeze every time they feel stressed or angry. This will help release the child's anger. Praise and acknowledge when the child makes the right choice and squeezes the ball (Morgan and Ellis, 2011b).

- Catch the child behaving well and provide immediate, positive feedback, and the behaviour will start to diminish.
- Provide the child with a 'Quiet Time' card, which they can show when they feel angry. This card allows them five to ten minutes of quiet time either within the classroom or within a partner classroom. When the child shows the card they are rewarded for making the right choice (Morgan and Ellis, 2011b).
- If necessary implement the whole-school correctives policy.
- Devise a behaviour plan with the child to help them take control of their own conduct.
- Make sure the child knows you care about them. Remember, the child took a long time to develop this unwanted behaviour, so be consistent and patient as the conduct sometimes takes time to change.
- If the behaviour continues, a meeting with the parent(s) or carer(s) may be advisable to establish the cause.

Activity to help with anger management

This idea has been adapted from *A Kit Bag for Promoting Positive Behaviour in the Classroom* (Morgan and Ellis, 2011b).

Can You Cool Off?

Ask the children to find a space and stand with their eyes closed. Ask them to think of something in the past that has made them angry. Ask them to imagine that anger turning into a hot red lump in the centre of their bodies and if they don't do something they will explode. Now ask them to feel soft cold snow falling on their heads. As the snow touches them their body absorbs it and begins to cool their anger, and after a while their anger is so cold it disappears and they are back to normal. Ask the children to use this method next time they feel angry.

Summary

In this chapter we have considered how to respond to and deal with a range of different behaviours which children might manifest in the classroom, including challenging behaviour. In Chapter 10 we switch our attention to managing pupils' behaviour in the playground.

Positive behaviour in the playground

In this chapter we will consider how to manage pupils' behaviour in the playground, a topic which can all too often be neglected.

The importance of play

Emotional, physical and cognitive skills are developed through play as well as through healthy brain development (Shonkoff and Phillips, 2000). Engaging in play enables children to discover more about themselves and the world. Play provides opportunities for children to learn through imitation, imagination and fun, and to learn about experiencing the consequences of their actions.

Play also has an effect on children's stress levels. Stress chemicals are lowered in the body, which enables the child to deal with exciting or challenging situations more successfully by playing imaginatively and creatively. Gentle rough and tumble play and laughter are also known to have anti-stress effects as this form of play activates the brain's emotion-regulating centres and causes the release of opioids, the natural brain chemicals that induce feelings of pleasure and well-being (Sunderland, 2006). Evidence has shown (e.g. Heck *et al.*, 2001) that children who engage in co-operative games (non-competitive games) are less likely to engage in aggressive behaviour.

Resolving conflict and building resilience are two important skills for children to learn and experience as they enable them to successfully deal with future challenges. These can be learnt through unstructured play as this is when children learn to develop their social skills, self-awareness, self-regulation and empathy in a 'real' context.

Playtime

Creating a well-structured playtime can help tackle the inactivity, boredom and poor behaviour of children who spend approximately one-quarter of their school day in the playground. An unstructured playtime can sometimes be the cause of a range of behavioural incidents. These unstructured events can not only impact on the health and well-being of other children but also have an adverse effect upon the morale of the playtime supervisors. If these are not dealt with appropriately, such incidents can carry on after playtime and impact on teaching and learning in the classroom.

It is therefore extremely important to create a well-structured playtime with trained playtime and midday supervisors. One of their tasks is to ensure consistency between classroom and playground approaches towards behaviour. This is one reason why involving playground assistants in school-based behavioural management training is very important. Incidents must also be dealt with effectively and immediately to prevent them escalating and recurring.

There are a number of possible reasons why children display unwanted behaviour during playtime. These include:

- unstructured playtimes;
- the duration of playtime/lunchtime;
- bad weather;
- lack of appropriate space to play;
- lack of play equipment;
- pupils being unfamiliar with playground rules;
- disagreements, e.g. over a game of football;
- bullying;
- pupils lacking social skills.

In order to encourage the right conduct, staff training on playground procedures is an essential part of a school's behaviour management policy and staff development.

Playground survey

Involving the children and all staff in creating a positive playground environment is also important as it helps the pupils to enjoy their 'free' time more. One way of achieving this is by creating a simple questionnaire to establish current playground behaviour, how the children feel about playtime and what, if any, changes they would like to see taking place during playtime. Here are some suggestions for such a questionnaire:

- How do you feel during playtime?
- What activities do you currently take part in?
- What activities would you like to take part in?
- Where do you go if you don't have anyone to play with?
- Where do you go if you feel upset and/or angry?
- What makes you feel upset and/or angry during playtime?
- Do you think playtime/lunchtime is too long or too short?
- What problems are there in the playground?

Keeping a log of incidents during playtime is also essential. A log will help identify areas of the playground which require more structure, supervision, etc. The log should include the following information:

- the behaviour, e.g. pushed a child into the fence;
- the location, e.g. on the football pitch;
- the reason for the incident taking place, e.g. inappropriate tackle.

Creating a positive playground environment

Playground rules

A school's staff should be included in writing the guidance on playground behaviour. This should include guidance on appropriate and inappropriate behaviour, with written definitions and examples so that all staff are clear on the expectations required of the children.
  To achieve positive playground behaviour:

- make sure pupils understand the playground rules;
- reinforce the rules on a regular basis, for example during PE, circle time, assembly;
- ensure playground monitors are consistent and fair when enforcing the behavioural expectations;
- ensure pupils are given regular praise for positive behaviour;
- ensure teachers reinforce good playground behaviour in the classroom;

- deal with incidents before pupils return to class.

Playground routines: lining up

Asking the pupils to line up after play ensures a calm transition from outside to inside the classroom. When the bell is sounded, encourage the children to freeze on the spot. When the playtime supervisor has the children's attention, the whistle can be blown, signalling for the children to line up. When they are appropriately lined up, reinforce their good behaviour by awarding a raffle ticket or token to two or three of the children who did it best or most quickly. This will help focus everyone's attention. The class teacher will then be ready to lead them into class for the start of the next lesson in an orderly manner.

Returning to class: refocusing

When the children return to class it is important they are focused, calm and ready to learn. Playing a calming and refocusing piece of music can help achieve this goal. The children sit either on the carpet or at their tables and listen and follow the instructions on the CD. Research has shown that children who feel relaxed:

- have the ability to think more constructively and positively;
- feel happy and more caring;
- develop self-confidence;
- are better able to manage their feelings and take responsibility for their actions;
- have improved listening skills, concentration and memory;
- feel calm and are able to problem-solve situations;
- develop imagination, creativity and self-expression;

Another way to help certain children to refocus is to send them to a partner class for no more than ten minutes. This works well with older children being sent to key stage 1 classes to help with the younger children, for example to read a story or to organise a quiet activity. Not only does this help to refocus the child but it also gives them an element of responsibility to help boost their self-esteem and build a positive relationship with the class teacher/teaching assistant.

Positive reinforcements

To ensure consistency, the use of positive reinforcements must be transferred from the classroom to the playground to help pupils internalise the effects and consequences of their own behaviour. As with all positive reinforcements, they need to be included in the behaviour policy, which should be reviewed on a regular basis in order to maintain pupils' interest and support. Here are some suggestions of playground positive reinforcements:

- *Praise*: giving genuine praise that is specific, descriptive, spontaneous and well deserved encourages positive behaviour. It also decreases competition amongst children.
- *Lunchtime helper*: choosing children as lunchtime helpers not only boosts their self-esteem but also gives them a position of responsibility, for example helping the younger children open their food packages.
- *Special helper*: reward a child by nominating them as 'Today's Special Helper'. As well as wearing a special badge, they can also help with certain playground routines such as ringing the bell. This is most effective with younger children.
- *Star certificate*: reward children with a certificate for displaying, for example, an act of kindness during playtime. These certificates can be presented during the end-of-week assembly.
- *Stickers*: stickers are great rewards to promote good lunchtime behaviour.

- *Tokens*: reinforce positive behaviour by rewarding a child with a raffle ticket or token. At the end of the day/week these tokens can be exchanged for x minutes to take part in a special activity in a designated area of the playground such as, for example, using sand and water. Alternatively, the tokens can be entered into a school draw, which may take place in a morning assembly or at a special Friday afternoon event.
- *Special table*: to help promote good manners during lunchtime have a special table in the dining hall. Make the table look special and enticing by laying a tablecloth, placing a vase of flowers in the centre, having a jug of juice and maybe some biscuits. Children who display good manners such as, for example, saying 'please' and 'thank you' can be chosen to dine at this table.
- *Extra play*: the class which lines up in the most sensible fashion at the end of playtime is chosen to have an extra five minutes of play when the rest of the children return to class.

Correctives

To ensure continuity and sustainability both inside and outside the classroom, all the staff and classroom and playground assistants must apply the rules, routines, correctives and positive reinforcements to both environments equally well and effectively. This ensures a consistency of approach when dealing with behaviour both in class and in the playground. Without this consistent approach children learn to respect only the areas which implement the policy, i.e. the classroom. There are a range of potential correctives which can be adapted for the playground. These include a Thinking Time Area.

Thinking Time Area

There will be occasions when a child displays unwanted behaviour in the playground and in some cases the child may need to spend time thinking about their actions and/or consequences. Setting up a Thinking Time Area away from any distractions is an ideal way to address this concern. The area can involve the child sitting or standing on a spot in the playground or sitting or standing in a classroom supervised by an adult. The Thinking Time Area allows the child to reflect on their behaviour, to come to understand what happened, how they reacted and what they could do differently next time. It is important that before the child returns to play they convey their reflections upon these three points to the member of staff who responded to the unwanted behaviour.

The Thinking Time Area can be located within the Quiet Zone of the playground. It is important that all children understand where the area is and why it is used.

Playtime activities

It is important to teach children fun and exciting ways to interact with one another in the playground. Children's early experience of play stems from their family. Different families have different expectations and levels of tolerance regarding their child's behaviour. Explicitly, for some families rough play is an acceptable form of interaction for their child. For other parents, it is not. Rough play is never acceptable in school as, inevitably, this form of play causes a variety of concerns amongst teachers and pupils alike.

There are a number of resources and physical activity initiatives for teaching new, fun and exciting games to play in the playground and, if the weather prevents outdoor play, inside the classroom or wet weather area. Local authority physical education instructors are often available to teach the children (and playground buddies) a range of co-operative games and activities. Charities such as the British Heart Foundation and leading supermarket chains have great physical activity ideas and resources for schools.

A teacher, teaching assistant or midday supervisor can co-ordinate these games every playtime and encourage all the children to participate. Games which will allow the children to burn off excess energy will probably benefit them more. These games can change every day, week or month to maintain the children's interest and attention. However, some pupils prefer regular games such as soccer or rounders.

Children love playing games and using them provides a wide range of psychological and physiological benefits as well as providing simple entertainment. Games are an excellent way to promote children's well-being, as well as providing valuable learning opportunities in a safe environment. Using games can teach pupils the following:

- how to 'take turns';
- patience;
- teamwork;
- the concept of sharing;
- the ability to express appreciation;
- how to develop motor skills;
- listening skills;
- concentration;
- educational concepts, e.g. Boggle teaches basic reading and phonics;
- how to strengthen relationships;
- good sportsmanship.

Lunchtime inter-school and intra-school tournaments

Running a lunchtime tournament is a great way for not only the participants to have a rewarding experience but also the spectators. Some primary schools divide pupils into houses in order to organise and manage inter-house competitions. These events can take place at lunchtime or during the school day, or both. It is important that these events offer a wide range of sporting, cultural and aesthetic activities. Involving as many different children as possible should be one of the main objectives. Therefore, in addition to sport, music, singing, drama, gardening and painting competitions should be organised, amongst others.

The school competition should start at the beginning of each school year and be completed by the end of the summer term. A special award ceremony is often an enjoyable and timely way to end the school year. Over the course of the year, individual and team prizes can be awarded. Running totals of points should be kept and displayed on a designated noticeboard. Equally, the performance of individuals and teams in inter-school events can be celebrated at the end of year prize-giving event, as well as the achievements of those who may have represented the school at county level or at a tournament or festival. It is also a good idea to award a few fun prizes for 'best effort at{...}' etc.

Co-ordinating a game

When introducing a new game to a group of children there are a variety of factors to take into consideration to avoid misunderstanding and potential disagreements:

- choose a suitable area to play the game;
- explain the rules, aims and objectives simply and clearly;
- train the children to use the equipment safely, demonstrating where possible;
- create a code of practice, for example that everyone can play regardless of age, gender, ability, etc., that children have the opportunity to play in different positions, taking turns, fair selection.

If there are disagreements the member of staff must stop the game and ask the children to problem-solve the incident amongst themselves. This is an invaluable learning process and one which encourages teamwork, responsibility, communication and respect.

The proper supervision of games is important, especially when children are learning to play new games, as inevitably they will encounter difficulties or situations in which they become unsure regarding game-play. When the children are more confident with the game, play leaders and playground buddies can be given the opportunity to support the activity.

Fair team selection

Here are some suggestions for ensuring fair team selection:

- *A Bag of Names*: children who want to be involved in a game place their names in a bag. The person supervising the game randomly picks out names and places them in teams.
- *Apples and Pears*: children stand next to their friend and are asked to choose 'who is the apple' and 'who is the pear'. All the 'apples' are then called to one area and all the 'pears' to the other, thereby forming two teams.
- *One, Two, One, Two*: children stand in a line. Each child in sequence is given a number one or a number two. All the 'number ones' are then called to one area and all the 'number twos' to the other, so forming two teams.

Case study: Introducing games

Primary school, South Wales

The school identified that behaviour at breaktimes and lunchtimes was generally good. Occasionally, there were isolated incidents of inappropriate behaviour. The school decided, therefore, to make a positive response to the problem by providing more structured activities for the children to participate in and enjoy. This was achieved by:

- contacting the organisation Torfaen Playworkers to teach the children games;
- encouraging pupils to take part in sporting activities;
- allocating to each class some play equipment to use at break and lunchtimes and enabling the children to pre-book the equipment in the morning;
- training midday supervisors in a variety of games which they could teach the children;
- introducing the staff on playground duty to new games for the children to play.

After these more structured playground activities were introduced, the incidents of inappropriate behaviour decreased.

Playground zoning

Playground zoning provides space for different activities, ensuring fairness and safety. Zoning the playground is ideal if space is restricted within a school and it also encourages children to recognise the importance of sharing and respecting space. This allows children to enjoy a variety of different activities, from sport to quiet reading. These activities can be divided into designated zones to address the needs of all children so even children reluctant to participate would eventually find an activity they enjoy. A rota system can be created to introduce a variety of activities throughout the year. Below are some ideas for zones:

Ball Zone	Quiet Zone	Games Zone	Creative Zone	Environment Zone
Football Dodgeball Netball Basketball Baseball	Friendship Stop Reading Listening to music Thinking Time	Board games Cards Skipping Hopscotch Skittles	Art and craft Construction Sand and water Dancing Drama	Eco Club Litter picking Identifying bugs and flowers Recycling Growing seeds

Developing a Ball Zone Agreement

Ball games such as football can cause a variety of problems during playtime if the activity is not well managed. If these problems remain unresolved they can inevitably overflow into or impact on the pupils' behaviour when they return to class. Properly structuring these types of games by establishing clear rules and procedures should ensure a positive outcome not only for the players but also for the other children sharing the playground.

The first stage in creating a Ball Zone Agreement is to involve the children, giving them ownership so that they are more likely to comply. Here are some suggestions on what to include:

- the identified Ball Zone area;
- rules, routines and correctives;
- a timetable to ensure all players are included;
- appropriate use of equipment;
- code of conduct: fair selection, respect for the playtime supervisor's decisions, rules for the conclusion of the game at the end of playtime.

Lunchtime clubs

Running lunchtime clubs is a great way to offer children more activities in school and gives them a lot of additional fun and pleasure. It also provides children with a variety of different experiences and the chance to learn new skills. Lunchtime clubs can operate both indoors and outdoors depending on the activity.

A general indoor or wet weather club can prove advantageous for children who sometimes feel overwhelmed with outdoor play and/or are unable to participate outside, for example if they are using crutches. This type of club can take place in a room with soft furnishings, a television, board games, construction kits and other toys. As with all clubs, there must be adult supervision and interaction to help maintain a safe and positive environment as well as helping the children to develop their social skills. For children who display emotional and behavioural difficulties in the playground, this type of club can often help. Some young children, for example, dislike going outside when the weather is very cold.

Outdoor displays

Some pupils enjoy making outdoor displays. Encouraging the children to paint and create murals etc. improves the attitude of pupils towards their school and increases their 'ownership' of the school.

Wet play

If wet playtimes are not adequately supervised and planned it is likely that incidents of inappropriate behaviour will increase. Playtime supervisors can be equipped with a report book which they can use to inform the class teacher of any unwanted behaviour. The teacher can then tackle the issues at a suitable time that will not hinder the teaching and learning in class.

Each classroom can be equipped with a labelled wet playtime activity box. Here are some suggestions on what to include:

Reading	Games	Creative
Comics	Board games	Paper and pens
Magazines	Card games	Colouring books
Books	Jigsaws	Activity books
Word search	Skittles	Collage
Brain teasers	Velcro darts	Plasticine
Plays	Juggling balls	Construction

A Wet Play Agreement can be formulated, setting out the class's expectations during this session, which helps to reinforce the rules and routines and reduces the incidence of unwanted behaviour. Here are some suggestions for the agreement: during wet play we:

- play with the items in the wet play box;
- always share and take turns;
- take turns on the computer;
- use the interactive whiteboard only when supervised;
- tidy up when the member of staff asks.

Playtime supervision

Buddy Schemes

Buddy Schemes, Playground Pals, Playground Squads or Playground Friends involve older children in primary schools being used as mediators for minor disputes, befriending lonely children, helping those who are hurt or frightened, mentoring in minor disputes, teaching games to children and looking after playground equipment.

The children involved in the Buddy Scheme are required to set an example and encourage the younger pupils to make positive behavioural choices. During their training they must understand the importance of using caring language, listening to both sides of an argument, and being consistent and fair.

Buddies are not members of staff. Therefore they should not have the authority to punish younger pupils, for example by putting them in time out, or be entitled to remove them from the playground. Instead, they must inform whoever is on duty about the situation and the adult in charge will then take the appropriate action.

Benefits of Buddy Schemes include:

- reducing incidents of inappropriate behaviour;
- encouraging more children to play together;
- promoting anti-bullying;
- enabling children to resolve play and friendship problems in a fair way;
- helping children find friends;
- making the playground a happier and safer place;
- helping to raise the self-esteem of children;
- providing positive role models for younger children;
- supporting staff.

Sustainability

As with all initiatives, sustainability is vital. There should be regular meetings and refresher training sessions for all buddies and their reserves with members of staff responsible for the playground policy's implementation. This includes lunchtime supervisors. It also makes sure new buddies are recruited when buddies leave and ensures continuity at the end of each year as new buddies come on board.

Friendship Stop

If children don't have anyone to play with or feel lonely they can go to a Friendship Stop, which can be located in the Quiet Zone. Children sometimes make friends with other children at the stop or they can be supported by a playground buddy who will help them find friends. Include the school council in setting up a Friendship Stop and in organising where it is to be located and its purpose. For example, should the Friendship Stop be beside a bench or a wall, or should there be a designated sign that can be used as the Friendship Stop? There are advantages and disadvantages to making the Friendship Stop visible to all.

Playtime/lunchtime supervisors

The role of playtime supervisors is to look after the welfare of school pupils during playtimes and lunchtimes. Their duties and responsibilities can vary according to the school. A typical list of their responsibilities during playtime might include the following:

- ensuring pupils don't leave the school premises;
- dealing with misbehaviour;
- reporting unresolved problems to the duty teacher or head teacher;
- tending to pupils who are sick or injured;
- reporting any serious accidents;
- being aware of responsibilities under child protection legislation;
- assisting with play activities if required.

Dinner time

Creating a calm atmosphere during dinner time is important to help children relax, socialise with their peers and enjoy their food. It is also an important part of the day where they can develop their social skills by practising their manners, which not only makes a good impression on others but also helps to boost self-esteem.

In order for this to happen, sound and effective organisation is important. Appropriate rules and routines must be implemented and understood by both staff and pupils alike. At dinner time the needs of vulnerable pupils such as those who are disabled or have special needs are particularly important and should be prioritised. Depending on the number of pupils within an individual school, getting the timings right can be crucial during this part of the day and smooth transitions are essential. Therefore head teachers need to take the following issues into consideration:

- How are the children entering the dining hall?
- Are there too many children in the dining hall at any one time?
- Is lining up for food organised?
- Are the queues too long?
- Are the pupils waiting in line too long for their food?
- What is the routine for clearing away cups and plates?

- How is the noise level regulated?
- How can good table manners be positively reinforced?
- What's the routine for slow eaters?

Getting their attention

There are occasions in the dining hall when a member of staff will need to get the pupils' attention, for example if the noise level becomes too high. There are a number of ways of achieving this depending upon the number and age of the pupils. A method which is used successfully in a number of schools is the teacher on duty or any member of staff raising his or her hand to signal for attention. The pupils are taught that when the member of staff raises his or her hand they also raise their hands and remain silent. This exercise can also be used when the member of staff wants to positively reinforce excellent individual and/or group behaviour in the dining hall.

Summary

In this chapter we have provided some suggestions on how to manage behaviour in the playground. In Chapters 11 and 12 we will consider some extremely important ideas on how to involve parents and children's families in school life.

Chapter 11

Effective partnerships with parents and families

School success must look beyond the school door. During the last 15 years education has concentrated on course curriculum, instructional methods and teacher training. Academic achievement is shaped more by children's lives outside the school walls, particularly their parents and home life. When parents and families are involved in school life there is a higher likelihood of better performance and a more positive attitude to school life.

(Bogenschneider and Johnson, 2004)

Teachers and pupils are the two key components of learning and school-based relationships. But there is a third party in the equation: their parents and families. In this chapter, we will first consider some of the evidence and rationale for involving parents and carers in their children's education. We will then consider in more detail one of the best and most successful approaches to involving parents in their children's schools and learning, which we ourselves have used. This is based on the Family Values Scheme (Ellis *et al.*, 2012). Finally, we will suggest some other practical ways of involving parents and carers in schools.

Parents are the child's first and most influential teachers. Therefore engaging parents and the children's wider and extended family is a very powerful tool in helping to build a child's success both in school and at home. Research shows that excellent home–school links have a significant and positive impact on a child's performance at school (Fan and Chen, 2001). The involvement of parents or carers in their children's learning leads to greater problem-solving skills, greater enjoyment of school, better attendance, fewer behavioural problems and greater social and emotional development (Melhuish *et al.*, 2001). A child's life is greatly influenced by their parents, grandparents and other care givers.

Before we develop this chapter, it is first necessary to give it some context. Family life in Britain, the United States, Canada, Australia and many other parts of the world is very different from, say, a hundred years ago. The influence of the extended family can be much less in some homes, although cultural traditions still differ widely. Divorce and parental separation have increased several times over since the 1950s, when divorce was rare. The number of children being brought up in single-parent families seems to increase in every new survey. In fact, it is probably no longer possible to describe the typical family because so many different versions apply. Likewise, whilst it was unusual for both parents to work in the 1940s and 1950s, there has been a gradual change and increase to the point that it is the norm for both parents/carers to work to support the family home and lifestyle.

For all these reasons, it has become even more important for the school to be aware of the home circumstances of each of their enrolled pupils. Other reasons include:

- for reasons of health and safety;
- for reasons of contact, as when, for example, pupils miss school without good reason;
- in order to comply with both the law and local authority regulations;
- so that the head teacher and/or local authority are aware of who the initial person for the home contact is and what the daily home collection arrangements are.

Involving families in school life

Epstein (1988) believes that schools and organisations should share responsibility for the socialisation of the child. This theory is based on the three most important contexts in which children develop and grow:

- the family;
- the school;
- the community.

Epstein states that for teachers to form good relationships they need to be actively involved not only with their schools and organisations but also with the family unit. She devised a framework of six ways that teachers can be involved in school life. These are:

- by supporting families with parenting, helping them to understand their child's development and by being aware of their home conditions;
- by communicating effectively with families about the curriculum and by keeping parents up to date with their child's progress through parents' evenings, open days, after-school activities and newsletters, etc.;
- by involving parents in school activities such as by encouraging them to be engaged as volunteers or by providing appropriate training to improve their parenting skills or knowledge;
- by involving families with their children in learning activities at home, including homework and other curriculum-linked activities and decisions;
- by including families as participants in the decision-making of the school through membership of the PTA, school councils, committees and other parent-led organisations;
- by co-ordinating resources and services to families, pupils and the school with businesses, agencies and other interested support groups, and by providing appropriate services for the community.

Benefits of involving families in school life

Researchers report that family participation in a child's schooling has many benefits. These include:

1   Benefits for the child:

- a positive child–parent relationship;
- improved emotional literacy skills;
- improved basic skills in reading, literacy and numeracy;
- opportunities to take part in activities inside and outside school;
- increased self-esteem seeing the family take an interest in their education;
- improved learning and academic achievement;
- a more positive attitude towards school;
- a sense of security.

2   Benefits for the family:

- improved parent–child relationships;
- improved parent–teacher relationships;
- networking with other families;
- promotion of positive attitudes towards school;

- more understanding of the school process;
- improved confidence and skills to help their child at home;
- the satisfaction of knowing that they are contributing to their child's education;
- fostering of a positive learning environment at home;
- encouragement of family-based learning.

3   Benefits for the school:

- improved child behaviour, attendance and academic achievement;
- benefit from families' skills and expertise through volunteering and other forms of school-based and external supportive activities, including fundraising, etc.;
- provision of more support within the classroom and for school/class trips, events, etc.;
- involvement of parents or carers with homework;
- a better understanding of the local community;
- an increased and better interaction within the family support unit, including good home–school communication and co-operation.

Family-centred approaches

Studies show that families spending quality time together can improve a child's learning performances by up to 60 per cent. It is the little things that families actually do together which achieve the best environment for learning. This process is described by Sheridan and Kratochwill (2007) as the 'Curriculum of the Home'. This means that parents who are actively involved in their child's development and learning act as a major contributor to creating a positive learning environment. It is important that this is supported by continuity, i.e. 'closing the gap' between home, school and organisation. The integration of values and beliefs is one of the ways of narrowing the gap between home and school.

> Early Intervention is an approach which offers our country a real opportunity to make lasting improvements in the lives of our children, to forestall many persistent social problems and end their transmission from one generation to the next, and to make long-term savings in public spending.
>
> (Allen, 2010: vii)

There are four ways in which partnerships between home and school can be created and these are outlined below.

Approach

The approach is the framework for schools to work with families to achieve a shared goal, for example successful educational outcomes for the children. This type of framework involves:

- effective communication between home and school;
- problem-solving between home and school.

Attitudes

Attitudes are the perceptions that families and schools have of one another. It is important to identify and acknowledge each other's strengths and, taking responsibility for the education and the children, together achieve individual potential.

Atmosphere

Schools and organisations need to become family-friendly communities, creating an atmosphere that welcomes all families and encourages active involvement. A welcoming atmosphere can be created by:

- having regular home–school communication;
- using formal and informal methods of communication;
- encouraging activity and event participation;
- showing an appreciation of family diversity.

Actions

Putting in place the above elements will lead to positive learning partnerships which actively include families in school life.

Hard to reach families

Unfortunately for some families, engaging with school may not be as straightforward as it may seem for other families due to a number of influencing factors. Desforges and Abouchaar (2003) identified the following factors as influencing home–school relationships: social class, maternal level of education, material deprivation, maternal psycho-social health, single parent status and, to a lesser degree, family ethnicity.

> Not all parents are angels. All are individuals – accept the real person in front of you. Be prepared to work where each one is. The way they were treated in the past, and the way the present is bearing down on them makes some parents appear negative. Get past that wall with your acceptance and sincerity.
>
> (Peterson, 1982)

There are many misconceptions among the general public and in teachers' minds about why some families are 'hard to reach'. Below we illustrate a few of these kinds of statements:

- Her mother was hopeless at school, so what can you expect?
- If parents don't attend school events it shows they don't care about their child's education.
- Parents who are illiterate and/or unemployed can't help their child.
- Children from working class backgrounds and certain estates are all troublemakers.
- Considering how Amy performed in school, is it any wonder that her sister's academic performance is so dreadful?
- Families who are non-English speaking in the home don't understand how to help and support their child's learning.
- It is acceptable only to contact families when a child has misbehaved.

These kinds of statements typify the low expectations which some teachers and members of the general public can hold about certain families when challenging situations occur. These views tend to be held by professionals who always blame pupils or their parents' shortcomings in the home rather than questioning their own or their school's actions. Research has consistently shown since the research of Rutter *et al.* (1979) that what happens inside individual schools and classrooms really matters and makes a significant difference to the performance of pupils. At the same time, Dalziel and Henthorne (2005) found that certain families, such as those containing a persistent school absentee, did hold more negative views towards teachers and their schools and made fewer voluntary visits to schools to foster and promote good home–school relationships.

Family initiatives

There are many initiatives which involve families in sound home–school links. Desforges and Abouchaar (2003: 2) state that 'good parenting in the home, including the provision of a secure and stable environment, intellectual stimulation, parent–child discussion, good models of constructive social and educational values and high aspirations relating to personal fulfilment and good citizenship; contact with schools to share information; participation in school events; participation in the work of the school; and participation in school governance' are all important.

A Family Involvement Policy

Developing a Family Involvement Policy is a great way to ensure a sustainable and effective approach to engaging all different kinds of families. The policy should include information on how the school will address the following issues: communication, parenting, skills, children's learning, volunteering, school decision-making and community involvement. This means via:

- *communication*: creating effective communication channels between the home and the school in order to provide information about the children's curriculum, progress, behaviour, attendance, interests, activities and other school-based events, including any external trips or visits;
- *parenting*: providing information and training for families on how to create a positive learning environment at home as well as on the best ways of supporting their school and schooling;
- *children's learning*: providing information and training for families to help with their child's education on such issues as, for example, homework;
- *volunteering*: creating opportunities for parents or carers to volunteer through participation in supportive roles, activities and events in school;
- *school decision-making*: providing opportunities for parents or carers to become involved in educational advocacy and decision-making on issues which affect their children's education, such as invoking and implementing new school policies;
- *community involvement*: creating links with community support groups, agencies and initiatives to help strengthen family and school partnerships.

Ways to engage families

It is important to make all parents or carers feel valued as some may have reservations about their own ability, participating in school life and the response they may receive from members of staff. Below is a bank of suggestions to help engage parents, carers and their wider families in their home–school links and, in particular, a discussion of the Family Values Scheme (see Chapter 12).

Effective home–school communication

There are various ways to communicate with families and to keep parents or carers updated about events, activities and other information. Within a minority of homes some parents' poor language skills and their inability to read can prove a barrier to home–school communications. This can be overcome in a number of ways, for example by phoning the home or videotaping the message. Home visits are also very effective. Written communication such as newsletters needs to be brief, be jargon free and whenever possible use bullet points. It is good practice to involve parents in improving the design and content of written communications and it is always wise and good practice to advise them of the home–school communication policy when their children start at the school. In some parts of the country it may be necessary to provide a translation service to assist non-English speaking families.

Here are a few suggestions to try to manage effective home–school communication:

- *face to face*: parents' evenings, open days, home time, special events;
- *telecommunications*: telephone, mobile, text messaging, radio services;
- *online*: school website, group/individual email, invitation-only social networking sites, PowerPoint presentations in the foyer;
- *printed materials*: brochures, message board inside/outside school, newsletters, flyers, letters, personalised invitations, reports, newspapers.

Ask parents or carers for their preferences and whether they have any particular needs.

Welcoming new parents: a school welcome pack

Making new families feel welcome and supported is very important for any school. A school welcome pack can provide key information on the school, its organisation, rules, activities and achievements. These can include:

- the school brochure;
- a copy of the home–school agreement;
- a calendar of events, e.g. school fete;
- a list of after-school clubs;
- a list of activities taking place within the area;
- details about the family drop-in centre;
- related home–school activities, e.g. the Family Values Scheme;
- guidance about how to become a school volunteer, parent governor, member of the Parent–Teacher Association, etc.

Welcome back to school

At the beginning of the new academic year organise a get-together to help re-engage families. This event can be held at a convenient time to ensure a good turnout, for example during the early evening for working parents. The event provides an ideal opportunity for families to meet the staff, take a look around the school and have an overview of the forthcoming year. It also provides an opportunity to re-establish the school's expectations on, for example, attendance, behaviour, uniform, equipment, etc. The event can be given a theme, for example:

- quiz hour;
- bingo and prizes;
- cheese and wine evening;
- coffee morning.

Tell them about yourself

Introduce yourself to your pupils' families by creating a flyer informing them about your job, responsibilities and tasks within school and any interests outside school which you may wish to share. You can also include a photo of yourself. This is a great way to break down barriers and make families feel more at ease, and you may also find you have a few things in common. If families feel they have an activity or interest in common with their child's teacher, they are much more likely to engage in conversation and form a good working relationship and will feel more at ease when visiting the school.

Tell us about your family

It's surprising how many different interests members of a family have and share. If you invite them to complete a 'Tell us about your family' questionnaire, the data gathered can provide the school with a wealth of information. For example, by collating the information the staff may decide to ask parents to:

- help set up and maintain a community garden;
- help choreograph the school play;
- paint a mural in the school hall;
- talk to a class about running a sanctuary for injured hedgehogs;
- help design and build a role-play area, e.g. a Viking ship;
- coach a football/rugby/netball team.

Home time

The end of the school day is an ideal time to interact with families. Informing them of their child's achievements during the day helps to lower barriers and encourages engagement. Some parents have formed barriers due to receiving negative comments regarding their child and also their own level of parenting. These barriers take time to break down, but try greeting a parent with, for example, 'Hi, Mr Harris. Jenny has had a great day today with all her friends and she created a very colourful flower out of Plasticine.' Such little titbits of easily relayed conversation can make a big difference and ease the process of relationship building.

Class/school assemblies

Whole-school and/or class assemblies are another great way of bringing everyone together, including families, thereby creating a sense of community. There are a number of ways to engage families in an assembly. Here are a few simple suggestions. Why not invite families:

- to an end of term/year celebration of their child's work;
- to talk about their job and/or interest;
- to watch their child, for example, perform, recite a poem.

Special events

A range of different events can be arranged in order to target different members of the family at different points of the day, term or year. The timing of these events is important. For example, dads are often more likely to attend in the evening and so offering soup and a roll with the activity may make it more tempting. If the school is located in a multi-cultural community such events can also include different food, costumes, traditions and heritage. Here are a few suggestions for possible school-organised activities:

- afternoon tea;
- historical talks;
- vegetable growing;
- orienteering;
- jewellery making;
- henna designs;
- international dinner;
- World Book Day;
- meet your child at the local library.

Open days

Invite families into school to see their child's work and meet the staff and other parents. Invitations can be written by their child so that they are personalised. These open days can also involve the families participating in an activity, for example:

- building the tallest tower using newspaper and masking tape;
- creating a bookmark using beads, ribbon and card;
- using ICT to research origami.

At the end of the open day, the families can be sent a thank-you note from their child, teacher or whole class. The note can also include information regarding the next activity/ event on the school calendar.

Mega-challenge evening

Once a month hold a mega-challenge evening and involve the families in a series of fun and exciting activities they can also do at home. To create an inviting atmosphere, provide refreshments and music. At the end of the mega-challenge hand out certificates for all those who have participated. Here are some ideas for a mega-challenge evening:

- an obstacle course;
- a board game challenge;
- a treasure hunt, using map-reading skills;
- a fashion show, creating an outfit from recycled materials;
- creating a family crest, using paint, paper, card, glitter, etc.;
- kite making, using ICT to design the kite, then making and flying it.

Get creative for parents' evening

To ensure good attendance for a parents' evening invite parent(s)/carer(s) to an art exhibition at the school where they can view and buy their child's work. Choose a school/class theme such as a sunset for the children to paint. These works of art can then be framed and displayed with the children's names engraved on them.

My portfolio

At the end of the week, month, term or year pupils can compile a selection of their best work, which can be displayed in a portfolio and taken home to show their family. The portfolio can include work from all subjects, including written documentation, photographs (of models made), drawings, etc. For children whose families have never seen their work, this provides a great opportunity for the child:

- to have their efforts acknowledged within the home;
- to talk to their family about what they have learnt;
- to recognise their achievements and develop self-esteem;
- to internalise what it feels like when their family takes an interest in their education.

Your child is a star!

Rewarding positive behaviour doesn't have to be time consuming or expensive. A simple positive note or phone call home can make such a difference to the child and family. Some families perceive a phone call from the school as likely to contain negative content.

Therefore receiving a positive communication helps to break down these perceptions. It shows also that the school cares about their child and the family and that they value the family's involvement.

Family drop-in service

There are occasions when families need to use a computer, find out information or just have a chat. School is a great place to capitalise on this need. Enlisting the help of a volunteer co-ordinator to be available at certain times of the day to help parents, carers or other family members and, if possible, providing a room equipped with a computer, leaflets and information about organisations, local initiatives, charities and support groups which are readily accessible all helps. This service can also offer resources which allow users to borrow items such as books, games, DVDs and CDs to help with family learning.

Information evening

Why not send out a questionnaire to establish what families are interested in or would like more information about from the school? For example, such issues might include: homework strategies, healthy eating, behaviour management, internet safety and adult learning, to name but a few. This can be achieved either by arranging an evening once a month with a guest speaker to present practical information on each chosen subject or by arranging with the local authority to set up an adult learning centre within the school. Here are some suggestions:

- understanding my child, stages of child development, parenting strategies, etc.;
- reading with my child, strategies, tips, etc.;
- helping my child through divorce, bereavement, remarriage;
- being a single parent/co-parenting.

Getting involved

Encouraging families to volunteer at school provides a potentially useful and supportive resource and also demonstrates to the children the value and importance of participating in the larger community. Informing families how they can get involved in the running, organisation and supervision of the school is an essential part of the process. Encouraging them to get involved with the Parent–Teacher Association or by becoming a classroom assistant or by applying for a position as a school governor are amongst a wide range of potential options. Parents can also get involved by contributing to other school schemes, campaigns and collections. Here are some possible options:

- collecting vouchers for schools from local supermarkets and petrol stations;
- being a classroom helper;
- helping to organise a fundraising event;
- being a playground supervisor;
- becoming a school/class trip helper;
- organising and/or assisting after-school clubs, e.g. chess;
- coaching the school team, e.g. football, netball;
- becoming a library assistant;
- working with the school orchestra choir;
- participating in the walking bus scheme;
- helping administration staff, e.g. with press releases;
- helping to judge competitions;
- speaking at events on a specific subject, e.g. World War II;

- helping with art and craft projects;
- creating costumes for school performances.

Volunteer training programmes

A volunteer training programme can be run at certain times of the year to provide on-site training for members of the family who are interested in supportive roles such as being a library assistant, reading buddy, classroom assistant, playground supervisor, family drop-in service co-ordinator. The training would provide them with key skills, confidence and an insight into each role. Once trained and experienced in their role they can then be invited to become a contributor or trainer on future programmes. This type of training would ensure retention and job satisfaction for all involved.

Crèche facilities

Some families' involvement is restricted due to the lack of childcare provision available. For key activities and events a crèche service is important.

Feedback

Encouraging families to feed back on different aspects of school life not only provides valuable information on what the school is doing well and on what needs to be improved but also encourages families to be actively engaged with the school. Opportunities to provide feedback can be displayed on the school website, with a suggestion box, in a newsletter, and in other documentation and correspondence.

Summary

In this chapter we have considered a wide range of ideas aimed at encouraging or improving parental participation in the classroom. We now develop this theme even further in Chapter 12 with a concise consideration of our own Family Values Scheme (Ellis *et al.*, 2012).

The Family Values Scheme

An example of effective partnerships with families

One of the ways of engaging families in schools is through a published scheme called Family Values. The scheme is highly successful in creating partnerships in a fun and active way and is based on the philosophy of values-based education. The Family Values Scheme was created by Gill Ellis and Nicola S. Morgan in 2009; it won the Leading Aspect Award in 2010 for its innovative way of engaging parents with schools and organisations, and was also a finalist for the TES National School Awards 2011. The scheme is also published by Routledge as *Better Behaviour through Home–School Relations: Using Values-Based Education to Promote Positive Learning* (Ellis *et al.*, 2012). Research has shown that healthy families spend quality time together, listen to one another, provide encouragement and love, share chores and decisions and plan ahead. The Family Values Scheme is designed to promote these ideals, as Figure 12.1 illustrates.

Aims of the scheme

By utilising the Family Values Scheme, teachers and their schools can significantly improve their relationships and communication with parents and carers, raise attendance, reduce bullying and help to nip in the bud potential or actual behavioural problems manifested

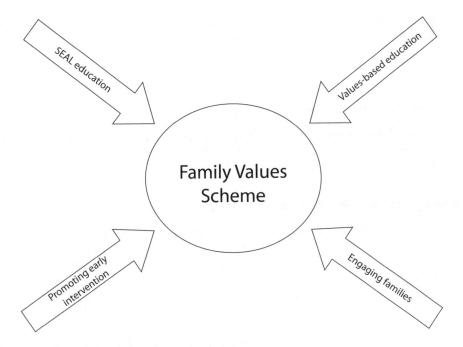

Figure 12.1 The Family Values approach

by their pupils in either the early or later stages with the full knowledge, participation and co-operation of their parents. In order for effective partnerships to be established, the scheme aims for individual families and schools to:

- raise standards in the basic skills of reading and writing;
- strengthen relationships and increase interaction between the family, the school and the local community;
- use appropriate 'values' to inculcate appropriate standards as an intrinsic way of life both at home and at school;
- improve behaviour and attendance;
- complement and enhance existing personal and social education (PSE) and parental programmes, e.g. by using SEAL;
- raise self-esteem.

Types of parents

The scheme is a useful tool for a wide range of schools and organisations and caters for all types of parents. Research by Smit, Driessen, Sluiter and Sleegers (2007) carried out in 500 schools identified six different types of parents and their characteristics:

- *supportive parent*: is satisfied with the school or organisation, always readily available and likes to be involved in their child's education;
- *absentee parent*: doesn't like to make a contribution, is impossible to contact and is generally introvert and unapproachable;
- *politician parent*: loves to be involved and make decisions, often a school governor;
- *career-maker parent*: is businesslike, loves responsibility but generally does not have time for school events;
- *tormenting parent*: can be cold, aggressive and impatient;
- *super-parent*: is loyal, inspiring to others and very good at communication; contributes to events and usually has good ideas.

Where child learning becomes family learning, and where educators understand that they cannot meet the needs of children and young people alone, true engagement and shared understanding are developed.

(NCSL, 2010)

Theoretical model partnerships

The Family Values Scheme is based on sound theoretical principles and models of effective partnerships. It was created to support schools and organisations to engage families in a fun and interactive way but with maximum benefits.

Family Values theoretical concepts

Family Values is based on four theoretical concepts, as illustrated in Figure 12.2:

- ecological theory;
- behavioural theory;
- a family-centred approach;
- values.

Together these four concepts form a partnership-centred approach. The Family Values Scheme believes that by focusing more on a partnership concept schools and families will

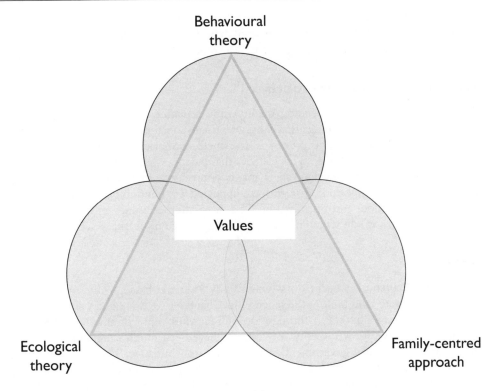

Figure 12.2 The Family Values approach model

achieve more of an equilibrium, one in which the family, school and organisation feel valued and recognised.

Ecological theory

Ecological theory is concerned with the multiple interdependent, inseparable systems or environments and contexts that surround children's development and education. This approach is well explained by Bronfenbrenner (1979), who categorises the systems into four basic areas and needs:

- *microsystem*: the family home and classroom;
- *mesosystem*: the interrelation of the microsystem;
- *exosystem*: factors which influence the microsystem, e.g. the level of parental involvement, the parents' working environment;
- *macrosystem*: the cultural setting, including external factors of social and national educational policies.

The key input taken from this theory is the importance of the mesosystem, the interaction of the two most important microsystems in education, i.e. the link between the family home and schools and organisations.

Behavioural theory

The second theoretical concept for Family Values is based upon behavioural theory, which focuses on the importance of 'learning' as a contributor to influencing interaction between families, schools and organisations. The learner who is exposed to positive role-modelling in the home and school environment will adopt these learnt behaviours themselves. In practice, pupils in a values-based education setting will experience this from their own peers and staff in the school. This practice will then be transferred to the home.

The family-centred approach

Studies show that families spending quality time together can affect learning by 60 per cent. To reiterate, it's the things that families actually do together which achieve the best environment for learning. This process is described by Sheridan and Kratochwill (2007) as the 'Curriculum of the Home'. This clarifies that parents who are actively involved in their child's development and learning are a major contributor to creating a positive learning environment. It is important that this is supported by continuity, i.e. 'closing the gap' between home, school and organisation. The integration of values and beliefs as a way of narrowing this gap is one which has the greatest influence on learners' achievement.

Values

The fourth theoretical concept on which Family Values is based is the intrinsic way that values are integrated throughout the scheme. In Chapter 1 we described values-based education's principles and philosophy through Dr Neil Hawkes, but Professor Terry Lovat and his colleagues at Newcastle University, in Australia, have been monitoring and researching the effects of the Australian government's Values Education Initiative. The university published its final report for the Australian government, which looks at the evidence concerning the impact of introducing and developing values education in schools (Lovat et al., 2009).

The research describes how values-based schools give increasing curriculum and teaching emphasis to values education. As a consequence pupils become more academically diligent, the school assumes a calmer, more peaceful ambience, better pupil–teacher relationships are forged, pupil and teacher well-being improves and parents are more engaged with the school.

Explicit teaching of values provides a common ethical language for talking about interpersonal behaviour. It also provides a mechanism for self-regulated behaviour. An important outcome is a more settled school that enhances quality teaching and enables teachers to raise expectations for pupil performance.

The Family Values Scheme and emotional literacy: links to SEAL

The Family Values Scheme enhances SEAL (Social and Emotional Aspects of Learning), with each month's and term's values being supported by the SEAL themes.

	Autumn	Spring	Summer
Values	Freedom Peace Co-operation Tolerance Responsibility Hope Honesty Friendship	Quality Simplicity Thoughtfulness Appreciation Humility Patience Happiness Trust	Caring Unity Courage Love Respect Understanding
SEAL	New beginnings Getting on and falling out (say no to bullying)	Going for goals Good to be me	Relationships Changes

Values-based education

One of the core principles of the Family Values Scheme is values-based education. It is through this concept that the Family Values Scheme is founded. The values themselves permeate the scheme and make it an effective tool for any school or organisation. Schools which are not values-based will still find the scheme just as productive to use in their setting.

The Family Values Scheme and the basic skills

The Family Values Scheme aims to improve the basic skills of reading, writing and numeracy through its four elements: Family Gathering, Family Essentials, Family Activities and Family Reflection. In the Family Essentials part of the pack there are lots of activities that reinforce the basics of everyday family life, including the basic skills of reading, writing and numeracy. The scheme supports the learning of the basic skills of reading, writing and numeracy through a range of related activities.

Reading

Supporting children at home with their reading is one of the best ways that parents can help their child. Schools and organisations support children with their reading at home through their home–school links policy. The scheme does not look to replace this support but seeks to enhance existing good practice, which is already available to the family. In this section we aim to give strategies that the whole family can be involved in.

Family reading time

Families need to be encouraged to dedicate some quality time to reading during the week or at the weekends. Creating the correct environment is essential if reading is going to be enjoyed by all the family.

Reading environment

Once a family reading session is planned the following ideas can be just the thing for a comfortable, relaxing reading session:

- get the whole family involved, including grandparents and younger brothers and sisters;
- families can read together or in pairs or individually;
- have a family DEAR (drop everything and read) time;
- have a dictionary and simple thesaurus readily available for the reading time, and a picture dictionary for younger readers to check the meaning of tricky words;
- make visiting your local library a regular family essential;
- read any material that stimulates or interests the reader, which can be jokes, riddles, poetry, facts, fiction or even plays.

Family reading strategies can be given to families to help them support their child with reading at home.

Writing strategies

There are lots of opportunities in the Family Values packs which encourage writing. Here are some simple ways to encourage writing in the home through the scheme:

- encourage young children to make marks as this is the early stages of writing;
- support younger children by writing a sentence and asking them to copy the words;
- encourage children to keep a writing journal to write down their daily events or record their moods;
- contribute to writing the family and personal goals;
- contribute to completing the STAR evaluation at the end of the month;
- create opportunities for writing from any of the activities, e.g. after a family walk or writing recipes;
- create experiences which stimulate and encourage creative writing.

Developing confidence in number

Encouraging children to be confident in number work will make them confident in the basics, e.g. addition, subtraction, multiplication and division. Building number into day-to-day family living will reinforce mathematical concepts taught at school and will raise confidence and improve self-esteem. Here are some ways we can support this in the home:

- regularly measure the height of younger members of the family to see how much they have grown;
- measure the height and record the progress of any Family Values activities which need to be grown, e.g. plants;
- use a visit to the shops to practise using the concept of money, e.g. weighing fruit and vegetables, budgeting for pocket money.

How the Family Values Scheme works

The Family Values Scheme is based around a set of twenty-two values. Each month a different value such as respect or co-operation is chosen for endorsement. The twenty-two values are made up into monthly packs which encourage parents or families to participate in a series of fun tasks and challenges which they plan and carry out together within the flexibility of their own home. All the activities reinforce the selected monthly value and every pack explains in detail to the family exactly what the value is and what it means, for example the value courage.

TIP: What is courage?

To have courage to try something which is different and that you are not familiar with is a real challenge in itself. Courage is not something that you are born with as it comes from within but it is very easy to care for. All you need to do is give it daily attention and it will grow big and strong! Having courage is persevering when things maybe don't turn out as they should or it could be having the confidence to stand up to someone or something you believe in.

(Ellis and Morgan, 2009)

Rewarding families

There are two ways to encourage family members to complete their tasks and to reward them for doing so:

- *Certificate of participation*: a certificate is awarded to a family who have completed one or more tasks from the pack;
- *Point system*: each task has a set number of points and there are three levels of award:

1   bronze award: 500 points;
2   silver award: 1000 points;
3   gold award: 1500 points.

Each family decides together at the beginning of the month what level of award they wish to achieve. This is entirely up to the family and is agreed by everyone. For example, if a family is particularly busy one month they can choose a lower level of award or if they really feel strongly about the value, and feel that it is one which they need to reinforce within their family, they can choose a higher level of award.

At the end of the month the family totals up the number of points they have achieved and they are awarded with a bronze, silver or gold certificate/rosette/badge.

Providing evidence

There are two ways a family can provide evidence that they have participated in the Family Values Scheme:

Log file

Evidence is gathered by the family during the month and placed in a log file. This can be a lever arch file or simple scrapbook. There are several ways that families can gather their evidence. These might include any of the following:

- photographs of the event or activity;
- video clips;
- written evidence;
- presenting participatory outcomes on the activity, e.g. through a painting or by making a friendship bracelet, whichever chosen outcome fits the theme best;
- writing a book review.

At the end of each month the parents or families are given a date to hand in their log files and/or the STAR (stop, think and reflect) evaluation sheets so that each family can be given the award for their efforts and achievements. The log files or scrapbook need to show evidence for the activities that they have completed. The log files can be either returned to the individual family or retained in school for display or self-evaluation purposes.

STAR evaluation

Families can choose to complete the STAR sheets to evaluate how they have reinforced the value of the month and how they have achieved their individual and family goal. When we stop, think and reflect, we learn something about ourselves.

Celebrating families' achievements not only reinforces the scheme but also raises their self-esteem and motivation. These achievements are celebrated and shared with the rest of the school. These celebrations and awards can involve a variety of prizes, which might range from stickers, rosettes or certificates to participation in a Family Values assembly, or, for a lucky few, winning a Family Values Cup.

Family Values assembly

Families are invited to an assembly to receive their end of month award, i.e. at bronze, silver or gold level. Rewards such as rosettes, certificates or badges are given to each family, a different colour for each award level.

Family Values Cup

Each month the family who has worked the hardest to achieve their goal is nominated for the Family Values Cup. This is not necessarily the family who has achieved the gold award. The cup is presented during the Family Values assembly, with the winning family holding the cup for a month. This achievement is then displayed on a Family Values Roll of Honour chart showing which family has won month by month.

The Family Values Scheme packs

There are four sections to the monthly values packs, with each section having a different number of points. Families are encouraged to complete all sections of the pack to achieve the maximum benefit. Below are the four different sections:

- *Family Gathering*: focusing the family on the month ahead;
- *Family Essentials*: motivating the family to participate in everyday tasks;
- *Family Activities*: including fun and exciting activities for the family;
- *Family Reflections*: focusing the family on what they have achieved.

Family Gathering

The Family Gathering section is the first part of each monthly pack and gives a step-by-step guide on how to start the tasks. The main aim of this section is for the family to begin the month by deciding on their family and personal goals and how to achieve them.

Family goals

Setting goals as a family brings everyone together, enabling the family to keep their values, focus and motivation rather than getting sidetracked. The process is a collaborative one which encourages the family to discuss what they'd like to achieve and to work together as a team by offering encouragement and support to achieve the goals.

Many parents, when asked, would like to spend more time with their family but everyday obstacles such as work commitments and the day-to-day running of the family home sometimes prevent this from happening. Setting goals to spend more time with the family must be planned out with a conscious effort toward that outcome. By planning an activity and completing it the parents not only achieve the goal of more family time but also achieve or participate in something fun. Here are some examples of family goals:

- go for a family walk;
- have a family meal once a week;
- plan a holiday;
- organise a monthly family fun night;
- grow vegetables in a vegetable patch.

Personal goals

Learning to set personal goals is an important life skill which helps us to focus and achieve at school, work and home. Setting realistic goals which challenge us but are also attainable helps to improve our concentration, self-esteem and motivation, as well as helping us overcome everyday challenges. Setting realistic goals can be achieved by using the SMART approach (see pp. 98–99). Here are some examples of individual goals:

- learn to ride my bike;
- read my book every night;
- arrive at school on time;
- spend more time with Grandad.

To kickstart the month the family hold a meeting with as many family members as possible. This can include parents, carers, grandparents, extended family members, aunties and uncles. They choose someone to chair the meeting and set a time and a date for the meeting to take place. Below are examples of discussion activities which take place before they start the tasks.

TIP: Family Gathering: the value of courage

Read together the 'What is courage?' section on the front of the pack and discuss what this value means to you as a family. Using a large sheet of paper, write the word 'simplicity' in the centre and write down everyone's responses. Pair together any answers which are related to each other. Use a dictionary if necessary to make sure that everyone understands what it means.

Together, discuss all the courageous things that each family member has done. Make a list. What does it mean to show courage? What qualities do you need to be a courageous person? Is it always easy to be courageous? Why? Discuss this together.

Now you are ready to decide on what your family goals are for this month. Together, answer the following questions:

- What do you want to achieve on your own?
- What do you want to achieve as a family?

Complete the 'Family goals' page and put a copy of it where everyone can see it. Keep reminding yourselves throughout the month what you want to achieve and be determined to find the time to do it! Think about how you will all feel when you have achieved what you set out to do.

Family Essentials

Routine family tasks are the core principles of Family Essentials; they are how families organise themselves on a day-to-day basis. Family Essentials is designed to help family members set clear routines so that everyone knows what they need to do, by when and how often. Providing routines enables all family members to feel safe, secure and valued and as a result able to overcome daily challenges more successfully. When routines become consistent they help to develop healthy habits, for example going to bed on time, brushing your teeth.

It is through the completion of these everyday essentials that bonding is strengthened during the process, thereby enhancing family relationships. By completing these tasks together families are embedding essential requirements into their everyday life so that, in due course, they start to become routine. These Family Essentials change from month to month to encourage the family to achieve each of the basics.

> In families, routines have been shown to increase health and psychological well-being, as well as improve social adjustment and academic achievement for children.
>
> (Dr Sian Rawkins, head of ambulatory psychiatry at Toronto's Mount Sinai Hospital)

Routines help children:

- develop healthy habits, e.g. brushing their teeth, going to bed on time;
- develop a sense of responsibility and a feeling of 'belonging';
- strengthen their bond with their parent(s)/carer(s) through predictability and the element of fun;
- spend quality time with their parent(s)/carer(s).

Routines help parent(s)/carer(s):

- feel more in control and more organised;
- complete daily tasks such as preparing a meal;
- share the responsibility of household tasks;
- spend more quality time with the family.

Creating routines

Every family is different and it is important that they understand what it is they want to achieve and design routines to help support this. For routines to be effective they need to be well planned, consistent and predictable. Routines also need to be fun, light-hearted and adaptable to change to ensure everyone's on board and motivated.

Below are examples of Family Essentials routines.

TIP: Family Essentials

Family meals

Plan to eat a family meal together. Laying the table, serving and washing up are all part of having a family meal together. How many family meals can you do?

Time for school

Can you get to school on time? How can you achieve this? Plan and prepare the night before to make your mornings go with a swing! If getting up is a struggle set your clock forward by ten minutes. This is a great trick that really works.

Family Values book club

Plan time for a family reading session. Choose a book together which you will all enjoy! Sit down in a circle and take turns reading. Discuss characters, the plot and the illustrations (if any). At the end of the story discuss your favourite parts and write a family book review.

Let's clean up

Housework is never a chore if all the family gets in on the act. Make a list of all the housework to be done during the week and divide the jobs up between all the members of your family. Dusting, washing, ironing and cleaning are essential to a clean home.

Turn the lights out

Are all the lights on in everyone's rooms – even if no one is in them? Turning the light off when you leave an area will help reduce your electricity consumption and it's also very good for the environment.

Be organised

This is the time to be organised. Sort through your belongings and anything you no longer need or use. This is your chance to donate them to charity or give them to someone else who could get a benefit from them.

Sleep! Sleep! Sleep!

Is it hard to get out of the bed in the morning? Are you yawning by lunchtime? Making sure you get enough sleep not only will make you feel more energetic but is also an important part of looking after your body! So go to bed on time to make sure you have plenty of sleep!

(Ellis and Morgan, 2009)

Family Activities

Spending quality family time is important to help build strong relationships as well as having fun and experiencing new and exciting things. The time spent together builds up an abundance of shared experiences and memories, which are a great source of conversation around the table.

Taking part in a variety of different activities helps to build skills, whether physical or mental, which enable us to understand and develop what we are interested in and maybe have a talent for. This section of the pack is bursting with lots of hands-on activities suitable for all the family. All the activities in this section reinforce the monthly value and family members can choose activities which interest them. For example, Grandad may choose to grow vegetables with his grandchild. Every month the activities change to suit the value of the month. Here are some examples of Family Activities:

TIP: Family Activities: the value of courage

Try something new

Have the courage this month to try something new! Do something new as a family or individually. This could mean meeting up with an old friend, trying a new hobby, wearing a different colour or trying a new food.

Blindfolded obstacle course

Together design an obstacle course in your back garden or local park. One family member plays the guide, the other is blindfolded. The one blindfolded must navigate the course by following the commands of the family member. The guide yells commands like 'Left', 'Right' or 'Straight on', along with warning the blindfolded partner about any obstacles. The aim is to complete the obstacle course successfully.

Be creative, as the more interesting the course is, the more courage one of you will have to complete it. Use paddling pools filled with water, blankets to climb under and objects to climb over.

Make a courage pennant

You will need cut-out pennant shapes (triangle shapes) made out of card. Each family member will need three pennant shapes, crayons, markers and glitter glue.

Each family member will need to complete three tasks. The first task is to think of something that will make you feel powerful, e.g. 'I feel strong. I can do it!' Write this on your first pennant and decorate it using crayons, markers and glitter glue. The second task is to write your name on the second pennant and be creative. For example, if you have an 'O' in your name you could turn it into a smiley face. Why not make your name into a rainbow or a happy shape? On the third pennant draw something that you enjoy doing, something that you are good at achieving. For example, select a favourite sporting event or animal to draw. Decorate this pennant with something that makes you smile.

Once you have completed your three pennants, be confident in what you can do and display them as a mobile for everyone to see.

Make a family scarecrow

Design and make your own adorable scarecrow using recycled materials. Why not put your scarecrow in the garden and see if it frightens the birds away. If you need some ideas on how to make a scarecrow, look on the internet or go to the library.

Family Reflections

The final part of the pack is designed to encourage the family to reflect on what they have learnt and achieved during the month. Families need time to understand what they have accomplished and also how to overcome problems which they have encountered along the way. This is brought about through reflection. Reflection is another word for learning, one which grows out of experiences. It is a process designed to promote cognitive learning. The reflective process helps the family stop, think and reflect on the month by asking certain questions:

- What did your family learn about this month's value?
- What was your family's favourite activity and why?
- What activity did your family least like and why?
- How has this month's value benefited your family?
- Have you noticed any changes in your family since taking part in Family Values?

This is achieved through a number of activities:

TIP: Family Reflections: the value of courage

Family meeting

At the end of the month it is time to hold a family meeting for everyone to reflect on how well they have done the following:

- demonstrated the value 'courage';
- communicated with each other;
- interacted with school and the community;
- participated in individual goals;
- achieved their family goals.

Time to evaluate

Evaluate your success using the checklist below:

- I/we have shown the value 'courage' this month by{...};
- I/we have communicated well with each other by{...};
- I/we have interacted with school and the community by{...};
- I have achieved my individual goal this month by{...};
- we have achieved our family goal this month by{...};
- I/we feel that we could improve{...}

Family nominations

Together decide who deserves your Family Values trophy. The nominations can be discussed around the table or written on a piece of paper and placed in a box. Pretend you're at the Oscars and present the winner with the trophy.

Families who are able to reflect and problem-solve are able to overcome a multitude of issues, which inevitably strengthens the family unit. Children develop resilience when they learn how to problem-solve from their parent(s)/carer(s).

> Problem-solving is the family's ability to resolve problems on a level that maintains effective family functioning.
>
> (Epstein *et al.*, 1993)

Problem-solving is a skill which can be learnt by working through the following stages:

1 *Identify the problem*: this can be achieved through discussion and listening to other members of the family.
2 *Generate options to deal with the problem*: discuss and brainstorm a variety of options.
3 *Agree on an option*: the family collectively chooses an option which they all agree to work with.
4 *Implement an action plan*: decide what each member of the family is going to do and by when.
5 *Monitor the action plan*: the monitoring process is very important as it allows the family to keep track of their progress and achieve their goal.

Summary

In this chapter we have considered the Family Values Scheme (Ellis *et al.*, 2012), which provides a structure and is a fun way to involve parents, pupils and their families in school life. Interested readers may wish to read the full text, which is also published by Routledge. We will now conclude this Handbook by examining the vexing but important issues of improving school attendance and preventing bullying.

Chapter 13

The link between pupils' non-attendance and their behaviour

In this chapter on pupils' non-attendance in the primary school, we will consider the following five important issues:

- the need for much earlier identification;
- reasons why primary pupils miss school;
- the causes of primary pupils' non-attendance;
- significant issues;
- managing attendance in the primary school, including strong and weak features.

It is proving to be an increasing cause of concern that a rising number of primary pupils at key stage 2 are appearing to miss school for reasons of unauthorised absence (truancy) throughout the UK and in some other parts of the world, including the United States.

The need for early intervention

Teachers in primary schools should be keenly aware of the importance of monitoring pupils' attendance for several reasons. The first is because under the terms of the 1944 and 1996 Education Acts (amongst others) parents are required by law to ensure their child or children attend school on a daily basis unless they have a good reason not to do so such as illness (Reid, 1999). The second is because pupils missing school in the primary phase often indicates that something is seriously wrong and psychologists often regard such behaviour as 'a plea for help'. Others appear to regard it as a 'defence mechanism' caused by unhappiness at home, school or both. The third reason is because it is important for classroom teachers and head teachers to monitor their attendance on a daily basis and to regularly analyse attendance data for any significant trends or patterns.

Existing evidence suggests that approximately 35 per cent of absentees begin their history of non-attendance in the primary school. Unless their non-attendance is assessed and investigated at the earliest possible opportunity, some or many of these pupils will start to miss school more regularly, and perhaps by the time they reach adolescence they will become persistent school absentees. Research indicates that pupils normally have one initial reason for missing school. Thereafter, the number of reasons they give increases significantly and it becomes more difficult to resolve the issues and to reintegrate pupils into their classes or school. Similarly, pupils' learning tends to deteriorate; not least their literacy and numeracy levels, but also their academic attainment and progress. It is for this reason that early intervention in school attendance cases is so important.

There are, however, other sound reasons for early intervention as well, particularly in the primary phase. Foremost amongst these may be that the initial reason for the non-attendance is serious and needs a home visit, case review or interdisciplinary meeting. Examples of such pleas for help might include potential child abuse, bullying, serious family rifts or emotional distress, amongst a whole raft of potential reasons. In fact, in a very high percentage of cases, especially amongst younger children, non-attendance is a manifestation of other serious problems rather than purely a case based around non-attendance per se. Often these initial reasons for a pupil's non-attendance become blurred and, over time, drift into 'generalised' absence cases, especially if early identification and intervention strategies are not used.

At least in theory, in cases where there is a genuine concern about the reasons provided for an absence, the education welfare service will arrange to make a home visit. This visit is not only to clarify the reason but also to check up on the welfare of the child. It is especially important to follow up cases of 'unauthorised' absence in younger school-aged children as soon as possible. Increasingly, in some parts of the United Kingdom, more learning school mentors, classroom assistants, home–school liaison officers or other school staff (including head teachers), health care and/or social service personnel are beginning to make these preliminary visits alongside or instead of education welfare officers.

Regrettably, although they are improving, early intervention strategies are often normally a key weakness and failing in existing school and local authority attendance strategies in the United Kingdom, alongside sound reintegration techniques, which can be virtually non-existent in some parts of the United Kingdom and in other parts of the world; this is generally an area of professional 'weakness'. Again, there are several reasons for this state of affairs: first, the lack of appropriate training given to teachers, head teachers, learning school mentors, classroom assistants and other caring professionals on the implications of school attendance and the need for early intervention (NBAR, 2008); second, the shortage of key professional staff such as education welfare officers and education social workers, which means that many primary head teachers have little or no available support to help them with initial detection or later more persistent cases; third, the 'confusion' caused by the introduction of the Children Act, 2004, and the Every Child Matters (2003) agenda, which has changed the emphasis in how many schools and local authorities now manage school attendance cases, with major organisational changes taking place between the systems in place in England and those in Scotland, Northern Ireland and Wales (Reid, 2010). In fact, since the advent of devolution, the management of school attendance is now the responsibility of the four 'home' administrations and their assemblies/parliaments, with the divergence in how they 'manage' school attendance beginning to increase significantly.

Reasons for missing school

Missing school in the early years or during key stage 1 is usually done for genuine reasons such as illness. Most younger children go through a phase when they start to 'catch' a series of infectious illnesses, often from other pupils, and this is perfectly normal. Nevertheless, it is often the youngest children who are most prone to child abuse, whether physical, psychological or through neglect (e.g. malnourishment). In such cases, missing school often provides the first (and sometimes only) clue.

Increasingly, however, more primary-aged pupils are missing school for reasons of 'unauthorised' absence or truancy. Reasons for unauthorised absence include: truancy (irrespective of cause), taking family holidays in term-time without the prior consent of the head teacher, parentally-condoned absences and specific day or lesson absence (although this occurs much less in primary schools).

It is never easy for teachers to ascertain whether absences are 'authorised' or 'unauthorised'. The system relies on parents being truthful in their 'absence notes' sent to the school or when teachers phone them up, whether this occurs for first-day absences or in follow-up calls. The system relies on both parental and school honesty when registers are marked and attendance statistics collated. But some parents and schools are often less than honest in this regard. Generally speaking, the reasons provided by parents and/or carers tend to be more honest and accurate at the primary phase than those often given at the secondary stage. This is one reason why national, local and school attendance data and statistics should carry a health warning! Either way, it the head teachers' responsibility to ensure that school registers are marked twice daily and schools are compliant not only with the law but with the school inspection regulations on attendance.

Occasionally, following home visits, it may be necessary for the education welfare service, school staff or other agencies to refer the child to other agencies such as health, social services or the police. Another important link is to the educational psychology service within the local authority. Here again, though, professional staff shortages and time delays often prevent the best and most immediate service from being provided; sometimes because certain professionals wrongly perceive attendance referrals as being less important than other types of cases. Sometimes this too is indicative of professional training deficiencies.

Increasingly, as well, interdisciplinary or multidisciplinary case conferences need to be held to discuss and consider an absentee's own or family circumstances and follow-up action will be agreed. Sometimes monitoring of the progress of such pupils will need to take place at regular periods, with detailed records held of the meetings and action agreed to comply with the Children Act, 2004, requirements.

The causes of pupils' non-attendance

Why pupils truant or skip school

The main reasons given by primary-aged pupils for missing school for 'unauthorised' reasons include: bullying, dislike of a particular teacher or aspects of the curriculum, poor relationships with teachers and/or fellow pupils, 'It's cool to miss school', feeling 'bored' at school and not feeling safe either at school or on the way to or from school.

Other causes include pupils who have psychological difficulties such as low self-esteem, school phobia, ADHD and related syndromes, learning difficulties (whether SEN, or having literacy or numeracy problems), or those with emotional, social or behavioural difficulties. It is for these reasons that a skilled assessment of the 'unauthorised' absent pupil is often advisable and in the child's own interest.

Research indicates that pupils who experience home difficulties are more likely to truant from school. Reasons related to home background factors include: lack of parent/carer support for children's learning, parent-condoned absenteeism, poor parenting skills, second/third-generation truant families, lack of home discipline, bullying or victimisation in the home, taking holidays during term-time, home–school communication difficulties or breakdowns, parental divorce or complex and/or unusual home care arrangements, poverty, lack of sleep (too much PlayStation or watching television beyond midnight!), a lack of parental supervision (e.g. parents or carers who leave the home early and are not there to support the child or to provide a breakfast) (Reid, 1985, 1999, 2000, 2002, 2008).

Unauthorised absence

There is abundant evidence from research to indicate that the vast majority of 'unauthorised' absences from primary schools are condoned by parents. Technically, parent-condoned absence is still truancy! Sometimes parents or carers fail to understand the importance of regular attendance at school or the legal requirements placed upon them. Some parents simply prefer to have their child at home for company or cannot be bothered to send their child to school. These and other reasons are why it is important for schools to liaise with the education welfare service to ensure that a home visit is made, with a detailed follow-up report.

Sometimes when a mother keeps her child at home it is for more serious reasons. Perhaps, for example, the mother is afraid of her husband or partner, is herself a victim of abuse and so feels safer with her child at home.

Research also suggests that there are different 'types' of pupils who miss school for 'unauthorised' reasons. Some pupils are naturally shy or quiet. Some may have 'phobic' tendencies. Others may be disruptive pupils who are often in trouble at school. Some pupils will talk 'openly' about their reasons for missing school. Others will not. Some will provide genuine reasons for missing school. Others will do the opposite (see pp. 13–17).

Significant issues

This section focuses upon a few significant features which teachers, parents, education welfare officers, educational psychologists and other caring professionals would be advised to take account of when dealing with school absentees and truants. The evidence is taken from the research literature on school attendance (Reid, 1985, 1999, 2008).

Literacy and numeracy

All the available evidence suggests that absentees come mainly from among pupils whose literacy and numeracy levels are two or more years behind their chronological age (see, for example, NBAR, 2008: 19–21). Therefore one of the best ways to prevent pupils from falling behind with their schoolwork or dropping out is to ensure that they catch up when they fall behind. This can be achieved through one-to-one support, however this is achieved. Such strategies include the use of LSMs, CAs, home–school liaison officers, voluntary agencies or by using voluntary parental school support systems. All the available evidence suggests that once pupils feel 'comfortable' in school and within their classrooms they will attend school normally.

Self-esteem

Closely related to pupils' literacy and numeracy levels are pupils' levels of academic self-concepts and self-esteem. Reid (1982) found that the greatest single difference between both boy and girl persistent school absentees when compared and contrasted with regular attenders was their general levels of self-esteem and academic self-concepts as measured by the Brookover and Coopersmith Scales. Therefore, if teachers wish pupils to attend school regularly, they should focus on raising their self-esteem. Of course, improving their literacy and numeracy levels facilitates this process.

Recent differences

Recent research suggests that truancy is starting increasingly younger within schools. We do not know why. Some people believe this is related to the modern-day pressure upon both parents and carers to need to earn and work. Others suggest it is related to ever higher rates of family breakdown and the increase in the number of single-parent families. Still others suggest it is related to the changing school curriculum, to increased 'testing' and to 'pressures' exerted upon children and young people in society to grow up sooner. What is clear is that fifty years ago most truants from primary schools (and there were very few then) were male. Today, there is a slight preponderance of girls.

Non-attendance and challenging behaviour

Concern has been mounting in recent years that more pupils with attendance problems exhibit behavioural problems upon their return to schools and, in so doing, can disrupt classes and other pupils' learning. Often it is better to facilitate returning pupils in catch-up classes or groups until they are ready to be reintegrated into formal lessons. Increasingly, both challenging pupils and truants can become candidates for fixed-term exclusions, sometimes all too easily, which is at best counterproductive.

Social class and socioeconomic background

There is overwhelming evidence that most school non-attendees, such as truants, come from lower socioeconomic backgrounds which are both disadvantaged and often live in difficult economic circumstances, often defined as being below the 'poverty line'. In some primary schools, a clear majority of non-attendees are on free school meals, whilst their parent(s) or carer(s) are on a range of income- and housing-related benefits (Reid, 1999). Despite this, we should never forget that the vast majority of pupils from working-class backgrounds attend school regularly.

Parents and parenting skills

In an important study, Dalziel and Henthorne (2005) found that the parents of school absentees and truants differed markedly from those of regular attenders in a whole variety of ways. These included having an anti-school and teacher attitude, which sometimes could be hostile or aggressive, poor experiences when they went to school themselves and general anti-education attitudes. These could be contrasted with the parents of regular attenders, who wished to help their children to do as well as possible and supported them in every way they could (including financial support, help with reading, etc.). It should also be remembered that some children who become non-attenders are the children of third- or fourth-generation 'truant families'.

Bullying

Recent research is finding an increase in the relationship between bullying (both verbal and physical) and, more recently, cyber bullying and truancy and other forms of non-attendance (Reid, 2008). This bullying may take place in school, out of school or on the way to or from school.

Managing school attendance in the primary school

Positive features in managing school attendance

Evidence from research and school inspection reports in England and Wales indicates that schools can do a lot themselves to improve pupils' attendance as well as their own rates of attendance. Some head teachers and classroom teachers do everything possible to manage and improve school attendance. Many schools make school attendance a priority. All schools should do so. Research evidence shows that schools which prioritise attendance can often improve their own rates of attendance by anything between 2 and 8 per cent a year. Thereafter, you cannot afford to take your foot off the gas! By contrast, schools which do not prioritise attendance can often inadvertently make things worse. Examples of comments made about key elements of good practice taken from research evidence and school inspectors' reports include the following:

- managing first-day absences well;
- pupils enjoying their lessons, getting on well with their teachers and learning satisfactorily;
- parents supporting schools on attendance matters in a positive manner;
- pupils liking their schools and therefore attending;
- giving rewards for regular or 100 per cent attendance (e.g. attendance certificates, prizes or other forms of incentive);
- holding 'praise' assemblies to award attendance prizes;
- organising a successful nurture group;
- having an effective whole-school policy on attendance;

- utilising pupils' views on attendance;
- forging good links with external agencies;
- having good relationships between the school and the local education welfare service;
- helping absent pupils catch up with work missed;
- sound use of learning school mentors, classroom assistants, attendance or administrative assistants and the education welfare service;
- providing parents with accurate school attendance data, including unauthorised absences;
- providing challenging benchmarks on attendance and responding to data showing natural or local norms;
- positive leadership by the head teacher and/or deputy head on attendance issues;
- interviewing parents or carers automatically in cases of prolonged absence;
- preventing the link between bullying and attendance and, when it's prevalent, acting upon it;
- arranging medical appointments within schools whenever possible by prior agreement with the local medical practice;
- making transport arrangements for pupils with travelling difficulties or with special educational needs or disabilities;
- using the police fastidiously;
- establishing a learning support centre to deal with return-to-school issues, reintegration and subsequently to meet pupils' needs, especially in cases of long-term absence.

Case study: Tammy

Tammy is nine years old. She started missing school at the age of five without good reason. Her mother always condoned her absences and made plausible excuses for her. Following the intervention of her school after the absences became more frequent and prolonged, Tammy was found by the education social worker to be living in a caravan with her mother and her mother's boyfriend some thirty miles away from the school's catchment area.

The conditions inside the caravan concerned the education social worker so much she reported the case to the social services department. Subsequent interventions found it necessary to rehouse the mother and to provide regular support to Tammy and her mother from social services. The mother was found to need Housing Benefit and Income Support, while Tammy was awarded free school meals. Tammy is now attending more regularly, although she is being constantly monitored by both the school and social services and it is likely that she will need to be regularly monitored throughout her school career.

Weak features in managing school attendance

Evidence from research and school inspectors' reports in England and Wales suggests that the weaker features found amongst primary schools in managing school attendance include the following:

- not paying sufficient attention to lateness, poor punctuality and poor parental attitudes towards regular school attendance;
- allowing too many unauthorised holidays;
- allowing too many holidays in term-time without the prior consent of the head teacher;
- not having any focused monitoring of pupils' attendance and/or not using appropriate attendance data wisely, including the failure to undertake comparative exercises;

- failing to analyse attendance patterns by gender, year group, term, day of week or, in certain cases, ethnicity;
- failing to implement first-day responses to absence;
- using recording codes for absences inconsistently;
- not checking the accuracy of data marked by supply teachers;
- not recognising that a school's poor rate of attendance is leading to declining standards at the school and acting accordingly (one of the key reasons for a school being found to have 'weaknesses', being placed in special measures or in 'challenging circumstances');
- marking registers inaccurately or not following Welsh Assembly government guidelines;
- recording certain categories of absences inaccurately (e.g. term-time holidays, illness, etc.);
- not taking action when the poor attendance of a few persistent non-attenders is having a marked adverse impact on a school's overall rates of attendance;
- not doing enough to emphasise the importance of regular and punctual attendance to parents;
- failing to act upon the link between bullying and attendance;
- failing to act upon the link between a school's poor internal facilities (e.g. dirty toilets) and pupils' attitudes and attendance;
- not understanding the consequences of high staff turnover and constantly requiring the use of supply teachers;
- having no follow-up procedures in place for long-term absentees;
- not using the education welfare service wisely or appropriately;
- not referring serious cases of absence either to the education welfare service or to other external agencies;
- not following up on pupils who fail to turn up for their in-school assessments;
- poor leadership by the head teacher and/or deputy on attendance issues;
- not being aware of the link between non-attendance and pupils with free school meals, special educational needs, disabilities and pupils in other minority categories.

Case study: Wayne

Wayne suddenly started having temper tantrums in class. These lasted for a few minutes at a time. He then calmed down. Suddenly, at the age of ten, he started missing school, at first only for a day or two, then for several days at a time. He complained of feeling unwell. After the school referred him to the education welfare service, he was taken to see his general practitioner and the local educational psychologist. Subsequent investigations found that Wayne was suffering from diabetes and had hearing loss. After medication was prescribed and a hearing aid fitted, Wayne's attendance improved. Although academically slower than some of his peers, he is enjoying school more; he needs a lot of support and encouragement on a daily basis.

Summary

In this short but specific chapter, we have considered several major issues concerned with managing pupils' attendance in the primary school which we hope will provide you with some useful information and give you a few good ideas. We will conclude our Handbook on managing behaviour in the primary school with a consideration of how to manage bullying.

Chapter 14

The link between bullying and pupils' behaviour

Introduction

Bullying, in all its forms, is perhaps the most malicious and malevolent form of anti-social behaviour practised in our schools. Bullying takes many forms. It can be physical. It can be mental. These days much of the most insidious forms of bullying take place on the internet or through specialist websites. This is now called cyber bullying. One reason for the latest concern about cyber bullying is that contact is sometimes unsolicited and can be sent to numerous contacts at the same time, often without redress. For pupils in school, totally private or false information can be sent to classmates, school peers or people in the local community. Many people tend to believe these false assertions and it is often difficult for victims to shake off the resulting false beliefs, so that they affect the lives of victims indefinitely.

Bullying incidents in primary schools often include such features as name calling, teasing, jostling and punching, pinching, hair pulling and kicking, intimidation and extortion. In more serious cases physical assaults take place.

The victims are often too ashamed or fearful to report the actions of the bullies. They may suffer the physical and psychological abuse in silence. They often feel isolated, lonely, insecure, anxious and unhappy. At its most insidious, bullying may focus upon vulnerable children who are regarded as being different from their peers. This may be for comparatively 'minor' reasons. Examples could be having unusual hair, being smaller than their peers or not having good clothes sense. Worse, it can focus upon pupils because of their ethnic origins, race, physical or mental disabilities.

Bullying equally affects those other children who may witness the violence and aggression, the subsequent distress of the victim(s), but who may choose to do nothing about it.

Head teachers need to ensure that all their staff and pupils are 'trained' about bullying and follow the school's policy code. Bullies need to understand that their behaviour will not be tolerated. Bullied pupils need to know that when they come forward they will be supported and can approach staff with confidence. It is important that bullied pupils feel that their allegations will be treated with respect and in confidence and they will not face any recriminations because of their actions.

When issues of bullying are reported, schools need to ask themselves some basic questions:

- How extensive is the problem?
- What are the characteristics of the pupils involved?
- Why is it occurring?
- Can the school do more to get rid of or minimise the problem?

Serious cases of bullying should always be logged and reported to local authorities and the appropriate follow-up action taken. The most serious cases may need to involve either the social services or police, or both.

It is not really known why some schools experience more incidents of bullying than others. Bullying in schools has always taken place. Some pupils appear to react worse to being bullied than others. What one person regards as teasing may be experienced as bullying by someone else. Research indicates that many school bullies have themselves been victims of bullying in their homes. Therefore, are they trying to get their own back on others or do they believe this is 'normal' behaviour?

The intensity of bullying can range from horseplay to a vicious assault. The bullying can be occasional and short-lived or it can be regular and longstanding. Cases have been found of children who have been systematically bullied for years at school or at home or both. Often, these serious cases have been undetected for several years.

Some bullying is premeditated and person specific. Other bullying is thoughtless, even accidental. It can be carried out by a single child or by a gang. It can be both boy- and girl-group based or cross the gender boundary. Research suggests that with boys the motive is often power related. For girls, it often has more to with affiliation as the victim is often excluded, scapegoated and victimised for not being part of a group activity or for behaving differently from her peers (e.g. going to church on a Sunday or not attending house parties).

Factors inside the school which may affect bullying in the school setting include the size of school and class, teachers' attitudes and behaviour, school climate and ethos, rule enforcement procedures and the effectiveness or otherwise of the school's bullying policy and school council.

External characteristics of potential victims and bullies include physical handicaps, obesity, language problems and physical characteristics such as hair colour, feet size, physical strength and weakness, gender traits, ethnicity, religion and disabilities, amongst others.

The psychological behaviour and characteristics of victims and bullies include such facets as pupils' attitudes towards violence, aggression, anxiety, self-esteem and punctuality. Pupils who react badly to either physical or verbal bullying are more likely to receive further bouts of bullying.

The socioeconomic background of pupils also plays a part in bullying and bullied behaviour. Parents and carers act as role models in this regard. Therefore conditions in the home, the child-rearing practices and the parents' or carers' own personal experiences as children or pupils at school can all play a part in the equation.

Assessment and intervention

The general principles which apply to the assessment of young children and later juniors in primary schools are the same for both bullies and their victims. In particular, it is important to:

- ascertain, as precisely as possible, both the nature and the context of the difficulties presented;
- draw up a profile (often a case study) of the various aspects of the child's development observed over a period of time, gathered from as many sources as possible;
- link assessment closely to intervention;
- involve the parent(s) or carer(s) and, in so doing, get to know something of the child's home background;
- enlist, if necessary, the aid of the appropriate support services, which may include the LA's Education Psychology Service or social services.

The way intervention is conducted is important. Short-term measures may include the following steps:

- the teacher talking to the bully, making it clear that bullying is unacceptable – depending upon the severity of the incident, the bullying should immediately be reported to the head teacher; from there, to the local authority;
- providing firm reassurance to the victim that action is being taken to stop the bullying;

- inviting (and expecting) the co-operation of the parent(s) or carer(s);
- increasing supervision by adults in school and the playground, and ensuring (if necessary) that the children involved are escorted to and from school and/or collected by a responsible family member;
- giving constructive tasks to the bully – this may or may not involve removing some privileges from him or her. In extreme cases, examples of serious or repeated bullying may require fixed-term or even permanent exclusion or removal to another school. It is important to ensure that it is the bully and not the victim who is punished further. Sadly, this does not always happen and can be a serious mistake on the part of a school or teacher;
- breaking up bullying gangs and not allowing gang bullying to take place within schools;
- using other members of the class (peer group) empathetically to support the victim – this can be just as important outside school as within a school's boundaries.

Longer-term measures can include:

- increasing adult participation in play situations to promote appropriate social skills;
- building up the self-confidence of the victim and, where necessary, the bully as well;
- ensuring that the bullied child's learning needs are being met in school;
- helping parent(s) or carer(s) to adopt more committed and positive child-rearing practices – sometimes this will require help and resources from external agencies;
- teachers, learning school mentors and even classroom assistants examining their own management style – this is often to ensure it does not provide a model of dominating behaviour; head teachers too may need to examine their own approaches to school discipline;
- utilising peer-mediated strategies – these measures can include rewarding the whole class for improvements in the behaviour of individuals or using small groups to promote and foster co-operation;
- watching and managing the language used by pupils in class or school and ensuring it is not too aggressive;
- if necessary, in schools with more serious or frequent problems, involving the education psychologist in, for example, behaviour modification programmes or sociometric techniques – the use by experienced educational psychologists of such processes as specialised repertory grid techniques can be especially helpful.

Using pupils

In order to identify pupils being bullied, sometimes it is necessary to utilise the school council or carry out in-depth class or school-based studies. Simple questions need to be asked, such as:

- Does anybody in your class bully other children?
- Does anybody in your class get bullied by other children? If so, who?
- Would you tell anybody if you were being bullied? If so, who? Where does the bullying usually take place? Does this happen within school or outside school?
- What do you think should be done about bullying in the school?
- Is there anyone you know who requires help from staff in the school because they are being bullied or victimised?

Surveys of schools on bullying have found that bullies account for as much as one in ten pupils. Usually, bullies are of average popularity (but often vocal or larger than their peers) with other children but they can exude overconfidence. A positive attitude towards violence rather than insecurity or unpopularity most likely underlies the behaviour. However, some studies have found that around one in five or six bullies are anxious about their own behaviour. These are often called 'anxious bullies'. They tend to be less secure and more unpopular than other bullies.

Between 7 and 10 per cent of bullied children experience being a victim during a typical school day. One survey found that 22 per cent of the victims never told their teacher; 59 per cent 'occasionally' told a teacher they were being bullied. Some of the most serious victims of bullying never tell anyone, in school or at home. Sometimes these are amongst the most high-profile suicide victims as the scars of being bullied can run emotionally very deep. 'Proactive victims' (children who actively seek to be victimised or provoke antagonism) can account for as much as one in five or six cases. In a small minority of cases, pupils bully and are themselves bullied in turn.

It used to be the case that bullying was considered the purview of boys. This is certainly no longer the case. The rise of girl gangs is one of the new phenomena of the last decade. Some studies have now found that more girls than boys are bullied in and out of school. Girls have been found to be less tolerant and even more aggressive than boys in some studies, especially in early adolescence.

In research into truancy and school absenteeism, Reid (2000) has found that incidents of bullying influence the attendance of pupils in up to one in five cases. Some schools have no absentees who have been bullied. In some others, it is the leading cause for pupils' non-attendance. No one fully understands why individual schools vary so much in the degree or intensity of bullying-related activities. The leadership of the school is obviously an important aspect. Some schools, however, seem to be better at making successful interventions than others. Some school staff appear to be better trained and more confident about using their school bullying policy and implementing its intervention strategies than others. Is this solely down to training, teachers' personalities and confidence or ability levels? Some schools apply zero-tolerance strategies towards bullies earlier than others and often exclude them for a short period whilst solutions are found. Some bullies end up being permanently excluded. More research is needed in this field, but school ethos, ethnicity, teachers' attitudes, location, size, socioeconomic factors, disabilities and the number of pupils with SEN or emotional, social or behavioural disorders seem to be amongst the causes which are linked to bullying.

Most schools now utilise whole-curriculum and whole-school approaches to combating bullying. The key issue is to involve both teachers and pupils in this training and in drafting the policy documents on bullying.

Some research has found that bullied pupils tend to experience more health problems, lower social class membership, poor peer group relationships, larger families and higher levels of economic and social disadvantage in their families. They also tend to live in poorer housing, have more educational disadvantage, be disabled and have some form of special educational need. But variations abound and some bullied victims come from affluent families, which may, in itself, be a cause.

In summary, bullied pupils can be helped to feel safer and to cope with bullying through:

- the introduction of a specific social skills programme such as SEAL;
- appropriate interventions to support the bullied child in (and out of) school, where necessary, sometimes involving external agents such as educational psychologists or social services or, in extreme cases, the police;
- implementing appropriate school-based strategies and policies;
- action taken by the school to change its own practice, identification of the problem and, sometimes, school ethos.

A zero-tolerance approach towards bullying is always a prerequisite to successfully managing the problem. Research indicates it is possible to teach children to feel valued and not to bully by:

- making a thorough assessment of the in-school factors giving rise to the behaviour;
- taking planned action to support the victim and to prevent the bully from repeating the behaviour;
- demonstrating support for the victim, often utilising the help of the peer group and classmates;
- a school revising its own practice and making appropriate changes, including amending its own bullying policy document and seeking the advice of external agencies.

Recording information

Teachers need to take care at all times to look out for any external signs of bullying and to know what action to take when it is identified. Advice from your head teacher can be paramount in this regard. Teachers should use appropriate bullying incident logs such as the examples shown in Figures 14.1 and 14.2.

Case study: Darren

Darren is ten years of age. He started missing school occasionally at the age of seven. He was reported for making repeated absences at the age of nine. His parents repeatedly made excuses for him claiming that he was ill, often with colds or flu. Eventually, the school contacted the education welfare officer, who made a home visit. She spoke to Darren and his mother. It turned out that Darren was being repeatedly bullied both physically and verbally. He was often too afraid to go to school. Further investigations showed he was also the subject of bullying on the school bus to and from school and in the playground during playtimes. His mother had taken him to see her general practitioner twice following bouts of physical bullying. Darren believed that if he reported the boys who were bullying him he would be subjected to more serious bullying. His mother was also concerned about being victimised within the local community. The bullying started because Darren was smaller than his peers, overweight and less good at sporting activities.

After the intervention of the education welfare officer and once the school had taken appropriate action, the bullying stopped. Darren is now attending well and making better progress with his schoolwork.

Summary

This chapter has focused upon key issues surrounding the understanding, management and prevention of bullying in the primary school. It is the final chapter in our Handbook. We hope you have enjoyed reading it and will find the details and practical advice helpful in your professional lives.

Alleged Bullying Incident Log

	Name(s), Age, Gender	Setting
Child(s) alleged to be experiencing bullying behaviour		
Child(s) alleged to be engaging in bullying behaviour		

Reported by:	Date:
Investigation by:	Date:

Account of individual(s) alleged to be engaging in bullying behaviour: (use separate sheet if required)

Looked After Child? Yes No	Ethnicity:

Action: (use separate sheet if required)

Review date:

Account of individual(s) alleged to be experiencing bullying behaviour: (use separate sheet if required)

Looked After Child? Yes No	Ethnicity:

Action: (use separate sheet if required)

Review date:

Was alleged bullying confirmed? (please circle)	Yes	No	Insufficient evidence to decide

Was the matter resolved? (please circle)	Yes	No	Details:

Future action (if appropriate)	

Figure 14.1 Alleged bullying incident log

Confirmed Bullying Incident Log

	Name(s), Age, Gender	Setting	How many times have they	
			Bullied others before?	Been bullied before?
Child(s) experiencing bullying behaviour				
Child(s) engaging in bullying behaviour				

Reported by: Date:

Reported to:

Investigated by: Date:

Details of bullying incident:
Those experiencing bullying behaviour: (use separate sheet if required)

Looked After Child? Yes No	Ethnicity:

Those experiencing bullying behaviour or those being bullied: (use separate sheet if required)

Looked After Child? Yes No	Ethnicity:

Action: (use separate sheet if required)

Review date:

Monitoring (you may circle more than one)

Physical	Verbal	Indirect	Cyber

Racial	Homophobic	Sexual	Appearance	Disability	Ability	Gender	LAC	Other

Figure 14.2 Confirmed bullying incident log

Further reading

Arthur, J. and Cremin, T. (2010) *Learning to Teach in the Primary School*, London: Routledge.

Bentham, S. (2005) *A Teaching Assistant's Guide to Managing Behaviour in the Classroom*, London: Routledge.

Bishop, S. (2008) *Running a Nurture Group*, London: Sage Publications.

Boxall, M. (2002) *Nurture Groups in Schools: Principles and Practice*, London: Paul Chapman Publishing.

Chaplain, R. (2005) *Teaching without Disruption in the Primary School*, London: Routledge.

Charles, C. M. (2008) *Building Classroom Discipline*, Boston: Pearson.

Cooper, P., Smith, C. J. and Upton, G. (1994) *Emotional and Behavioural Difficulties: Theory to Practice*, London: Routledge.

Cross, M. (2004) *Children with Emotional and Behavioural Difficulties and Communication Problems*, London: Jessica Kingsley Publishers.

Docking, J. and MacGrath, M. (2002) *Managing Behaviour in the Primary School*, London: David Fulton.

Ellis, G., Morgan, N. S. and Reid, K. (2012) *Better Behaviour through Home–School Relations: Using Values-Based Education to Promote Positive Learning*, London: Routledge.

Faupel, A. (ed.) (2003) *Emotional Literacy: Assessment and Intervention*, prepared by Southampton Psychology Service, Slough: NFER.

Fay, J. and Funk, D. (1995) *Teaching with Love and Logic*, Golden, CA: The Love and Logic Press.

Greene, R. W. (2010) *The Explosive Child*, New York: HarperCollins Publishers.

Griffiths, A. and Jones, K. (2006) *101 Essential Lists on Managing Behaviour in the Primary School*, London: Continuum International Publishing Group.

Haydn, T. (2006) *Managing Pupil Behaviour: Key Issues in Teaching and Learning*, London: Routledge.

Hook, P. and Vass, A. (2004) *Behaviour Management Pocketbook*, London: Management Pocketbooks.

Hopkins, B. (2004) *Just Schools: A Whole-School Approach to Restorative Justice*, London: Jessica Kingsley Publishers.

Hunter-Carsch, M., Tiknaz, Y., Cooper, P. and Sage, R. (eds) (2006) *The Handbook of Social, Emotional and Behavioural Difficulties*, London: Continuum.

Kay, J. (2006) *Managing Behaviour in the Early Years*, London: Routledge.

Moir, A. (2008) *The Behaviour Management Toolkit for Primary School Teachers*, London: Wizard Publishing.

Morgan, N. S. (2009) *Quick, Easy and Effective Behaviour Management Ideas for the Classroom*, London: Jessica Kingsley Publishers.

Morgan, N. S. and Ellis, G. (2009) *The 5-Step Behaviour Programme: A Whole-School Approach to Behaviour Management*, Cardiff: Behaviour Stop Ltd.

Morgan, N. S. and Ellis, G. (2011) *A Kit Bag for Promoting Positive Behaviour in the Classroom*, London: Jessica Kingsley Publishers.

Roffey, S. (2004) *The New Teacher's Survival Guide to Behaviour*, London: Sage Publications.

Roffey, S. (2006) *Helping with Behaviour in the Early Years: Promoting the Positive and Addressing the Difficult*, London: Routledge.

Roffey, S. and O'Reirdon, T. (2003) *Plans for Better Behaviour in the Primary School*, London: David Fulton.

Rogers, B. (2006) *Classroom Behaviour*, London: Paul Chapman Publishing.

Rogers, B. (2007) *Behaviour Management: A Whole-School Approach*, London: Sage Publications.

Rogers, B. (2009) *How to Manage Children's Challenging Behaviour*, London: Sage Publications.

Rosenberg, M. B. (2003) *Non-Violent Communication: A Language of Life*, Encinitas, CA: Puddle Dancer Press.

Rosenthal, R. and Jacobson, L. (2003) *Pygmalion in the Classroom*, Carmarthen: Crown House Publishing Ltd.

References

Allen, G. MP (January, 2010) *Early Intervention: The Next Steps. An Independent Report to Her Majesty's Government*, London: HMSO.

Allen, G. A. and Smith, I. D. (2008) *Early Intervention: Good Parents, Great Kids, Better Citizens*, a report for the Centre for Social Justice by Graham Allen, MP and the Rt Hon Iain Duncan Smith, MP, London: The Smith Institute.

Association of Teachers and Lecturers' Survey (2010) *Challenging Behaviour in School*, London: ATL.

Bishop, S. (2008) *Running a Nurture Group*, London: Sage Publications.

Bogenschneider, K. and Johnson, C. (2004) 'Family Involvement in Education: How Important Is It? What Can Legislators Do?' In K. Bogenschneider and E. Gross (eds), *A Policymaker's Guide to School Finance: Approaches to Use and Questions to Ask* (Wisconsin Family Impact Seminar Briefing Report No. 20, 54 pages), Madison, WI: University of Wisconsin Center for Excellence in Family Studies.

Boxall, M. (2002) *Nurture Groups in Schools: Principles and Practice*, London: Paul Chapman Publishing.

Bronfenbrenner, U. (1979) *The Ecology of Human Development: Experiments by Nature and Design*, Cambridge, MA: Harvard University Press.

Brookes, G., Gorman, T., Harman, J., Hutchinson, D., Kinder, K., Moor, H. and Wilkin, A. (1997) *Family Literacy Lasts*, London: Basic Skills Agency.

Cazbah Report (2008) *Delivering Children and Young People Focus Groups as Part of the National Behaviour and Attendance (NBAR) Review*, Cardiff: CAZBAH.

Children and Young People's Commissioner's Report for Wales (2007) *Unofficial Exclusions*, Swansea: Children Commissioner's Office.

Children and Young People's Consortium for Wales (2006) *Blast Off Guides to Increasing Participation of Children and Young People*, Participation Unit, Cardiff: Welsh Assembly Government/Department for Education and Skills (DfES).

Cole, T. (2007) *A Review of Attendance and Behaviour: Reports and Guidance Issued by Government and Government Agencies in the British Isles*, Penrith, Cumbria: SEBDA.

Dalziel, D. and Henthorne, K. (2005) *Parents'/Carers' Attitudes towards School Attendance*, Research Report 618, London: DfES.

Desforges, C. and Abouchaar, A. (2003) *The Impact of Parental Involvement, Parental Support and Family Education on Pupil Achievement and Adjustment: A Literature Review*, DfES Research Report 433, London: DfES.

DfES (2003) *Every Child Matters* Green Paper, Norwich: HMSO.

DfES (2005) *Learning Behaviour: The Report of The Practitioners' Group on School Behaviour and Discipline*, London: DfES.

Dyer, W. (2001) *You'll See It When You Believe It*, London: Arrow Publishers.

Ellis, G. and Morgan, N. S. (2009) *The Family Values Scheme*, Cardiff: Behaviour Stop Ltd.

Ellis, G., Morgan, N. S. and Reid, K. (2012) *Better Behaviour through Home–School Relations: Using Values-Based Education to Promote Positive Learning*, London: Routledge.

The Elton Report (1989) *Discipline in Schools: Report of the Committee of Enquiry Chaired by Lord Elton*, London: HMSO.

Emerson, E. (1995) *Challenging Behaviour: Analysis and Intervention with People with Learning Difficulties*, Cambridge: Cambridge University Press.

Emerson, E. and Einfeld, S. L. (2011) *Challenging Behaviour*, Cambridge: Cambridge University Press.

Epstein, J. L. (1988) 'How Do We Improve Programmes for Parental Involvement?', *Educational Horizons*, 66: 75–77.

Epstein, J. L. (1995) 'School/Family/Community Partnerships: Caring about the Children We Share', *Phi Delta Kappan*, 76, 9: 701–712.

Epstein, J. L. (2001) *School, Family, and Community Partnerships: Preparing Educators and Improving Schools*, Boulder, CO: Westview Press.

Epstein, N. B., Bishop, D., Ryan, C., Miller, I. and Keitner, G. (1993) 'The McMaster Model View of Healthy Family Functioning'. In F. Walsh (ed.), *Normal Family Processes*, London and New York: The Guilford Press.

Estyn (2008) *Having Your Say: Young People, Participation and School Councils*, Cardiff: Estyn.

Fan, X. and Chen, M. (2001) 'Parental Involvement and Students' Academic Achievement: A Meta-analysis', *Educational Psychology Review*, 13: 1–22.

Farrell, C. and O'Connor, W. (2003) *Low Income Families and Household Spending*, DWP Research Report Series No. 192.

Faupel, A. (ed.) (2003) *Emotional Literacy: Assessment and Intervention*, prepared by Southampton Psychology Service, Slough: NFER.

Feinstein, L. and Symons, J. (1999) 'Attainment in Secondary School', *Oxford Economic Papers*, 51: 300–321.

Freedman, J., Jensen, A. L. and Freedman, P. E. (2001) *Handle With Care: Emotional Intelligence Activity Book*, Dallas: Six Seconds Publishers.

Funky Dragon Report (2007a) *Our Rights, Our Story*, Swansea: Funky Dragon.

Funky Dragon Report (2007b) *Why Do Children's Ages Go Up Not Down?*, Swansea: Funky Dragon.

Gibbs, G. (1988) *Learning by Doing: A Guide to Teaching and Learning Methods*, Oxford: Further Education Unit, Oxford Polytechnic.

Hallam, S., Rhannie, J. and Shaw, J. (2006) *Evaluation of the Primary Behaviour and Attendance Pilot*, Research Report RR717, London: DfES.

Hastings, R. P. and Remington, B. (1994) 'Rules of Engagement: Towards an Analysis of Staff Responses to Challenging Behaviour', *Research in Developmental Disabilities*, 15: 279–298.

Heal, K. (1978) 'Misbehaviour among School Children: The Role of School Strategies for Prevention', *Policy and Politics*, 15, 3: 283–299.

Heck, A., Collins, J. and Peterson, L. (2001) 'Decreasing Children's Risk Taking on the Playground', *Journal of Applied Behavior Analysis*, 34: 349–352.

Henderlong, J. and Lepper, M. R. (2002) 'The Effects of Praise on Children's Intrinsic Motivation: A Review and Synthesis', *Psychological Bulletin*, 128, 5: 774–795.

Hopkins, D. (2002) *Improving the Quality of Education for All*, London: Fulton Press.

Hopkins, D. (2004) *Every School a Great School*, London and New York: Open University Press/McGraw Hill.

Howe, C. and Mercer, N. (2007) *Children's Social Development, Peer Interaction and Classroom Learning*, Cambridge University Review Report 2/16, Cambridge: Cambridge University.

Humphrey, N., Kalambouka, A., Bolton, J., Lendrum, A., Wigelsworth, M., Lennier, C. and Farrell, P. (2008) *Primary Social and Emotional Aspects of Learning (SEAL): Evaluation of Small Group Work*, Manchester: University of Manchester.

Iszatt, J. and Wasilewska, T. (1997) 'Nurture Groups: An Early Intervention Model Enabling Vulnerable Children with Emotional and Behavioural Difficulties to Integrate Successfully into School', *Educational and Child Psychology*, 14, 3: 121–139.

Kane, J. G., Lloyd, G., McCluskey, G., Riddell, S., Stead, J. and Weedon, E. (2007) *Restorative Practices in Scottish Schools*, Edinburgh: Scottish Executive.

Laming Report (2003) *Keeping Children Safe, The Victoria Climbie Inquiry Report*, London: Crown Copyright.

Lovat, T., Toomey, R., Dally, K. and Clement, N. (2009) *Project to Test and Measure the Impact of Values Education on Student Effects and School Ambience*, final report for the Australian Government Department of Education, Employment and Workplace Relations, Newcastle, Australia: University of Newcastle.

McCluskey, G., Lloyd, G., Kane, J., Riddell, S., Stead, J. and Weedon, E. (2008a) 'Can Restorative Practices in Schools Make a Difference?', *Educational Review*, 60, 4: 405–417.

McCluskey, G., Lloyd, G., Kane, J., Riddell, S., Stead, J. and Weedon, E. (2008b) '"I Was Dead Restorative Today." From Restorative Justice to Restorative Approaches in School', *Cambridge Journal of Education*, 38, 2: 199–217.

McGee, P. (2001) *59 Minutes to a Calmer Life*, Reading: Cox and Wyman.

Melhuish, E., Sylva, C., Sammons, P., Siraj-Blatchford, I. and Taggart, B. (2001) *Social, Behavioural and Cognitive Development at 3–4 Years in Relation to Family Background. The Effective Provision of Pre-school Education, EPPE Project*, London: DfEE/The Institute of Education.

Morgan, N. S. and Ellis, G. (2009) *The 5-Step Behaviour Programme*, Cardiff: Behaviour Stop Ltd.

Morgan, N. S. and Ellis, G. (2011a) *The Good Choice Teddy Approach*, Cardiff: Behaviour Stop Ltd.

Morgan, N. S. and Ellis, G. (2011b) *A Kit Bag for Promoting Positive Behaviour in the Classroom*, London: Jessica Kingsley Publishers.

Morrison, B. (2007) *Restoring Safer School Communities*, Sydney: Federation Press.

National Behaviour and Attendance Review (NBAR) (2007) *Interim Report*, Chair: Professor Ken Reid, Cardiff: DfES.

National Behaviour and Attendance Review (NBAR). (2008) *Final Report*, Chair: Professor Ken Reid, Cardiff: DfES.

NCSL (2010) *Leadership for Parental Engagement*, Nottingham: National Leadership of Schools and Children's Services.

Office for National Statistics (2006) *Time Use Survey*, London: ONS.

Peters, M., Seeds, K., Goldstein, A. and Coleman, N. (2008) *Parental Involvement in Children's Education 2007*. Research Report, DCSF RR034.

Qureshi, H. and Alborz, A. (1992) 'The Epidemiology of Challenging Behaviour', *Mental Handicap Research*, 5: 130–145.

Reid, K. (1982) 'The Self-concept and Persistent School Absenteeism', *British Journal of Educational Psychology*, 52, 2: 179–187.

Reid, K. (1985) 'Truancy and School Absenteeism', *British Journal of Educational Psychology*, 52, 2: 179–187.

Reid, K. (1999) *Truancy and Schools*, London: Routledge.

Reid, K. (2000) *Tackling Truancy in Secondary Schools*, London: Routledge.

Reid, K. (2002) *Truancy: Short and Long-term Solutions*, London: Routledge.

Reid, K. (2003) 'Strategic Approaches to Tackling School Absenteeism and Truancy: The Traffic Lights (TL) Scheme', *Educational Review*, 55, 3: 305–321.

Reid, K. (2004) 'A Long-term Strategic Approach to Tackling Truancy and Absenteeism from Schools: The SSTG Scheme', *British Journal of Guidance and Counselling*, 32, 1: 57–74.

Reid, K. (2005a) 'The Causes, Views and Traits of School Absenteeism and Truancy: An Analytical Review', *Research in Education*, 74: 59–82.

Reid, K. (2005b) 'A Comparison between Inspection Reports on the Management of School Attendance throughout the Education Service', *Pastoral Care in Education*, 23, 4: 31–41.

Reid, K. (2005c) 'An Evaluation of Inspection Reports on the Management of Secondary School Attendance', *School Leadership and Management*, 25, 2: 121–139.

Reid, K. (2005d) 'The Implications of Every Child Matters for Schools', *Pastoral Care in Education*, 23, 1: 12–18.

Reid, K. (2006a) 'The Professional Development Needs of Education Welfare Officers on the Management of School Attendance', *Journal of In-Service Education*, 32, 2: 237–253.

Reid, K. (2006b) 'An Evaluation of Inspection Reports on Primary School Attendance', *Educational Research*, 48, 3: 267–286.

Reid, K. (2007a) 'An Evaluation of OFSTED Reports on LEAs' Management of School Attendance', *Education Management Administration and Leadership*, 35, 3: 395–413.

Reid, K. (2007b) 'An Evaluation of Reports on the Attendance of Pupils in Out-of-school Provision', *International Journal of Educational Management*, 21, 2: 144–157.

Reid, K. (2008) 'The Causes of Non-attendance: An Empirical Study', *Educational Review*, 60, 4: 345–357.

Reid, K. (2010a) 'Management of School Attendance in the UK: A Strategic Analysis', *Education Management Administration and Leadership*, 38, 1: 88–106.

Reid, K. (2010b) 'Improving Attendance and Behaviour in Wales', *Educational Studies*, 36, 3: 233–249.

Reid, K. (2012) *Disaffection from School*, London: Routledge.

Reid, K., Challoner, C., Lancett, A., Jones, G., Rhydiart, G. A. and Challoner, S. (2010a) 'The Views of Primary Pupils on School Attendance at Key Stage 2 in Wales', *Educational Studies*, 36, 5: 465–479.

Reid, K., Challoner, C., Lancett, A., Jones, G., Rhydiart, G. A. and Challoner, S. (2010b) 'The Views of Primary Pupils at Key Stage 2 on School Behaviour in Wales', *Educational Review*, 62, 1: 97–115.

Rutter, M. (1983) 'School Effects on Pupil Progress: Research Findings and Policy Implications', *Child Development*, 54: 1–29.

Rutter, M., Maughan, B., Mortimore, P., Ouston, J. and Smith, A. (1979) *15,000 Hours*, London: Open Books.

Save the Children Report (2007) *Stop, Look and Listen: The Road to Realising Children's Rights in Wales*, Cardiff: Save the Children.

Sheridan, S. M. and Kratochwill, T. R. (2007) *Conjoint Behavioural Consultation: Promoting Family–School Connections and Interventions*, 2nd edition, New York: Springer.

Shonkoff, J. P. and Phillips, D. A. (eds) (2000) *From Neurons to Neighborhoods: The Science of Early Childhood Development*, Washington, DC: National Academy Press.

Smit, F., Driessen, G., Sluiter, R. and Sleegers, P. (2007) 'Types of Parents and School Strategies Aimed at the Creation of Effective Partnerships', *International Journal about Parents in Education*, 1, 0: 45–52.

Smith, P. (1993) *Professional Assault Response Training*, San Clemente, CA: Professional Growth Facilitators, revised 2000.

SEAL (2005) *Guidance Pack*, London: DfES

SEAL (2006) *National Strategy for School Improvement: Guidance Notes and Advice*, London, DfES.

Steer Report (2005) *Learning Behaviour*, London: DfES.

Stott, D. (2009) *50 Top Tips for Managing Behaviour*, Milton Keynes: Speechmark Publishing.

Sunderland, M. (2006) *The Science of Parenting*, London: Dorling Kindersley.

Sylva, K., Melhuish, E., Sammons, P., Siraj-Blatchford, I. and Taggart, B. (2004) *Effective Pre-School Education*, Final Report. London: DfES/Institute of Education.

Walberg, H. J. (1984) 'Families as Partners in Educational Productivity', *Phi Delta Kappan*, 65: 397–400.

Webster-Stratton, C. (2006) *The Incredible Years*, Seattle, WA: Incredible Years.

Welsh Government (2009) *Behaving and Attending*, report of an Implementation Group established to respond to the NBAR Report, Cardiff: Welsh Government.

Witte, E. H. and Davis, J. H. (1996) *Understanding Group Behaviour: Small Group Processes and Interpersonal Relations*, vol. 2, Mahwah, NJ: Lawrence Erlbaum Associates.

Index

Better Behaviour through Home-School Relations

Using values-based education to promote positive learning

By Gill Ellis, Nicola Morgan and Ken Reid

- How can we create effective partnerships between home, school and the community?
- How can the relationships and communication between families and school be strengthened?
- How can families help schools to improve behaviour in their children, both at home and at school?

It has been proven time and time again, that the children of parents who are actively involved in their child's learning are the ones who make the most progress socially and academically. This highly practical book shows schools and organisations how to create effective partnerships with families and the community in a fun, exciting and sustainable way.

Using a tried and tested framework that has been successfully implemented throughout a wide variety of very different schools and settings, 'Family Values' is a scheme which engages and empowers families to work in close collaboration with schools and organisations, and results in long-term improvements in behaviour, communication, pupil achievement and relationships. Pupils become more academically diligent, the school assumes a calmer, more peaceful ambience, better pupil–teacher relationships are forged, pupil and teacher wellbeing improves and parents are more engaged with the school.

The authors' award-winning 'Family Values' scheme is underpinned by theoretical principles, and they show here how it has been successfully put into practice through case studies in real school settings. The book explores how the scheme promotes social, emotional and family system theories, and as it makes links effectively to SEAL (social and emotional aspects of learning), the scheme complements existing personal and social education programmes in all schools.

Contents

1. The Family Unit
2. Engaging Families
3. Values-based Education
4. The Family Values Scheme
5. How the Family Values Scheme Works
6. Implementing the Family Values Scheme in Schools
7. Promoting the Family Values Scheme
8. Implementing the Family Values Scheme in Organisations

2012
Paperback: 978-0-415-50417-1
Hardback: 978-0-415-50416-4

To order a copy please visit ...

www.routledge.com/education